# BAM The Next Wave Festival

# BAM

# The Next Wave Festival

Edited by **Steven Serafin** and **Susan Yung**

BAM **Brooklyn Academy of Music**
in association with **Print Matters Productions**

# The 1995 Next Wave Festival

Brooklyn Academy of Music

BAM's 1995 Next Wave Festival is sponsored by Philip Morris Companies Inc.

# Foreword

**As stewards** of this world-class institution, our responsibility is to make space for the creative artistry that defines BAM. And nothing embodies that electricity quite like the Next Wave Festival, which has been upending performance forms and conventions since its inception. Our dear friend and colleague—and current BAM executive producer—Joe Melillo was the producing director of the Next Wave from the inaugural season and will spearhead BAM's adventurous programming roster through 2018. His three-decade-plus vision for and dedication to the art of performance continues to astonish us and gives cause for celebration.

Readers of this book are likely familiar with the iconic artists who permanently altered the performance landscape via their participation in this groundbreaking festival: Pina Bausch, Philip Glass, Meredith Monk, Bill T. Jones/Arnie Zane, John Adams, and Robert Wilson, to name but a handful. It's also important to note what the Next Wave means to a new generation of artists and audiences. Today it means making and seeing work in the BAM Fisher, in addition to the Howard Gilman Opera House and the BAM Harvey.

Joe had a vision for a non-proscenium flexible performance space with single low-cost admission, and since that vision was realized in 2012 with the addition of the Fishman Space in the BAM Fisher the entire institution has benefitted from a galvanizing creative infusion from artists such as Nora Chipaumire, Kyle Abraham, Geoff Sobelle, Suzanne Bocanegra, Yoann Bourgeois, Company Wang Ramirez, and the Norwegian collective Verdensteatret. New names, new innovations—a new BAM legacy.

Every fall the metaphors fly around the BAM campus: the wave is cresting, crashing, and always all-consuming. It is familiar now: the rush, the discoveries. But this book serves as a powerful reminder that it wasn't always this way. It's an enduring testament to the many people—artists, administrators, producers, stagehands, executives, and, of course, our signature adventurous audiences—whose efforts have created and sustained the surge.

**Katy Clark**
BAM President

**Adam E. Max**
Chair, BAM Board of Trustees

OPPOSITE
Next Wave Festival brochure, 1995. Courtesy of BAM Hamm Archives

FRONTISPIECE
Chou Chang-ning in *Moon Water*, Lin Hwai-min/ Cloud Gate Dance Theatre of Taiwan, 2003. Photo: Jack Vartoogian

ABOVE
Isabelle Huppert in *Quartett*, Robert Wilson/ Odéon-Théâtre de l'Europe, 2009.
Photo: Stephanie Berger

# Preface

## Harvey Lichtenstein

The pattern we developed at BAM was to do things we thought important and worthwhile that were essentially not being done in New York. It could be a 17th-century Baroque opera or a repertory company doing Shakespeare or the Comédie-Française or Pina Bausch, but it had to be interesting and provocative—something that no one else was doing—it had to be new, innovative, and cutting edge.

In the late '70s, early '80s, we began thinking about the possibility of a festival, a venue just for the avant-garde—but I wasn't sure we could put together a full season and still attract an audience. At the time, we were curtailed by limitations and deeply in debt, so we decided to try it out on a smaller scale—a season that would package a contemporary opera with three modern dance companies.

So we came up with a name—the Next Wave—from the French "Nouvelle Vague" or New Wave, and in the fall of 1981 we introduced the Next Wave Series, which had Trisha Brown, with **Glacial Decoy** and **Son of Gone Fishin'**, Laura Dean and her dancers, Philip Glass with **Satyagraha**, his opera based on the life of Gandhi, and Lucinda Childs with the New York premiere of **Relative Calm**.

And I have to say, it was an extraordinary season, and it got the Next Wave off to an incredible start. It was like nothing we had ever done, and remember, the major core of the season was dance. Looking back at what happened in that first series, what we accomplished, and the level of work, it was just—extraordinary—and somehow or another we were able to turn a losing situation into something terrific.

With the second series—in 1982–83—we really picked up momentum, with music from Steve Reich and from Glenn Branca, then the Flying Karamazov Brothers, dance from Dana Reitz and from Bill T. Jones/Arnie Zane, with musicians Max Roach and Connie Crothers, and Laurie Anderson with **United States: Parts I–IV**, a true breakthrough work that was a huge, huge success for us.

On October 4, 1983, we launched the first Next Wave Festival with **THE PHOTOGRAPHER/Far From the Truth**—composed by Philip Glass—followed by performance artist George Coates, and Trisha and Laurie working with visual artists Donald Judd and Robert Rauschenberg, the Art Ensemble of Chicago, and Lucinda with **Available Light**—a signature piece for her—with music by John Adams.

And then more dance—from Carolyn Carlson, Molissa Fenley, Rina Schenfeld, and Nina Wiener—the "futuristic" opera **Victory Over the Sun**, and we ended with **The Gospel at Colonus**, with Morgan Freeman and the Institutional Radio Choir of Brooklyn, which for me was the highlight of the festival. It just transfixed me, the whole transformation of the Oedipus story into a gospel service, and the Five Blind Boys of Alabama—fantastic, just fantastic.

From "Harvey Lichtenstein (1929–2017): The Oral History," conducted by John Rockwell, June 20, 2007–March 18, 2008

The inaugural festival was exceptional and established our reputation as a destination for the nontraditional. And to be honest I was astonished by what took place. We were able to sustain all that activity—dance, theater, music and opera, performance art, multimedia—and it really captured the imagination. It got the audience to come, it got critical attention, and it was exciting. It really began to cross a divide for BAM, a divide that we hadn't crossed before.

In a way, the Next Wave put a label on what we were doing, and somehow, something came together that really put BAM on the map. It gave us a new kind of identity, what would come to define us as experimental, irreverent, and adventurous. And I don't quite know how in fact that happened, but it really did. There was the Left Bank of Paris, the South Bank of London, and now we had downtown Brooklyn. We had found our niche—the Next Wave.

Harvey Lichtenstein in the Lepercq Space, Peter Jay Sharp Building, 1987. Photo: Rob Kinmonth

# Introduction

Kristy Edmunds

Over the past 35 years, the Next Wave Festival at the Brooklyn Academy of Music has provided the New York cultural world with a litany of innovative, awe-inspiring, and provocative works of distinct vision and enduring value, and continues to stand as a bellwether for the modern legacy of the art of performance.

There are few American institutions where expanding the fence line of the familiar—in the context of the theatrical venue—is as emboldened for a broad public than through the Next Wave Festival. In the words of prominent theater and opera director and BAM artist Anne Bogart, cofounder of SITI Company, the Next Wave is "where one collects the world beyond one's known parameters."

Much has been written about the creation of the Next Wave Festival and its visionary instigator Harvey Lichtenstein, president and executive producer of the Academy from 1967 until his retirement in 1999. The stories that surround his impetus, and what it required of the staff and leadership of the institution from the outset, are spectacularly entertaining—literally, the stuff of legend. The principal term used to characterize his initial gamble is "risk," and it is typically offered with emphasis: "Risk" with a vibrating capital "R."

The history of the Brooklyn Academy of Music in the early years of Lichtenstein's tenure suggests that the institution's financial picture was not entirely rosy; more accurately, it was bleak and teetering on the brink of collapse. As anyone confronting the fiscal realities of a declining balance sheet can attest, fortitude and belt-tightening provide only a temporary reprieve from the undertow. Lichtenstein conceived of the Next Wave as a way forward for the institution, however contrary it may have seemed at the time.

Converting intuitive will into a strategic solution for an organization is no small feat, nor is the requisite ability to convince others to back it. In doing just that, his determination certainly carried risk, but the decision to redirect the institution's resources toward an international festival framework was also an impeccably timed expression of his artistic intelligence.

The nonconventional emphasis of the Next Wave Festival was supremely logical in the sense that Lichtenstein held an abiding loyalty to contemporary performance makers who had long woven their work throughout the alternative spaces of the "downtown" New York art scene, while finding far more supportive footing in Europe.

Today, it is hard to fully imagine a time when artists like Merce Cunningham, Robert Wilson, Philip Glass, Trisha Brown, or Meredith Monk were being embraced in Europe, but

*Reflections*, included
in *L.A. Dance Project*,
Benjamin Millepied, 2014.
Photo: Julieta Cervantes

remarkably underappreciated in the wider perspective of New York culture; when Laurie Anderson or Steve Reich, Bill T. Jones or Jawole Willa Jo Zollar were performing their self-produced projects in the lofts and spaces of friends, holding down part-time jobs and/or couch surfing, or the design genius of Jennifer Tipton was scaffolded in the confines of a gallery or church in lower Manhattan. Much of their collective output was being performed amid an audience of 50 to 100 people—quite possibly the same 50 or 100 people.

What these artists were developing required scale and financial ballast if it was to expand the literacies of audiences, or accomplish the fullness of what they envisioned in their art. They warranted access to institutional resources that were not constrictive—in form, nor content—had physical room for scale, and weren't inherently tied to box office receipts when making program decisions.

Before the Next Wave, unless you were a regular art world traveler heading to the major contemporary venues of Europe, the Edinburgh International Festival, or Festival d'Automne in Paris, there was limited opportunity for American audiences to experience the work of contemporary artists acclaimed in Europe—artists like Pina Bausch, Sankai Juku, Reinhild Hoffmann, Maguy Marin, and Anne Teresa De Keersmaeker—who would alter our perception and appreciation of the performing arts.

In talking with the many artists that I have subsequently had the pleasure of working with over the years, they describe in Lichtenstein a man who could fully perceive the substance of their artistic concepts and would remain undaunted by the challenges posed through the complexity of their vision. He was an advocate and disciple, and they entrusted their ideas to his thoughtful and strategic faculties. He had already championed many on the basis of their artistry. What he needed was a framework that could simultaneously elevate the visibility and capacity of the institution's support, while shifting the margins on the institutional forecast.

The Next Wave Festival would become the apparatus to achieve both, and in doing so Brooklyn became "home" to an international vanguard for the contemporary performing arts in the United States. Remarkably, this was not a slow build before taking hold. The impact was immediate.

It was a strategy that enabled the Brooklyn Academy of Music to reinvent itself in the mid-1970s as BAM—an acronym that came to represent an artistic renaissance that required a twofold approach: someone to provide the art and someone to make the art happen. And to that end, enter Joseph V. Melillo and Karen Brooks Hopkins.

Next Wave Festival poster for *Scenario*, included in *Cunningham Merce: Forward & Reverse*, Merce Cunningham Dance Company, 1997. Photo: Timothy Greenfield-Sanders

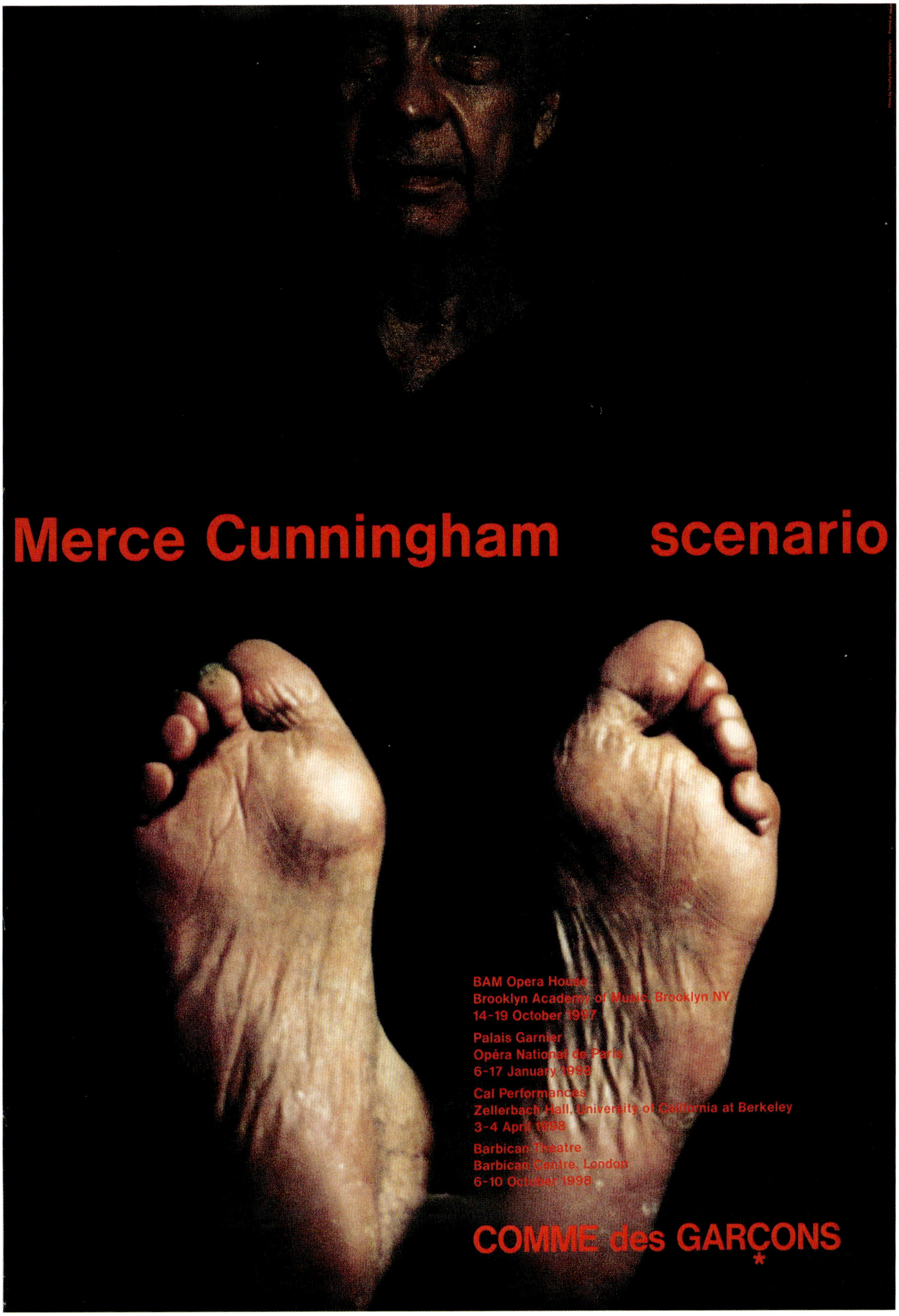
Merce Cunningham
scenario
BAM Opera House
Brooklyn Academy of Music, Brooklyn NY
14-19 October 1997
Palais Garnier
Opéra National de Paris
6-17 January 1998
Cal Performances
Zellerbach Hall, University of California at Berkeley
3-4 April 1998
Barbican Theatre
Barbican Centre, London
6-10 October 1998
COMME des GARÇONS

The fundraising machine created by Hopkins, who succeeded Lichtenstein as president, was critical to the survival of the institution as well as fusing the festival with synergy. Melillo was tasked at the onset to be the producing director of the Next Wave and remained at the helm since the foundational beginning. Known across the board informally as Joe, he presided over the festival with devotional commitment, and his contribution to the careers of countless artists is extensive to say the least.

Often when Joe is asked how he got his start at BAM, he tells the story of Harvey handing him "the List"—the artists he was tasking Joe to secure. It is a simplified encapsulation of the

Dominique Mercy in *Palermo Palermo*, Tanztheater Wuppertal Pina Bausch, 1991. Photo: William Gibson/ Martha Swope Associates "make it happen" version of mentorship, and a charmingly succinct description for how one succeeds as a renowned festival producer. Be that as it may, the Next Wave Festival's programmatic legacy became equally his own, and a testament to the value he placed on his relationships with artists, his esteem for Harvey Lichtenstein, and the guiding mission of the institution.

Within every annual edition of the Next Wave Festival there are hallmarks to Melillo's programming that carry forward a distinctive BAM signature, while assuring the festival's equilibrium across the wildly swinging pendulum of contemporary artistic output.

One is the consistent presence of master performance makers who remain highly adventurous in their creative practices. In form, cultural inquiry, and aesthetic predisposition, their resulting works for the BAM stages—the Howard Gilman Opera House, the BAM Harvey Theater, and the recent addition of the Fishman Space in the BAM Fisher—can be contrasted to the accomplished conventions upheld through major-scale cultural institutions. This is not to say that these artists stand at odds to the traditional; in fact, many are now fully embraced by the classical opera, symphony, and dance worlds. But the work that they have presented at BAM has tended toward cultural and artistic urgency while remaining liberally untethered from the linear.

For BAM audiences, access to the sustained work of these artists has generated a deepened recognition of their singularity. The Next Wave offers a consistent exposure that involves audiences in much the same fashion as that of experiencing a retrospective of an artist's work at a major modern art museum. In precisely this way, the festival attains a temporally elongated survey of major bodies of work over successive years and decades.

Another signature hallmark in the programming is the dimensional inclusion of multiple art forms—either through a collaborative team of artists developing a production together, or through the juxtaposition of blurred discipline categories in contemporary performance. Opera, dance, and theater are calibrated with cinema, literature, and design over the course of each festival, as are featured commissions by composers, visual artists, and interdisciplinary pioneers. The cross-referenced ideas of our time, and the currencies of each genre, are there for exploration with multiple literacies at play in every Next Wave platform.

What is equally true since the inaugural festival through to this day is the creative collision of experimentation by artists whose projects continue to be scaled upward from the lofts and smaller spaces they typically work within, along with the robust presentation of landmark productions from abroad. The Next Wave Festival becomes a global conversation whose participants cut across generational, cultural, and national boundaries, while fusing categories of artistic knowledge and practices, and it all happens in Brooklyn—what Harvey Lichtenstein deemed the Left Bank of New York City.

Like most of the pivotal discoveries in my life, I learned about the Next Wave Festival because of the artists that I greatly respected. These were the artists who shaped and defined the Next Wave—working, collaborating with other artists, seeking to be part of the BAM experience—or they were in annual attendance as audience members to see the work of their peers.

Regularly present within the Next Wave audience are also the individuals who make up a generation of curators and artistic directors, producers, programmers, and critics in the field of live performance. Although it is not the primary focus of the Next Wave to ignite the artistic

ABOVE
Meredith Monk in her *On Behalf of Nature*, 2014. Photo: Julieta Cervantes

OPPOSITE
*Kagemi: Beyond the Metaphors of Mirrors*, Sankai Juku, 2006. Photo: Jack Vartoogian

sensibilities of professional colleagues holding forth in our national urban centers, the impact of BAM on our work, our challenges, and our accomplishments is undeniably present.

Each of us can recount precisely when a Next Wave production first knocked us into a state of spectacular wonderment. Whether it was theater or dance or music isn't as important as the astonishing surprise of being suddenly and profoundly arrested by artistic perspective. And because of it, life can be grasped anew. For countless many, the Next Wave is where that first catalytic encounter took place.

Next Wave Festival poster for *The Mahabharata*, Peter Brook/Jean-Claude Carrière, 1987. Courtesy of BAM Hamm Archives

In 1987, while the Next Wave was undertaking the legendary American presentation of British director Peter Brook's **The Mahabharata** (requiring the refurbishment of a long-shuttered cinema known then as the Majestic and now as the BAM Harvey), I encountered the work of Robert Wilson for the first time. I was completing my film degree in what was then West Berlin, and my professor insisted that I attend a play at the Schaubühne theater titled *Death Destruction & Detroit II*. He asked if I had ever heard of **Einstein on the Beach**, which I hadn't, and he finally convinced me to take the time out of my busy schedule of being a 20-something by emphatically stating that I was unlikely to ever see this "kind of theater" in the United States—apart from BAM where Wilson had staged the remount of *Einstein* in the 1984 Next Wave.

This "kind of theater" was spectacularly distinct from the narrative storytelling I had seen previously. There was architecture, painting, cinematic progressions, soundscapes, light, and text coalescing into a sustained meaning that was completely held by the nonlinear.

At roughly the same time, audiences in Brooklyn were having a similarly epic experience while attending Brook's *The Mahabharata*. By all accounts, this too was a towering work of theater wherein the world was gloriously tilting on its axis of the known to offer something brilliantly other because of its existence.

Thirty-five years on, the Next Wave Festival can, and does, claim that it has permanently changed the artistic landscape. In equal measure, the festival has expanded the appetite of its audiences who have become the adventurous interlocutors of the BAM community each autumn.

Today, when you happen to be in proximity with other BAM aficionados, you'll find they are generously predisposed to sharing their experiences. Artists, productions, compositions, plays, and choreographies are rattled off without pause for breath, as if this was all as readily available as the masterworks of the Western classical canon, as accessible as the high amplification of popular entertainment, or as likely to be held "in common" as a recently trending video on YouTube.

Of course, these are not the names that have been lodged into popular consciousness through the proliferation of commercial distribution or mainstream exposure. They are the maverick authors that make up our cultural through-line within the arc of nonconventional performance. The Next Wave's audience and artists are akin to something of a living archive for the potent and accomplished lineage of the art of performance.

FOLLOWING PAGE
Jasper Newell, Caitlin Scranton, and Tomás Cruz in *Einstein on the Beach*, Robert Wilson/Philip Glass/Lucinda Childs, 2012. Photo: Stephanie Berger

The Next Wave Festival:

# An Artistic Journey

## Joseph V. Melillo

In conversation with **Anne Bogart**, **Karen Brooks Hopkins**, **Colleen Jennings-Roggensack**, **David Lang**, **Beth Morrison**, **José Parlá**, **Marianne Weems**, and **Jawole Willa Jo Zollar**

Joseph V. Melillo at Centro Cultural del Bosque, Mexico City, 2015. Photo: Bart Michiels

The creation of the Next Wave was transformational for BAM. Not only did the concept of a festival enhance the focus and density of the amount of work available to the public, it allowed us to initiate a more interesting and provocative journey through the contemporary arts scene. We could program our discoveries and shape the offerings in a way that would encourage our audience to step out of their comfort zones to try something they had never experienced. The Next Wave Festival endures and continues to be successful because it has always stayed on mission—to engage our audience as part of the artistic experience at BAM and to encourage the discovery of new ideas from a rich and diverse menu of possibilities.

## Karen Brooks Hopkins

President Emerita, BAM

My tenure as executive producer at BAM represents a personal journey that began as a teenager at the Shubert Theater in New Haven, Connecticut. As a theatrical novice, I wasn't sure what to expect and didn't have the critical faculties to fully understand or appreciate the performance—but what I remember is being totally mesmerized.

I found myself in the balcony of the Shubert as a spectator in direct proximity with the performers and to the physical stage, and what I encountered was nothing less than pure spectacle. And I knew then that an extraordinary world existed for me beyond the perimeters of my circumscribed life.

It was essentially what critic Eric Bentley would call a theatrical moment—a moment of engagement that serves as an intensification of your humanity. And for me that moment was further realized as a graduate student at Catholic University in Washington, D.C., where I earned an MFA in theater—and where I was launched on this journey of aesthetic development.

There are certain realities of human existence. You breathe. You walk. You talk. And theater became a reality that confronted the issue of the individual in society versus the needs of the community. I came to believe there was something about the theater that I needed to explore and something I needed to accomplish.

I began my professional career at the Guthrie Theater in Minneapolis, where I worked under artistic director Michael Langham, and my experience at the Guthrie was a turning point for me. I learned something very important from Michael. Being in the rehearsal studio, I would watch him explicate a text to his actors, assisting them to make the choices needed to get to the meaning of a scene. And it forced me to realize that he had a talent I didn't have, but it was a talent I could recognize, capture, and channel into my own work.

As the artistic director of the Next Wave Festival, there's always an element, an ingredient, of risk-taking that has a lot to do with intuition and instinct. You research a particular artist or production that you believe is appropriate for your work here at BAM, and then you fill in your itinerary with new discoveries, which is very much a part of the business of curating. As I think about these artists and as I look at your creative palette, it's been diverse, it's been gender diverse, and it's been diverse by sexual preference. And I wonder if this is a conscious effort on your part or a feature of the BAM personality because there are many institutions as renowned, as large, and as focused as BAM that don't fully accept that responsibility.

## Colleen Jennings-Roggensack

Curator and Arts Administrator

Within the context of academia, I understood what it meant to be a director, an actor, or a playwright, but I was searching for something different. My talent was being able to work with other talented people, and it was this ability that would eventually connect me to BAM—the ability to curate, to present, and to produce.

I moved to New York because there were opportunities for me here that provided a different kind of off-the-charts learning. It was about American cultural history happening right in front of me, and I needed to be a participant in that process. I became exposed to a tremendous amount of creativity, and my education grew exponentially in relation to the performing arts as well as ballet, modern dance, and symphonic music—knowledge built upon my own passion and commitment to American theater.

I think the most interesting lesson for me was confirming that great art is limited to only a few individuals. There are many well-intentioned artists and creators, but virtuosity is unique. Whether preordained or not, there are people who are just exceptionally gifted. The ingredients of what makes great art—first and foremost, virtuosity, then discipline, practice, and commitment to technique.

This was something I shared with my predecessor, Harvey Lichtenstein, and what continues to define my role as an artistic director. My entire personal and professional life is about the importance of community, and the theater provided me the opportunity to establish relationships and to do what I do best, which is to facilitate—being able to transfer the ideas of an individual artist or a collective ensemble who want to create something—and to find the means to successfully make that happen. I have the capability of participating in the cosmos of the artistic imagination, but I also have the skill set to speak in the civilian world, and to orchestrate the progress of a creative endeavor at a specific moment.

In the early 1980s, Harvey proposed the idea of creating a contemporary, nontraditional performing arts festival for New York City, and he was willing to dedicate his entire organization to make that happen. The context of the Next Wave was to engage an artist on a personal level and to understand who they are in relationship to their work. In very specific terms, the highest compliment that a cultural institution can give an artist is to invest in their creative imagination and to commission new work from them.

In the fall of 1981, Harvey presented the first of two seasons deemed the Next Wave Series, and the transition to a full-fledged, multidisciplinary festival was due in large part to the emergence of BAM as a mecca for modern dance and to the overwhelming success of landmark productions, the Philip Glass opera **Satyagraha** and Laurie Anderson's multimedia epic **United States: Parts I–IV**. It was essentially the response to the Next Wave Series that gave Harvey the confidence to consolidate the extraordinary amount of large-scale work from contemporary artists on the BAM stages. Once again, nothing less than a theatrical moment—and this was my introduction to BAM.

I have a vivid memory of my first day at BAM—walking into 30 Lafayette Avenue. When I arrived, Harvey handed me a single sheet of paper that contained a list of artists and productions, and my first act as the producer of the inaugural Next Wave Festival was to separate Harvey's list into two columns: column A for what we could do, and column B for what we couldn't do. And

*Einstein on the Beach*, Philip Glass/Robert Wilson/Lucinda Childs, 1984. Photo: Babette Mangolte

at the top of Harvey's list was **Einstein on the Beach**, a unique collaboration between Philip Glass and Robert Wilson, an extraordinary work that I knew would happen at BAM, but it wasn't ready for the first festival. It needed to be reconstructed from the original version performed in 1976 at the Avignon Festival, including new choreography by Lucinda Childs, so *Einstein* would have to wait.

One of the major objectives of the Next Wave was to give artists the opportunity to collaborate on what was referred to then as interdisciplinary work, and we opened the festival on October 4, 1983, with the production of **THE PHOTOGRAPHER/Far From the Truth**, a hybrid form of music-theater conceived by Dutch visual artist Rob Malasch and composer Philip Glass and performed in three parts: the first, a play, with a text by Robert Coe; the second, a mixed media presentation, with projections by Wendall K. Harrington incorporating animated photographs of the human body in motion; and the third, a movement-dance work choreographed by David Gordon. Based on the life of 19th-century British-born photographer Eadweard Muybridge and directed by JoAnne Akalaitis, with sets and costumes by Santo Loquasto and lighting by Jennifer Tipton, the BAM-produced collaboration yielded an extraordinary achievement that became

Next Wave Festival adhesive sticker by Keith Haring for *Secret Pastures*, Bill T. Jones/ Arnie Zane & Company, 1984. Courtesy of BAM Hamm Archives

In relation to multi-genre, multidisciplinary performance, BAM—and especially the Next Wave Festival—has become a robust platform for hybridity. Before the Next Wave, the experimentation taking place in Europe was mostly lost within American culture. We had to endure some 40 years of kitchen sink drama and one-dimensional storytelling without any real cross-disciplinary influence. My work seems to be a natural response to the progressive events of the late 20th and early decades of this century in which we had to navigate much of our identity through media. Media became the venue that stretched us, the venue that took us away from classical theater, and so integrating that into the vocabulary of storytelling seemed utterly natural and urgent.

**Marianne Weems**

Theater and Opera Director

a milestone of music-theater and signified an aesthetic, artistic ingredient for the festival. The BAM audience had never seen a performance work on such a large scale, and it established the reputation of the Next Wave as a showcase for contemporary nontraditional art.

This reputation was further enhanced in that same season with the production of **The Gospel at Colonus**, a hybrid work by Lee Breuer and Bob Telson. Based on an adaptation of a Greek play set within an African American Pentecostal environment, *Gospel* featured Clarence Fountain and the Five Blind Boys of Alabama as Oedipus, a relatively unknown off-Broadway actor at the time named Morgan Freeman as "The Messenger," and the Brooklyn-based Institutional Radio Choir playing the Greek Chorus.

Theater. Dance. Music. Visual art. All separate silos of artistic form, merged on the BAM stages. It was about different artists—in this case, American artists—crossing disciplines to tell a story. The Next Wave gave artists the opportunity to create work on a large scale. They were essentially challenging the aesthetic norm while focusing on different forms to harness content and storytelling.

Audiences were genuinely shocked by the Next Wave—the scale of *THE PHOTOGRAPHER* and the audacity of Breuer and Telson to stage a black Pentecostal work of music-theater based on Greek drama. It was something out of another world, something that didn't fit into any classification. And to be honest, we really didn't know if the Next Wave was going to have value or if we were having a party that no one was going to attend.

We learned that the exploration of what was new, innovative, and progressive would take tremendous energy as well as intellect. It wouldn't be a meditative moment. Given the context that many of these artists were performing in downtown loft spaces or art galleries, the Next Wave provided the unique opportunity to work on a full stage.

One of the greatest gifts given to BAM is that audiences come and see the unexpected—something different, disturbing, or challenging—and it does not shock them if what they see is not completely satisfying—because the BAM audience has been created to accept and appreciate risk. They have a broader sense about their relationship as listeners and participants in the artistic process. And that's not only good for BAM but good for the artist. What was interesting is that BAM became a home for revolutionary American productions that could previously only happen in Europe, and the Next Wave gave new composers the opportunity to show they were capable of having a powerful impact on contemporary music.

**David Lang**
Composer

From the beginning, dance played a significant role in our artistic programming. We had David Gordon collaborating with Philip Glass; Trisha Brown with the New York premiere of **Set and Reset**, a collaboration with Laurie Anderson and visual artist Robert Rauschenberg; Lucinda Childs performed **Available Light**, with sets by Frank Gehry and music by John Adams; and from the European community, we had a large-scale work by the Caroline Carlson Dance Theater of La Fenice.

Other highlights included Molissa Fenley and Dancers, collaborating with composer Anthony Davis and visual artist Francesco Clemente; Israeli choreographer Rina Schenfeld; and Nina Wiener and her dancers performing **Wind Devil**, a collaboration with composer Sergio Cervetti and sculptor Judy Pfaff, which illustrates the importance of collaboration as a vital part of the artistic process.

Building on the inaugural season of the festival came Meredith Monk with **The Games**, collaborating with theater artist Ping Chong, which opened the second Next Wave season, and since then, she has been a regular BAM artist. And you have Bill T. Jones and Arnie Zane performing **Secret Pastures** with music by Peter Gordon, working with visual artist Keith Haring and fashion designer Willi Smith.

And then, the wait for *Einstein* was finally over, and it was like nothing I had ever seen. I perceive the production as music-theater, but the creators self-describe it as an opera. However, I like the idea that they use the term because with three BAM iterations of this production—1984, 1992, and 2012—the concept of taking a non-narrative form with heightened visual material and animated dance sequences has greatly influenced opera in the late 20th and early 21st century.

Music has always been a key ingredient of our artistic platform, but it was a very different environment

at the time for music in New York City; and to use Philip as an example, it actually was art gallerist Paula Cooper who gave him his first concert in her gallery. The downtown Manhattan art scene provided access to a venue for composers to have their music performed. There was a series of galleries as well as loft and studio spaces on and off Canal Street that paved the way for the Next Wave, and it was Harvey who made BAM and the Next Wave Festival a destination for alternative art forms.

The third season of the festival opened with the residency of now iconic German choreographer Pina Bausch and her company, which introduced the BAM audience

*Rosas Danst Rosas*, Anne Teresa De Keersmaeker/ Rosas, 1986. Photo: Tom Brazil

PINA BAUSCH
WUPPERTALER TANZTHEATER

In many ways, my work as the artistic director of Urban Bush Women grew out of wanting to engage other artists in large-scale collaborative performance—various artists coming together or being put together for the purpose of learning from each other—and the Next Wave gave artists that ability, especially in dance. I was challenged by the element of risk—the high risk of failure and the high risk of success—that edge interested me. I've only learned recently to articulate what I like to create as an artist and like many others I have a broad palette. I love density and works that have complexity and layers. That's what I find in the Next Wave—a density of ideas that allows you to see the movement of storytelling.

**Jawole Willa Jo Zollar**

Dancer and Choreographer

Next Wave Festival program for Tanztheater Wuppertal Pina Bausch, 1984. Courtesy of BAM Hamm Archives

to tanztheater—her unique brand of dance-theater. Her work was daring and provocative—raw, physical, dream-like—and people either loved her or hated her. And I said to myself that this is what it means to introduce the concept of difference in relation to the aesthetic perspective that most people had about the performing arts—either the conventionality of American theater or the very precise modernism of dance.

The Next Wave Festival has evolved over these 35 years, but first and foremost our mission is to maintain the relationships between the institution and the artists. For example, the Brussels-based Belgium choreographer Anne Teresa De Keersmaeker—we introduced her in the 1986 Next Wave in the Lepercq Space (now the home of BAMcafé) with **Rosas Danst Rosas**, the first piece she created for her ensemble, Rosas. She then moved to the Carey Playhouse—a performance venue converted in 1998 into the BAM Rose Cinemas—and she now performs in the BAM Howard Gilman Opera House.

She is a practitioner who evolved from the 1980s to her present status as a BAM artist; her art has changed and we have grown as she's grown. So there are artists like Anne Teresa whom we refer to as "iconic." It's a coinage that works for us. The evolution of the Next Wave Festival has been a nurturing process to continue to find the right work from her current repertory that should be seen in New York City by the BAM audience.

When Harvey retired, he passed down his mantra to "follow the artist," and I live with that principle. It means that there is value for an arts institution to make long-term investments with individual artists who you believe animate your institution. And that has proven true for BAM. I'm pleased with my relationships with artists and listen to them and really try to digest what they're trying to accomplish, and not superimpose my values or deeds onto them. Having the experience of working with and knowing the individual develops a certain kind of trust.

I have learned a great deal during my tenure at BAM, and my concern is maintaining the core values of the institution as well as continuity and growth. Harvey's greatest gift to me was risk. He would risk everything for what he believed, and I learned from him to choose or accept risk but to think through the implications of my choices. I think of myself as the perfect representative of the BAM audience. I believe that I walk into performance venues, wherever they may be, without a bias, a tabula rasa as it were, and open myself to the experience.

I have also become something of a global citizen and appreciate other cultures and their importance to my work. There are individuals who see the world in unique and different ways, and my role as artistic director is to seek them out so that for the price of a ticket, others can make the same discovery.

New York City has a very vibrant art enthusiastic community of ticket buyers, so balancing the iconic artists with young emerging artists means that I go to other venues in Brooklyn, Manhattan, and anywhere else that services younger artists to see who they are and to become conversant about their work. BAM is both locally and globally responsive, and that is where the Next Wave Festival has to be in order to discover new artists.

Our physical neighborhood is profoundly changing with the rapid influx of new construction, and we need to acknowledge the responsibility we have to invest in a future that will constitute an active, animating aesthetic contribution to our growth and development.

The major transition for BAM in recent years was the impact of the Richard B. Fisher Building, completed in 2012, and specifically the Fishman Space, a 250-seat completely flexible theater. This has allowed engagement with a range of Brooklyn-specific artists who are participants in the contemporary pursuit of culture but are not necessarily performing artists. We're working with filmmakers as well as performance and visual artists whose work requires a smaller-scale performance space—among them, Jonah Bokaer, Nora Chipaumire, Faye Driscoll, and Kyle Abraham.

What I hope is that each artist would say that they were successful in presenting their work as part of our programming. Metaphorically, I am inviting you to come to BAM and do your best work and then to feel you've been successful. We don't measure success by box office receipts or critical reviews; we measure success by the individual artist saying, "Here—within the BAM environment—this is where I've done my best work."

My response is that the sum of the parts creates an aesthetic that I equate with taste. At the end of the day, I'm addicted to storytelling—I am not afraid of stories being told in new and unusual ways as long as I can understand the abstract, emotional, or psychological narrative. If I really understand, then I believe our audiences will connect with it.

Of most importance is that I've had the good fortune to work with an enlightened board of trustees and with two extraordinary colleagues, Karen Brooks Hopkins, president of BAM from 1999 until her retirement in 2015, and now Katy Clark, who have steadily supported my artistic vision. In addition, it has been my privilege to be part of what I lovingly refer to as Team BAM—the many dedicated hard-working BAM staff members who each have a role in making the work onstage possible.

Next Wave Festival brochure, BAM Fisher Opening Season, 2012. Courtesy of BAM Hamm Archives

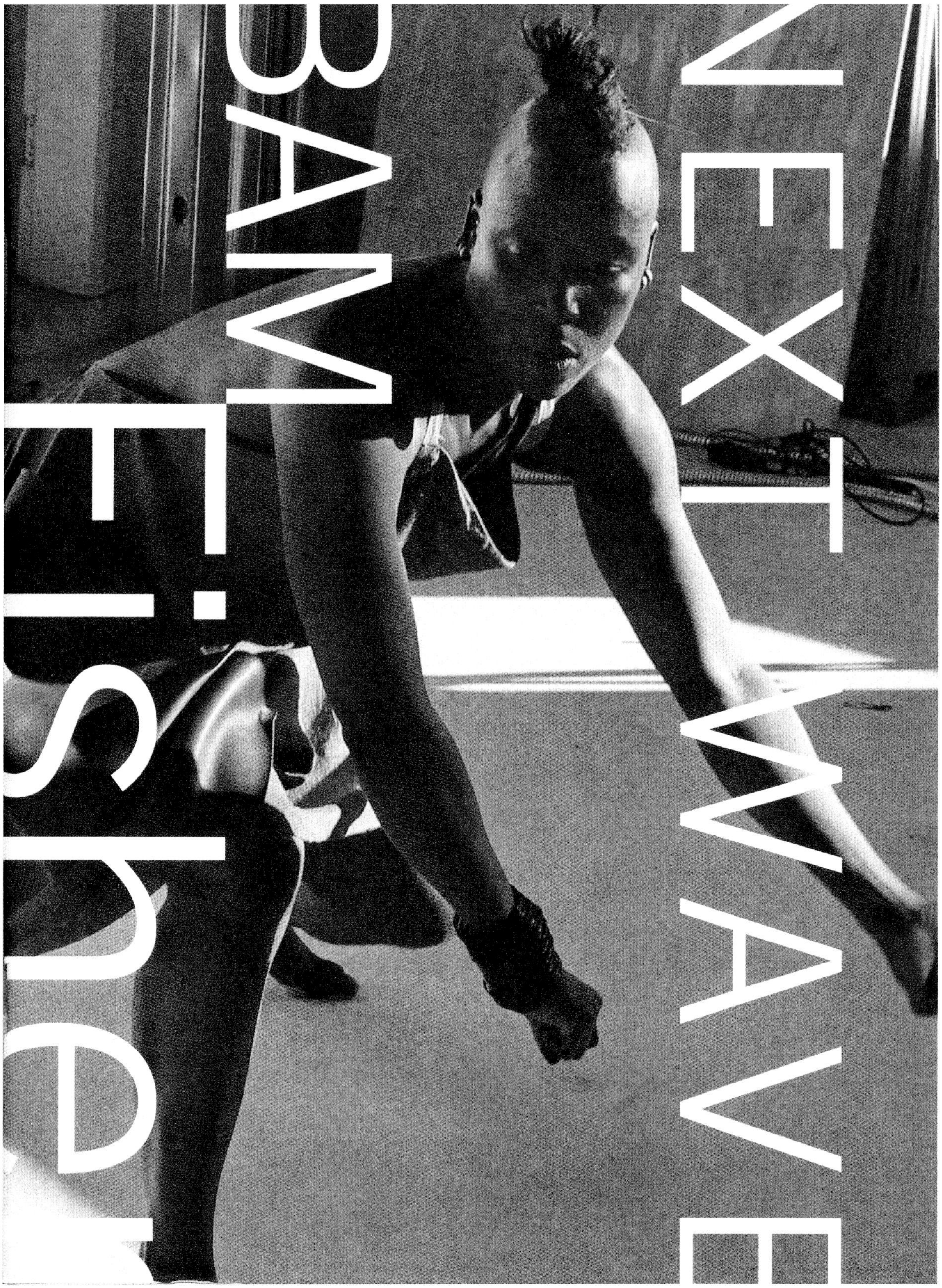
NEXT WAVE
BAM Fisher

As a director, I came of age with the Next Wave, and hybrid art seemed like a common language for me. I always thought that my aspiration would be to swim in that water and become a part of that tradition. Hybridity is a necessity, connecting the kind of esoteric technological work that we do and the performance venue, and I don't know what we would be doing as a culture and curatorial body—and certainly as artists—if we weren't able to cross over those lines. What made the Next Wave successful was not just putting all these threads together but that they were intertwined. And that creates a very specific collaborative method. Different artists were able to reach across boundaries to make something together because they were given the liberty to borrow from other forms.

**Marianne Weems**

Theater and Opera Director

Satchie Noro in *Au Revoir Parapluie*, James Thierrée/La Compagnie du Hanneton, 2007.
Photo: Julieta Cervantes

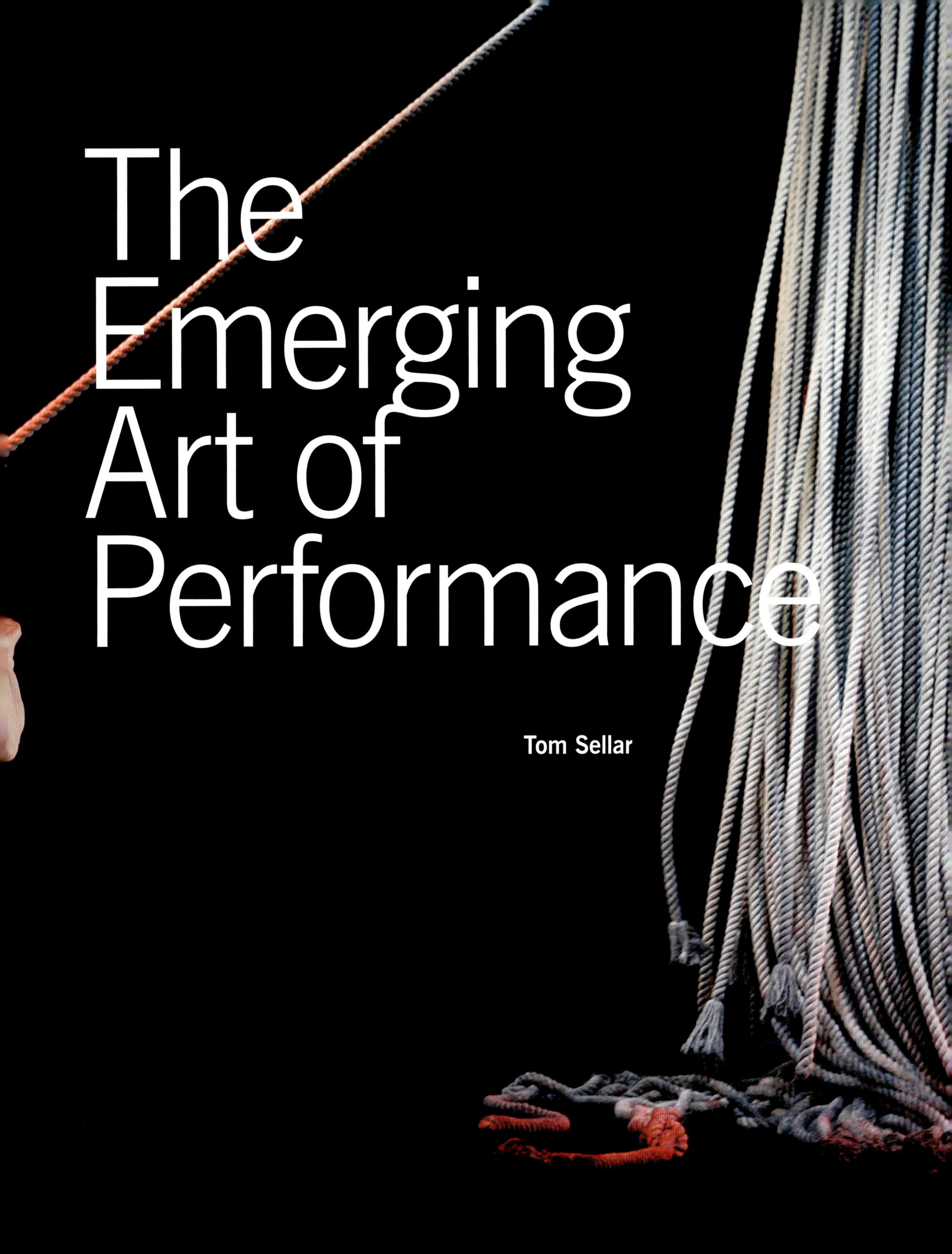

# The Emerging Art of Performance

Tom Sellar

"I bring good news," announces a speaker poised at a lectern early in the performance of **THE PHOTOGRAPHER/Far From the Truth**. "This is not life-like! This is not realistic!"

Rhapsodizing about a changing world, this Victorian-era lecturer proposes that in the future a new category of artists—photographers—will "animate the motion of all humanity." What new frames of mind will their pictures reveal? What future empires will be built upon images? How will the camera alter our perceptions of time and truth? She adds, "We stand at the dawn of a new age. . . . The loss of familiar references will not be an easy adjustment—not at all!"

Those prophetic, spine-tingling words might equally well describe another new age at hand—an era of borderless artistic forms, ushered in with this landmark production, which opened the inaugural season of BAM's Next Wave Festival.

Originally commissioned by the Holland Festival and performed in Amsterdam in 1982, the mixed media reconfiguration of the work that launched the Next Wave contained all the ele-

*THE PHOTOGRAPHER/Far From the Truth*, Philip Glass/ Robert Coe/David Gordon/ JoAnne Akalaitis, 1983. Photo: Beatriz Schiller

ments for which the festival later became renowned. Expressive and powerful, the production demonstrated the potency of collaboration: some of the most important artists of the century worked together to explore a potent subject in a new form. This masterwork was also a conglomeration of forms—on one hand, it was a music-theater piece, consisting of equal parts play, concert, and dance directed by JoAnne Akalaitis. But *THE PHOTOGRAPHER/Far From the Truth* combined these elements with a frenzy of movement, images, and sound. With a visceral, walloping score by Philip Glass, a charged theatrical book by Robert Coe, and choreography by David Gordon, this bold evocation of Eadweard Muybridge's passion-fueled life heralded, above all, the arrival of a radical, unprecedented medium, capable of capturing, concealing, and altering reality.

It's hard to imagine a better way to launch the Next Wave, a festival born of a desire to bring the rising pioneers of performance to wider exposure. After an initial two seasons as a smaller Next Wave Series, in 1981 and 1982–83, featuring predominantly young artists from the emerging avant-garde, BAM had formalized the commitment to change and innovation by designating it a festival, hiring a young producer by the name of Joseph V. Melillo, and making it the centerpiece of fall programming. The "Next Wave" name came from the staff, and reflected an ambition to make a current generation of genre-crossing artists visible on an unprecedented scale in New York.

Despite these lofty aesthetic goals, former BAM president and executive producer Harvey Lichtenstein largely avoided programming around ideas; he preferred to emphasize the experience and the excitement that a presentation could generate. In a 2008 interview with critic John Rockwell, he recalled that he never looked for thematic connectivity in programming the festival, not in the early days, and not later. "What I was more concerned about was having a big opening and a big closing," he recalled. "Early on, really more and more the stuff was what I saw and really responded to personally." Yet his instinct—that something significant was happening in the progressive precincts of theater and dance, deserving its own, new platform—turns out to have been remarkably prescient.

If modernism had meant investigating theater, dance, music, painting, and other forms to uncover and redefine their essential properties, the postwar generations, centered in New York, had begun another process, experimenting with collisions between art forms and with popular culture and other phenomena. In the 1960s and 1970s, New York's progressive performing arts scene came together in the downtown Manhattan neighborhoods where many artists lived, converting industrial spaces into studios and theaters, and using basements and rooftops and any other space that could be found. Experimental performance companies such as Robert Wilson's Byrd Hoffman School of Byrds, Richard Foreman's Ontological-Hysteric Theater, and Richard Schechner's Performance Group were based in SoHo lofts. In churches and storefronts, groups like the Judson Dance Theater and Judson Poets Theater, Squat Theatre, Mabou Mines, and countless others carried out fervent experimentation.

Melding and mixing of forms—dance, opera, music-theater, dramatic theater, circus, "happenings," poetry, rock, spoken word, quotidian activities, and amateur participants—was a crucial aspect of the advances in these decades. BAM had long supported the work of many of these artists, pioneers like Merce Cunningham—whose choreography lived in inventive interplay with visual artist Robert Rauschenberg and composer John Cage. BAM had also presented Robert Wilson's early epic performance spectacles, brought Julian Beck and Judith Malina's radical Living Theatre back to New York from international exile, and sponsored Jerzy Grotowski's Polish Laboratory Theatre, as well as encouraging artists from this "downtown" community such as Glass, Steve Reich, Twyla Tharp, and Trisha Brown.

At the time that BAM launched its young artist series and then the Next Wave Festival, the New York performance scene was entering an exhilarating new phase. Artists in the 1980s often spoke

Philip Glass during the production of *THE PHOTOGRAPHER/Far From the Truth*, 1983. Photo: Tom Caravaglia

of “intermedia” or “multimedia” art, as they sought to build on emerging technology and integrate video and prerecorded sound into live theater and dance. Their investigations into the limits and textures of live performance were nurtured and supported by critical theories of “postmodern” art—and by the simultaneous founding of “multi-arts” venues to support it in Europe. New York artists who wanted to work across disciplines on a large scale found themselves approaching European producers for help. Art critic Kay Larson, writing in *New York* magazine in 1981, summed up the situation when she decried the “national shame that both Glass and Wilson must go to Europe to find a sympathetic set of bureaucrats for their world premieres.”

In a statement prepared in 1983 laying out his vision for a festival, Lichtenstein cited the proliferation of cross-disciplinary experiments and identified a need. “By whatever name it is known—avant-garde, experimental, post-modern, etc.—this work embodies the current generation’s quest to extend the boundaries of artistic expression,” he wrote. “The nurturing of many of our most creative artists has been done by such groups as The Kitchen, the Walker Art Center, Dance Theater Workshop, P.S. 122, and other, mostly alternative, spaces in cities across the country. BAM is taking the next step in commissioning and producing large-scale work and in arranging for tours of some of that work.”

In June 1983, BAM held a press conference at the New York Public Library for the Performing Arts at Lincoln Center and announced the transition of the Next Wave Series into a full-fledged autumn festival, accompanied by a fund to encourage national tours of selected projects to take them to even wider audiences. “The exposure of this creative work is a crucial adjunct to the festival itself,” noted Lichtenstein.

Lichtenstein had observed the fluidity not only of these performance forms themselves, but also of audiences and venues, noting that Philip Glass and his ensemble could attract diverse audiences not only in concert halls but also in rock clubs and art galleries. “In conceiving this project,” Lichtenstein declared, “BAM is responding to substantial evidence that a significant audience has developed for these works.” BAM could offer these genre-crossers its large, landmark stages, an adventurous audience, and national exposure; in later years, the festival also extended art-world cachet and links to sophisticated corporate patronage.

It didn’t take long for creative visionaries from this scene to embrace the Next Wave as their own platform—a hospitable home for hybridity, for performances that couldn’t fit readily into other programs, and a chance to work on large stages for a broad public. Essentially, from the moment it was founded, the Next Wave had successfully institutionalized an avant-garde—at first from New York and later from abroad—that had previously been confined to more marginal, alternative venues or been forced to search for funding and recognition in Europe.

In the festival's early years, the very fact of the intermingling of forms was remarkable. But over the next decades, fusing genres and juxtaposing disciplines became accepted practice and then commonplace. Commentators came up with countless additional terms and applied them variously: live art, interdisciplinary performance, transdisciplinary, performance art, visual arts performance, devised theater, physical theater, ensemble-created performance—not to mention the explicitly hybrid forms such as dance-theater or tanztheater, circus theater or nouveau cirque, hiphopera, popera, rock-opera, and more.

Wisely, perhaps, given the scope and invention of BAM artists' work, the Next Wave Festival has never dwelled on nomenclature. Lichtenstein and later Melillo have long preferred to emphasize the experience, the encounter, and the excitement of a destination that itself suggests a new territory for many traditional patrons: Brooklyn. By the 21st century, the catchall term "performance" was in common use by artists, critics, and arts professionals. "Performance" was broad and unspecific, and thus useful as a word gesturing to this sphere of creative activity where genres are questioned, deconstructed, melted down, and merged with other forms and even with non-aesthetic fields like anthropology or science. Academic disciplines such as "Performance Studies" arose alongside this flourishing and gave the term further breadth and nuance. Meanwhile, for Next Wave audiences, the visceral charge, ambition, and surprising qualities of these unclassifiable performances is what truly matters.

## Collaboration

At the heart of these advances were collaborations, partnerships between singular artists who saw the possibility of breakthroughs together. From its inception, the Next Wave Festival embraced creative teams working across and between disciplines, facilitating collaborations through invitations, commissions, presentations, and promotion. In the first season, *THE PHOTOGRAPHER/ Far From the Truth* set the course for such genre-defying structures: Dutch artist Rob Malasch had conceived the project with composer Philip Glass, director JoAnne Akalaitis, choreographer David Gordon, playwright Robert Coe, media artist Wendall K. Harrington, and designers Santo Loquasto and Jennifer Tipton.

But another production in that same inaugural season showed just how far the producers could go and how much the traditional stage was transforming: Lee Breuer and Bob Telson's **The Gospel at Colonus**, a massive music-theater retelling of Sophocles' tragedy *Oedipus at Colonus* by Pentecostal preachers, who speak and sing of the king's suffering and redemption. In addition to a cast of five actors (including Morgan Freeman) in the tragedy's core dramatic roles, the character of Oedipus was represented in collective form by Clarence Fountain and the Five Blind Boys of Alabama. The Greek chorus took the form of a 40-member gospel choir from Fort Greene, Brooklyn—the Institutional Radio Choir. And it was this group—BAM's neighbors—who became the true hit of the show, along with a nine-musician band. As Melillo said, with 17 albums, a Sunday night radio show, and national touring recognition, "They were the obvious choice for the job. We didn't consider anyone else. They are known."

Breuer had developed the project in stages, first as a touring prototype version in 1982, then in a concert version at the Walker Art Center in Minneapolis in the fall of 1983, before premiering the full-scale realization at BAM. Drawing text from Sophocles' related plays, and joining scenes with Telson's songs, Breuer and his collaborators

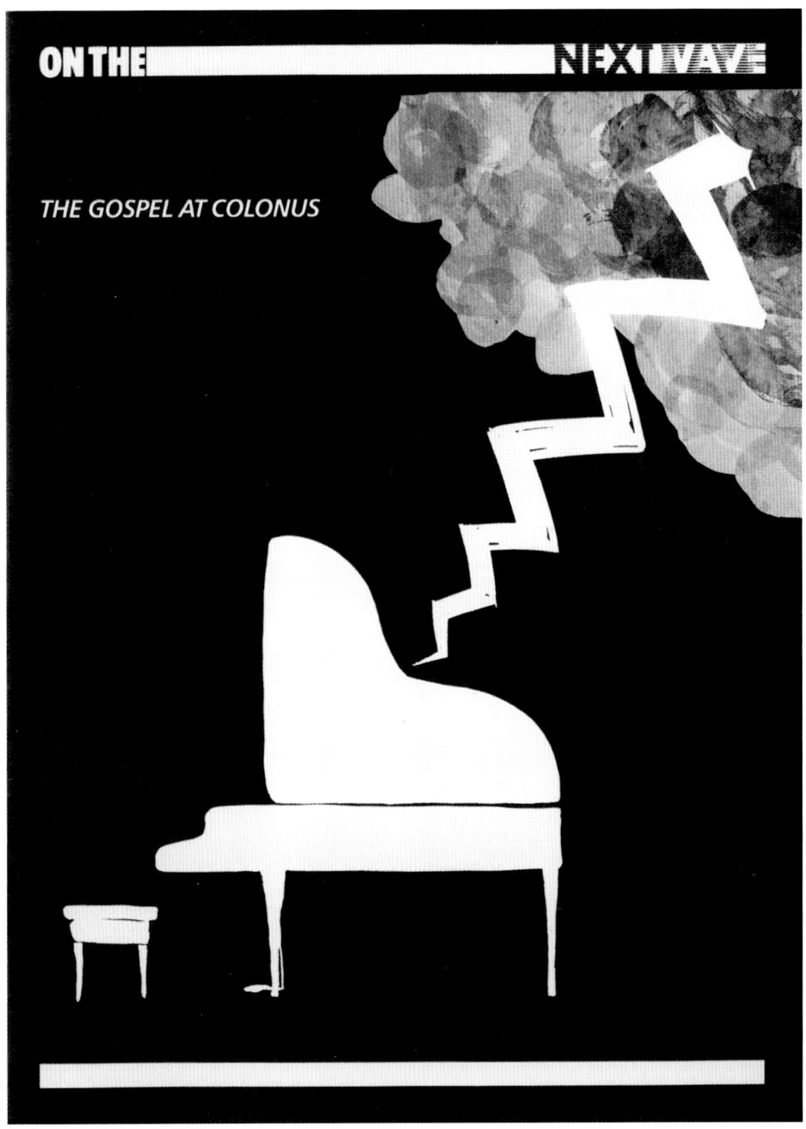


Next Wave Festival audience magazine *On the Next Wave* cover featuring *The Gospel at Colonus*, November 1983. Courtesy of BAM Hamm Archives

transformed tragedy into an ecstatic form; for this master director, *Gospel* brought "the idea of dying without dying, of being lifted directly to Heaven or taken directly into the bosom of God."

The production effectively, even startlingly, transposed the ancient myth to a Christian framework, joining ancient and modern Western traditions with stunning music and transcendent drama. The critically acclaimed production, which won an Obie Award and was a finalist for the Pulitzer Prize, eventually transferred to Broadway in 1988. Some critics struggled with its unusual approach, but the *Village Voice* raved about Telson's "soaring, ecstatic music" and *Artforum*'s David Frankel wrote that it is "full of *coups de théâtre*" in which Greek and Christian codes "dovetail seamlessly." He noted: "*The Gospel at Colonus* is a popular work; it raises the possibility of unifying in one audience people from many social spheres. This is not its least achievement."

As if orchestrated by divine will, during a particularly memorable performance, one of the pillars of the Carey Playhouse caught fire during a special thunder-and-lightning effect. Some mistook the fire for heavenly intensity, but according to news reports, actor Morgan Freeman stopped the show and directed the audience to the exits, and the choir resumed the show 15 minutes later with an improvised gospel number called "It's Out."

Critic James Leverett even called the production an example of a "new Classicism" taking shape across the arts, paralleling larger shifts in a national culture reinvigorated by "other cultures, other races, other sexualities" and paralleling cultural changes arising from changing demographics. He wrote, "Breuer gave the tables a complete turn by making the outside—the devalued, 'non'-culture into the inside."

Another collaboration, one of the most notable of the festival's early years, defined **The Birth of the Poet** in the 1985 season, pairing SoHo's experimental playwright-director Richard Foreman with the punk-influenced poet Kathy Acker, and adding a musical score written by Peter Gordon and sets by the artist David Salle. These collaborators were all major figures in the downtown experimental scene; here they joined forces for this wild, massively scaled production contemplating (among other themes) the spirit of the avant-garde in the face of encroaching apocalypse and in defiance of forces of conformity.

For Foreman, the American theater's reigning philosopher-king, who had mounted visually saturated projects exploring the frontiers of consciousness for decades in downtown Manhat-

*The Birth of the Poet*, Richard Foreman/Kathy Acker/Peter Gordon/David Salle, 1985. Photo: Leo van Velzen

tan lofts, the vast playing space of the Opera House posed a challenge. Salle's design saw giant set pieces constantly flying in and wheeling out, while the ensemble's movements brought to mind historical avant-gardes from Meyerholdian biomechanics to Futurism. Meanwhile, Acker's declarative, anatomically explicit text, with high-voltage feminist intimations of sexual dystopia and dehumanization, cast New York City in 1985 in the hallucinated twilight of ancient Rome's demise, a change "from Republic to Empire." Who are the rebel artists and who are the despots in this collapsing fantasy civilization? What satisfactions can they find—bodily, political, moral—as they wander in the fragmented ruins and journey in the mind's eye?

"As a collaboration, it fails decisively," wrote John Rockwell in the *New York Times*, labeling it "a well-intentioned, neatly crafted mess." Rockwell's response revealed a hidden assumption—often shared by audiences—that cohesion and alignment of disparate elements is the criterion for success. *The Birth of the Poet*, however, sought no such thing: it evoked the anarchic impulses of disaffected artists in an ailing Empire; if the radical collisions onstage proved inassimilable to spectators, they nonetheless formed the heart of this collaborative experiment.

**The Soldier's Tale**, adapted by the Flying Karamazov Brothers in the 1986 Next Wave from Stravinsky's *L'Histoire du Soldat*, was an early manifestation of an enduring tendency at the Next Wave: physical theater. Directed by Robert Woodruff—one of America's most searching stage directors—the production used jugglers, actors, and musicians. The composer Igor Stravinsky appears as a character in the show, and the stage of the Carey Playhouse (now the BAM Rose Cinemas) brimmed with eclectic set pieces. Comic business shared the stage with a narrator who fills in the contours of the modernist source. A loose, mutating narrative surfaces, involving an American G.I. (named "Joe King") returning home to search for the American Dream, a lost father, and his fire-eating fiancée ("Barbie Q"). Joe King faces a mad world he no longer comprehends, playing out in a series of Stravinskian interludes, physical comedy routines, and dramatic fragments. Falling somewhere between experimental theater and clowning, the production offered a new synthetic form with its own loopy logic, incorporating fiddlers, juggling, clowning, dioramas, and toy soldiers, engaging the audience with puns and antics while alluding to the starkest of themes.

Dance-theater, advanced by the major success of Tanztheater Wuppertal Pina Bausch in its many presentations at the Next Wave, became the site for many collaborative creations. **Can We Dance a Landscape? (Peut-on Danser le Paysage?)**, conceived by Karel Appel and choreographed and directed by Min Tanaka, received its American premiere at the 1989 Next Wave Festival in the Carey Playhouse, with sets designed and painted by Appel. (Tanaka also performed with the company.) Skaters swept back and forth across an upstage ramp in this apocalypse-tinged performance, with animal forms and live goats—some of them flying—contributing to an otherworldly, spellbinding tapestry. With a score of throbbing, pulsating, and ambient music, ravaged humanity confronts catastrophe in this haunting work. Similarly, **Land**, conceived and performed by the experimental dance legends Eiko & Koma with

OPPOSITE
*The Soldier's Tale*, Robert Woodruff/ The Flying Karamazov Brothers, 1986. Photo: Tom Brazil

ABOVE
*Can We Dance a Landscape? (Peut-on Danser le Paysage?)*, Karel Appel/ Min Tanaka, 1989. Photo: Nico Koster

music by Robert Mirabal and artwork by Sandra Lerner, was performed in the BAM Lepercq Space (now home to BAMcafé) in 1991 on an installation-like set—another formal expansion, in which kinetic motion and visual environment intersected.

Not all the collaborations were strictly aesthetic; lines between art and life sometimes blurred in performance too. **Still/Here**, a 1994 premiere integrating dance, video, and text, was choreographed by Bill T. Jones with music by the rock musicians Vernon Reid and Kenneth Frazelle (with folk vocalist Odetta). Bill T. Jones/Arnie Zane & Company had performed previously at BAM with **Intuitive Momentum** in 1983 and **Secret Pastures** in 1984. Zane died (of AIDS-related lymphoma) in 1988 and Jones had spent two years organizing workshops for survivors of life-threatening diseases. *Still/Here* integrated the participants' words and experiences into an aesthetic dance frame, supported by video and other multimedia elements by Gretchen Bender. Choreographed sequences expressing resilience, support, struggle, isolation, and community mix with sound and video clips from the workshop participants whose experiences directly inspired the company. Dancers sometimes interact directly with video testimonies. "Her eyes / her eyes, I remember it, I could see it in her eyes," a singer recalls as the dancers traverse the stage, recollecting in motion. Interviews with the afflicted recount moments of diagnosis; documentary-like monologues narrate their coming-to-terms with illness, despair, and mortality.

The production made a powerful expression of love, solidarity, compassion, and hope in the shadow of the AIDS epidemic, despite friction in its critical reception provoked by the

OPPOSITE
Bill T. Jones in *Still/Here*, Bill T. Jones/Arnie Zane Dance Company, 1994. Photo: Joanne Savio

ABOVE
Next Wave Series poster for *Intuitive Momentum*, Max Roach/Bill T. Jones/Arnie Zane/Connie Crothers, 1983. Courtesy of BAM Hamm Archives

*New Yorker*'s dance critic Arlene Croce in a highly controversial article in which she called the project "victim art" and refused to evaluate it as an aesthetic object. "My illness is not me / in my heart I know I will be cured / cured finally to be alive / alive alive alive." Such words, coupled with imagery from medical videos, voiceovers, and the dancers onstage, made multimedia performance part of a space between birth and death, full of transcendent energies.

Could there be a form called "popera"? Some critics and fans mused about this when a trio of genre-defying rock operas in the 1990s, created by Robert Wilson for the Thalia Theater in Hamburg, made a compelling case for a burgeoning form. Those productions hinged on the Next Wave's most famous artistic partnerships. Wilson worked with bluesy rocker Tom Waits on **The Black Rider: The Casting of the Magic Bullets** (1993), a production that captured popular imagination like few other Next Wave events. Created with legendary Beat author William S. Burroughs, the project was directed and designed by Wilson with Waits's distinctively dreamy music and lyrics alternating with Burroughs's sometimes hallucinatory texts. Originally mounted in Hamburg, it featured the Thalia's physically dexterous ensemble as flying birds, stags, skeletons, foresters, and other fantastical creatures in Wilson's signature whiteface. In a feat of aesthetic alchemy, Wilson drew on cabaret forms, elements of burlesque, biomechanics, and circus in a series of formal scenic tableaux.

Following this decided success, the Thalia produced a second Waits-Wilson team-up, **Alice**, based on Lewis Carroll's writings and life. The piece—presented in the 1995 Next Wave—drew on contributions by co-composer Kathleen Brennan and playwright Paul Schmidt, and spawned an album of songs recorded by Waits.

**Time Rocker**, Wilson's subsequent collaboration with Lou Reed, with text by Darryl Pinckney, was the last of the Thalia "trilogy" and its 1997 Next Wave presentation made a triumphant homecoming of sorts for these New York-based artists, who on a large stage found a wildly enthusiastic audience. Once again, the fluidity of Wilson's stage aesthetic allowed a nuanced collaboration to take root. Composed of short, episodic scenes, this uncategorizable music-theater work follows two lovers as they look for a time-traveling doctor across epochs. Reed's songs, performed in English by the German-speaking ensemble, range from breezy jazz to pumping disco romps to hard-charging, full-throttle rock ballads. Wilson fulfilled the fantastical tale with

shadow and hand puppets, a bowler-hatted ensemble in soft-shoe numbers, and living tableaux veering from intimate to panoramic—a futuristic vaudeville with eruptions of song. The lovers converge, singing suspended, upside down, in space and temporal motion: "If I had to, I'd call love 'time,'" says one lover. "Time has no meaning / no future, no past / and when you're in love, you don't have to ask / there's never enough time to hold love in your grasp / turning time around."

Wilson's exquisite stage picture, coupled with Reed's moving, original songs showed the soaring heights Next Wave collaborators could reach. It set a high bar for the festival, which to this day continues to promote extraordinary partnerships across art forms.

ABOVE, LEFT
Dominique Horwitz and Stefan Kurt in *The Black Rider*, Robert Wilson/Tom Waits/William S. Burroughs/Thalia Theater, 1993. Photo: Hermann and Clärchen Baus

ABOVE, RIGHT
Annette Paulmann and Jörg Holm in *Alice*, Robert Wilson/Tom Waits/Kathleen Brennan/Paul Schmidt/Thalia Theater, 1995. Photo: Dan Rest

## Nontraditional Performance

Under the artistic leadership of Harvey Lichtenstein, BAM and particularly the Next Wave Festival emerged as a top showcase for nontraditional and experimental performance. Early Next Wave productions in the 1980s and 1990s propelled the institution, bringing international renown for its programming in theater, dance, music, opera, film, and media. Among the artists closely identified with the early years of the festival were Lee Breuer and Bob Telson, Meredith Monk, Bill T. Jones and

*United States: Parts I–IV*, Laurie Anderson, 1983. Photo: Perry Hoberman

Arnie Zane, Robert Wilson, Pina Bausch, Lou Reed and John Cale, Mark Morris, Martha Clarke, John Kelly, and Elizabeth Swados—all making groundbreaking work, and all finding national exposure, access to performance spaces like the Opera House and the Lepercq Space, and a broader audience.

Of all these nontraditional artists, it was perhaps Laurie Anderson who became most explicitly identified with the Next Wave, eventually reaching a widespread international audience through her long affiliation. **United States: Parts I–IV**, her 1983 opus performed in the Next Wave Series, turned into a major event. It was a realization of Lichtenstein's ideal in every way: BAM provided a large-scale space for exactly the kind of multimedia performance it sought to encourage, an experimental aesthetic that Anderson had long germinated in SoHo's lofts and art spaces. The festival threw a spotlight on her extraordinary suggestive powers as a writer, vocalist, composer, and visual artist. For the 1989 festival, Anderson went on to reveal another dimension of her work, creating and performing **Empty Places** with computer animation, photography, original music, and commentary delivered in her inimitable offbeat style. For *United States*, Anderson anchored a team of onstage collaborators. But *Empty Places* was a true solo: one woman holding the stage alone, moving among a series of MIDI keyboards, using her violin, singing and speaking through electronic mediations but also, to surprising effect, unfiltered. Anderson offered stories and songs examining the behemoth state of Reagan's America, and its bewildering effect on the spirit, perhaps best captured in the song "Strange Angels."

Anderson's live multimedia performances blurred lines between rock concert, theater production, and art installation. They also tangled traditional categories of "high" culture and "pop culture," pleasing crowds as entertainment while introducing experimental vocals, electronic composition, and nonlinear narratives into the mix. Anderson's performances confirmed her status as a major American artist, whose work spans across genres, and who could command the Opera House stage as a soloist. As Catherine Texier wrote in the *New York Times*, "the biggest surprise is that she drops her electronic masks and sings." Anderson reliably filled the house at the Next Wave, but she remained a multifaceted creator in continual self-invention. She went on to present other Next Wave works such as **Songs and Stories from Moby Dick** (1999), based on the novel by Herman Melville, **Delusion** (2010), and **Landfall** (2014). Album recordings corresponding to these live presentations solidified and spread her fame.

For *Moby Dick*, mounted with the experimental director Anne Bogart, Anderson eclipsed herself with an intricate visual design (with Chris Kondek) and elaborate music and lyrics. She performed with her violin, guitar, and talking stick on a striking set with sleek projections conveying the sublime depths of the ocean; Anderson would settle into an armchair as a reader to recount aspects of the novel with electronic mediation. Additional performers—notably actor Tom Nelis who played the role of Ahab—expanded the scope, a massive spectacle with text, dance, scientific data, and literary dimensions. The piece was profoundly hybrid, an amalgamation of the source novel and Anderson's subjective response to its sensuous contours, delivered via dramatic monologues, projections, and a full musical score.

A subsequent breakthrough in live form came in 1993 with **The Cave**, conceived by composer Steve Reich and the video artist Beryl Korot. Directed by Carey Perloff, this technically virtuosic live performance explored the Cave of the Patriarchs in the West Bank, via biblical scripture and documentary film footage projected onto a series of large screens, synching rhythmically with Reich's astonishing score. In combination, these elements—with 17 musicians and singers—created a mesmerizing tapestry, tracing the lines of religious tradition back to Abraham, who was buried in the cave, and contemplated what ground might be shared by Islam, Judaism, and Christianity. Part concert, part video installation, the performance offered many overlapping and simultaneous layers even in the set's multiple

Laurie Anderson in her *Empty Places*, 1989.
Photo: Linda Alaniz/
Martha Swope Associates

tiers—a massive, epic-length spectacle with glimpses of history, geography, and faith in visual and sonic counterpoint. The transcendent temporalities of Reich's score brought ancient, modern, and present times into seamless interplay.

Another imaginative epic came from West Coast composer, saxophonist, and activist Fred Ho, who presented his **Journey Beyond the West: The New Adventures of MONKEY** at the Majestic Theater in the 1997 season. Adapted from a 16th-century Chinese adventure serial about a nervous priest dispatched to India to retrieve the Buddhist scriptures for China, Ho conceived the piece as a lively mix of martial arts, dance, theater, and music—a living comic book, with music. ("Martial arts," Ho once declared, "is going to kick the ass of modern dance.") His score for singers and a "monkey orchestra" fused Eastern and Western influences, ranging from traditional Chinese opera to raucous jazz. In an interview with music critic Kyle Gann, Ho called it "a kind of Tang dynasty Wizard of Oz." Ho described it this way: "What I'm trying to do is to try to change the American musical landscape . . . to develop a new American music that is anchored in the traditions of people of color in this society. To de-Europeanize the world." Ho returned to the Next Wave in 2001 with the New York premiere of **Once Upon a Time in Chinese America . . .**, another music-theater epic and martial-arts ballet using kung fu, tai chi, and hand-to-hand-boxing.

**Songs for 'Drella—a fiction**, Lou Reed and John Cale's 1989 tribute production celebrating the life of Andy Warhol, offered a collaboration between two of the most influential downtown rock musicians from the Velvet Underground, a band embraced and promoted by Warhol. But the piece also evoked and reveled in the spirit of New York's midcentury avant-garde: Warhol's open houses, his Factory circle, Brillo boxes, films, paintings, writings, his ceaseless self-invention and luminous personality. The composers of the song cycle also performed it, Cale at the piano and Reed seated with guitar; video projections upstage conveyed biography, the spaces of this disappearing New York, and the expanse of Warhol's mind. The songs (also released as an album) had a hard edge but a transcendent, elegiac spirit—the perfect eulogy.

"I'm sorry that I doubted your good heart / things always seem to end before they start," sings Reed in "Hello It's Me," reflecting on learning of Warhol's death. Depths of feeling emerged from this collaboration expressing affinities from two major artists for their lost contemporary. These two legendary iconoclasts looked utterly at home on the Next Wave stage, where they embodied the spirit of nontraditional performance.

## International Focus

In addition to promoting collaboration and fluidity of form, the Next Wave expanded the field of performance through its commitment to introducing significant international artists to audiences in the United States. In his 1983 announcement of the festival's founding, Lichtenstein wrote, "It is ironic that while America's artists are recognized as leaders around the world, it is mostly the European opera houses and theaters which have sponsored their work." The festival began with an impulse to give genre-crossing artists a native platform in the United States, but BAM's producers soon discovered the other side of that coin: New York also needed to see important artistic developments from abroad, and there were no major, consistent venues for large-scale experimental work where that could happen.

In its early seasons, the festival had immediately changed the landscape of American dance through its presentations of the German choreographer Pina Bausch and of the Flemish company Rosas, led by Anne Teresa De Keersmaeker. But a turning point for the Next Wave came in 1987 with the landmark production of **The Mahabharata**, staged by British theater director Peter Brook, a major event that firmly established BAM as a premier venue for international artists as well as for American iconoclasts.

In 1970, Brook had cofounded the International Centre of Theatre Research with Micheline Rozan in Paris, where he worked not with star actors but with ensemble members from all over the world, immersing in the modernist experimental aesthetics of Antoine Artaud and Jerzy Grotowski and traditional techniques from Africa and Asia. He initiated a long-standing relationship with BAM in 1971 with the presentation of his legendary Royal Shakespeare Company rendering of *A Midsummer Night's Dream*, so in 1973 Lichtenstein invited Brook and the new ICTR company to BAM for a series of workshops and performances. This included a staging of *Conference of the Birds*, based on a 12th-century Sufi story of a flock in search of God, journeying together through Africa, India, and elsewhere in search of storytelling methods. Rather than merely mimicking these narrative forms, the ensemble attempted to synthesize them into their own projects in their Paris laboratory, raising a number of exciting (and hotly debated) questions: What could happen in a self-consciously cosmopolitan crucible like ICTR? What would

a "world theater" approach to interpreting classical texts yield? Could the contemporary theater reach new forms by combining aspects of long-existing ones, with performers drawn from many backgrounds and training? How to address issues of cultural appropriation, while broadening the Western theatrical imagination by expanding influences, subjects, sources? Nothing less was at stake in Brook's ICTR work.

Lichtenstein continued to scout the borough for suitable locations for the company's work, which was highly responsive to site and sculpted to the architecture of playing spaces, trying schools, community centers, navy facilities, and other locations. A breakthrough finally came when Lichtenstein discovered the Majestic Theater (now the BAM Harvey Theater), an aban-

*Songs for 'Drella—a fiction*, Lou Reed/John Cale, 1989. Photo courtesy of BAM Hamm Archives

doned movie theater on Fulton Street near BAM that underwent a $4 million partial renovation with help from the City of New York.

The Majestic was perfect for Brook's company. The scale resembled the group's Paris base at the Théâtre des Bouffes du Nord, with an intimate relationship between the house and stage, and with a stately formality offset by its timeworn condition. BAM had found a theatrical ruin, and left key elements unrestored. As author Jonathan Cott put it in a reflection on *The Mahabharata*, the Majestic, like the Théâtre des Bouffes du Nord, offered "a tremendously warm, living atmosphere that a brand new theater can't have. Ours is like the subway... it's got all of the graffiti of a hundred years on it."

Jeffrey Kissoon and Tapa Sudana in *The Mahabharata*, Peter Brook/ Jean-Claude Carrière, 1987. Photo: Martha Swope

Lichtenstein invited the ICTR to open the space with its three-part, nine-hour adaptation of the ancient Indian epic. *The Mahabharata* was based on a 100,000-word, two-line stanza Sanskrit text, the longest poem in the world, depicting the dynastic struggle between two rival families. Among other things, it is a treatise on war, mortality, and power, and Indian and Indonesian culture have long roots in its language and stories. For Hindus, it is a book of life. For Brook and company, the text's long history of authorial permutations, additions, and evolutions was an invitation for the devising ensemble to arrange it in illuminating ways for the stage. The text was adapted by Jean-Claude Carrière, and the production—which had played to packed houses in Paris in 1985 and 1986 and could be seen at BAM either on successive evenings or in marathon presentations—included 28 actors and 5 musicians from 18 countries. The simplest forms of storytelling shared the Majestic stage with 35 cubic yards of mud, pools of water, and fiery pyres.

Audiences and critics were enthralled—and ultimately divided. The national press accounts were voluminous. Some spectators actually found the epic too compressed, its mysteries truncated, its message (with intimations of nuclear war) muddled. Others found astonishment at the reimagined act of storytelling and the spiritually invested qualities in the acting. *New York Times* critic Margaret Croyden wrote: "At the end of the performance, many in the audience . . . were full of wonderment and awe at what they had seen. For them, Mr. Brook's theatrical magic had worked, evoking the possibilities of live theater with grand themes in the hands of a master magician."

By spotlighting a multinational, multiethnic ensemble working across cultural traditions—and in an exciting

Marie Brassard in *Polygraph*, Robert Lepage/ Marie Brassard/Le Théâtre Repère, 1990. Photo: Martha Swope

new space full of historical resonance—the Next Wave had demonstrated a capacity to give national and even global exposure to innovative international artists. With this project, BAM audiences understood that the Next Wave wasn't exclusively about experimental formalism; the festival—now with a variety of stage spaces—could also be a place for discovering unfamiliar artists and companies from around the globe.

More experimental work from abroad followed from this milestone. Acclaimed Québécois director Robert Lepage made his Next Wave debut in 1990 with **Polygraph**, a live-action "metaphysical detective story" with film elements, designed by Lepage and coauthored with Marie Brassard. Lepage returned in the 1992 season with **Needles and Opium**, a solo performance moving from autobiography to the lives of Miles Davis and Jean Cocteau, via the mesmerizing, nuanced visual layers for which this young Canadian director was becoming celebrated. In 1996, Lepage and his Ex Machina company returned with a far larger project, **The Seven Streams of the River Ota**, which incorporated puppetry and cinematography into live theater. **Elsinore**, Lepage's high-tech reimagining of Shakespeare's *Hamlet*, was staged in 1997, and **Geometry of Miracles**, one of the director's masterworks, was presented in the 1999 program, offering a media-infused dreamscape surveying, among other things, Frank Lloyd Wright's architecture and the writings of George Gurdjieff. Other Next Wave

productions included **Lipsynch** (2009), a nine-hour epic about singers and the power of speech, and **The Blue Dragon** (2013), about a Canadian artist in China. Lepage returned to BAM in 2017 with the production of *887*, a visual autobiography contemplating 1960s Québec, among other threads of time. The director's use of media elements and his design-based aesthetic proved profoundly influential for U.S. theater makers and the sheer beauty of his stage compositions made Lepage a favorite of Next Wave audiences.

The Next Wave also made it possible for American audiences to glimpse the important postmodern performance experiments taking place since the 1980s in Belgium, Japan, and France. Following on the example of De Keersmaeker and Rosas—whose major Next Wave presentations included **Rosas Danst Rosas** (1986), **Drumming** (2001), and **Rain** (2003) in collaboration with composer Steve Reich—new ensembles were investigating temporality and presence onstage.

The Brussels-based Needcompany, under the direction of Jan Lauwers, was one such group, quickly becoming a festival staple for its humor and densely layered journeys in time and

OPPOSITE
Normand Daneau and Rebecca Blankenship (featured) in *The Seven Streams of the River Ota*, Robert Lepage/Ex Machina, 1996. Photo: Dan Rest

ABOVE
Cynthia Loemij in *Drumming*, included in *Steve Reich Evening*, Steve Reich/Anne Teresa De Keersmaeker/Rosas/Ictus, 2008. Photo: Jack Vartoogian

space. **Morning Song**, the ensemble's biographical performance tapestry of memory and mystery, brought them to the festival in 1999, followed in 2001 by **King Lear**, their wild rock-saturated dance deconstruction of Shakespeare. **Isabella's room** (2004) featured a tour-de-force performance by Viviane De Muynck, who played a blind woman in a science study allowing a camera to project images of objects into her brain. **The Deer House**, ruminating on tragic deaths in Kosovo across several media forms, was featured in the 2010 program.

**Noiject**, by the Japanese ensemble KARAS with choreography and design by Saburo Teshigawara, at the BAM Majestic Theater in 1994, was a rare opportunity for New York audiences to encounter the hybridity of a company traversing classical ballet, butoh, and modern dance. Moving from ambient evocations of industry to a sonic roar at its zenith, the breathtaking piece saw the company, clad in black, dance with fervor in front of large metallic panels—a postindustrial

ABOVE
*The Deer House*, Jan Lauwers/Needcompany, 2010. Photo: Richard Termine

OPPOSITE, LEFT
Viviane De Muynck in *Morning Song*, Jan Lauwers/Needcompany, 1999. Photo courtesy of BAM Hamm Archives

OPPOSITE, RIGHT
*Noiject*, Saburo Teshigawara/KARAS, 1994. Photo: Dan Rest

apocalyptic vision. The final sequences were particularly memorable—dancers ricocheted around the space at hyper speed like human pinballs as the walls lit up with flashing lightbulbs, to industrial pulsations shaking the theater's walls. *Noiject* culminated in an eruption of electrified, kinetic energy, amid dehumanized figures and intimations of dystopia. For U.S. audiences it was a rare chance to become immersed in Japan's avant-garde and its significant crossing of traditional lines.

Another foreign sensation came in the form of an equestrian theater troupe. The company Zingaro, hailing from France but drawing on a panoply of global popular traditions, presented two major works: **Chimère** (1996) and **Eclipse** (1998). BAM set up a special off-site venue for these horseback performances, erecting a bigtop tent at Battery Park City to make room for the 26 horses, their riders, a giant pool surrounded by candles, traditional Rajasthan and Korean folk musicians, dancers, and acrobats. With an air of mysticism and the panache of circus, Zingaro, led by director Bartabas, blended myth, athleticism, and spectacle into a dream-like evening—a mix of cultural traditions, and, like so much Next Wave work, far beyond national categories.

## The New Millennium

Joseph V. Melillo had served as the festival's producing director since its inception. Following Lichtenstein's retirement in 1999, he faced the daunting task of maintaining the Next Wave's commitment to the headliner artists who had helped define it—now accepted as the most important artists of their time—while also staying true to the festival's mission of presenting the new and promoting younger artists. Once again, the festival's capacities were greatly expanded with a new footprint; this time, opportunity came with the opening in 2012 of the Richard B. Fisher Building, and specifically the Fishman Space, a 250-seat completely flexible venue, purpose-built to accommodate hybrid performances of all kinds. A rising generation, increasingly interested in

*Chimère: Equestrian Theater by Zingaro*, Bartabas, 1996. Photo courtesy of BAM Hamm Archives

digital technology, object-based performances, and physical and visual arts performance, now had a designated space for their work. With fewer seats than the Harvey Theater or the Opera House, the Fishman Space offered a more intimate way to encounter these artists and their discoveries.

By now, certain kinds of formal experimentation were uncontroversial, accepted practice in the performing arts. A generation schooled in "interdisciplinary" approaches explored questions and themes with freedom to move among and between genres and forms, even as they uncovered new frontiers and embraced possibilities raised by new technology. Globalization and networks were omnipresent, but corresponding questions about cultural identity, race, power, and borders lingered, engaging many Next Wave artists.

With **Come home Charley Patton** (2004), writer, performer, artist, and choreographer Ralph Lemon completed his **Geography** series, a trilogy exploring the spaces and reverberations between Asia, West Africa, and the United States through dance, narrative, and installation. *Charley Patton* touched on embodied and enacted forms of memory, and personal and diasporic histories carried in the body, including Freedom Bus riders, ancient dances from West Africa, and lynchings in Lemon's Minnesota hometown.

Architectural set pieces, wheeled in and around the Harvey Theater stage—themselves fragments of larger structures—gave visual weight to the themes of cultural dislocation and immersion in local histories. Lemon's ensemble itself combined American and West African dancers; their collaboration, with Lemon, in investigating the traces and remains of disappearing and vulnerable histories, formed an essential part of the project. In a powerful sequence, Lemon was water-hosed by another performer as he danced to a blues track, later eclipsed by the ensemble's ecstatic elongated frenzy, the body continuing on in time and space after these echoes of violence perpetrated on civil rights marchers. The piece closes with a recording by James Baldwin (represented by a cartoon of the author on a screen mounted along the proscenium). "Something is happening in the Western world—everybody in one way or another feels this," says Baldwin, addressing another era's dislocation but now speaking for the globalizing era at hand. "In short, the center, what is presumed to be the center of the earth, has shifted, and the evolution of man has shifted with it."

Footage from the production reappeared in **How Can You Stay In The House All Day And Not Go Anywhere?** Lemon's subsequent work, which played the Harvey Theater in the

2010 festival. Here the choreographer references twin muses behind the earlier works, adding yet another, reflective layer to the granularity of the project—this one perhaps more introspective and personal. “After all the digressions into its particular matters of American culture and race, the end of our 2004 performance work *Come home Charley Patton* was an attempt at the beginning glimpse into some kind of liberation. A breaking down of an empirical dancing body in the theater. Perhaps after all the sincere tourism of the rest of *Geography* I arrived at a tourism of the other of myself.”

For **the 51st (dream) state**, conceived and written by Sekou Sundiata and directed by Christopher McElroen, the poet-composer performed along with vocalists and musicians on the Opera House stage in the 2006 festival. The piece raised questions about the American nation-state and the military empire it maintains: a projection in the early moments reads, “Will this cost America its soul?” The reflections that followed traversed the nation’s conscience and unmoored psychic landscape in the wake of 9/11 and the invasion of Iraq. Combining spoken word, monologue, political polemic, poetry, jazz, photo montage, and video art, the project excavated the contradictions of a country built on myths.

Another multimedia global travelogue traced lines across borders and proposed new maps: **Cast No Shadow** (2007), by Isaac Julien and Russell Maliphant, played in three parts on the Harvey stage: "True North" was performed by the Russell Maliphant Dance Company with a film installation by Julien; "Fantôme Afrique" was a film featuring on-screen choreography and dancer Stephen Galloway; and "Small Boats" was again performed by the dance company with Julien's film. In an indication of the festival's reach, the piece was co-commissioned with London's Sadler's Wells and the 2007 Performa biennial of visual arts performance, and was presented at the 25th Next Wave Festival. In the unforgettable third part, the dancers share the stage space with the film, inhabiting the shipyards and embodying the motion of passage. They cling to nets hanging from the ceiling, while projections of seawater and people floating in it

OPPOSITE
Ralph Lemon in his *How Can You Stay In The House All Day And Not Go Anywhere?*, 2010. Photo: Stephanie Berger

ABOVE
*the 51st (dream) state*, Sekou Sundiata, 2006. Photo: Stephanie Berger

and defying its grip, command the eye. One of the current century's great questions—migration of peoples—had been breached and beautifully evoked. Performa subsequently co-presented **The Humans** in the 2013 festival, a performance piece by the British artist Alexandre Singh incorporating theater, music, and sculpture. Originally conceived as an installation (at the Witte de With Center for Contemporary Art in Rotterdam), *The Humans* drew from Aristophanes' comic narratives to follow two spirits, Tophole and Pantalingua, opposed to the creation of the Earth. Their objections shadow humanity as it develops, evoked in the sculptural scenic design by Singh and Jessica Tankard, in choreography by Flora Sans, and in costumes evoking classical traditions from ancient Athens to commedia dell'arte.

**red, black & GREEN: a blues**, presented in the 2012 program, also embedded themes of global circulation into an architectural visual structure. The project's creators—including Marc Bamuthi Joseph, director Michael Garcés, the Living Word Project, and sets designed by visual

Sam Crane (featured) in *The Humans*, Alexandre Singh/Witte de With Center for Contemporary Art/Performa, 2013. Photo: Richard Termine

artist Theaster Gates—used a range of African American musical styles and forms to explore questions of geography, race, and urban environmentalism. The audience entered via the stage, moving among the performers; the house in which they perform breaks apart into four mobile architectural units—a project highlighting the Fishman Space's flexibility, while meditating on sustainability and what it might mean for cities.

Performed in the 2013 festival, **Bodycast: An Artist Lecture by Suzanne Bocanegra Starring Frances McDormand** challenged spatial parameters, too, but in a completely different way, departing imaginatively and purposefully from the standard limitations of an artist's talk. Created by the visual artist Suzanne Bocanegra with director Paul Lazar, composer David Lang, singer Theo Bleckmann, and the actor Frances McDormand, *Bodycast* merged personal narrative and aesthetic commentary.

Frances McDormand in *Bodycast: An Artist Lecture by Suzanne Bocanegra Starring Frances McDormand*, Suzanne Bocanegra/ Paul Lazar, 2013. Photo: Rebecca Greenfield

---

Twenty-first century audiences have become noticeably more comfortable with ambiguities of genre and outcome. Their openness was rewarded in **Inside Out**, a 2009 production by Sweden's Cirkus Cirkör with live music by the rock band Irya's Playground and directed by Tilde Björfors. The Howard Gilman Opera House stage looked at times like a multi-ring circus, with a white-faced, white-suited, white-wigged ringmaster alternating between philosophizing on the eternal mysteries and playing pranks on audience members and conducting magic tricks. Cirkus Cirkör combined dance, video projections, and grotesqueries with hoop acrobatics, juggling, trapeze acts, and pop songs. The silly shared the stage with the wondrous and profane.

Jens Engman in *Inside Out*, Tilde Björfors/ Cirkus Cirkör, 2009. Photo: Jack Vartoogian

Looking at Next Wave productions over the decades, it is striking how technology brought fluidity to the mixed media elements. In early productions, dance might have co-existed with video; theater alternated with film sequences. But increasingly sophisticated digital systems for projection and sound made their integration more holistic.

**Persephone**, a 2010 production by Ridge Theater, demonstrated the transformed artistic horizons made possible by technology. The piece, directed by Bob McGrath, used the company's lush, intricate projections by Laurie Olinder, and film by the

acclaimed filmmaker Bill Morrison to recast the myth, time-traveling in 19th-century pictorial, presentational theater tableaux and integrating them into a 21st-century mediascape. (Warren Leight supplied the show's book, and Ben Neill and Mimi Goese wrote the original music.) Time-lapse photography was juxtaposed with classical, sculptural acting, inviting spectators to watch closely as the performers inhabited many realms simultaneously.

In the many productions Melillo traveled to see in this era of digital revolutions, he noticed a striking tendency: a resurgence of artistic interest in physical objects for live performance. This phenomenon seemed all the more remarkable to him in an era where identities and lives were increasingly found online. Whether objects in live time and real space are antidotes to the technologies dominating our lives or further expressions of it, artists in Europe were thinking very differently about the transformative powers of technology than Americans were, Melillo noticed.

*Persephone*, Bob McGrath/
Ridge Theater, 2010.
Photo: Stephanie Berger

Part of his mission was to bring their perspectives and innovations to New York. "Somehow, we now once again understand the visual and the physical in live performance, in a social space of the theater, just as we instinctively understand it on our screens."

French director Aurélien Bory fused physical-theater and nouveau cirque in **Les sept planches de la ruse (The Seven Boards of Skill)**, a performance in the 2008 Next Wave by his Compagnie 111. Chinese acrobats and Peking opera performers push, scale, topple, and move a series of three- and four-sided wood blocks, some of them weighing 500 pounds. The mix of circus arts and inventive visual geometries illuminated the elegant playful spirit of art and human ingenuity. **Timber**, presented in the 2012 season, was billed as an "evening-length percussion sextet" by composer Michael Gordon. But the sound and the visuals both derived from six hardware-store variety wooden 2x4s, cut to different lengths for varying pitches, captured by microphones along with other suspended objects. Structures in motion also provided the artistic engine of **Hans was Heiri** (2013), by the Swiss directing duo Martin Zimmermann and Dimitri de Perrot. An open-walled, four-room unit turned and rotated, taking five tumbling performers with it in an antic physical spectacle.

Some productions proposed striking new approaches to stage space or to audience configurations. **Roman Tragedies**, a theater production by director Ivo van Hove (with his ensemble Toneelgroep Amsterdam), transformed the Opera House in order to immerse and implicate the spectators in this trilogy about corruption of the body politic. Van Hove boldly adapted Shakespeare's *Coriolanus*, *Julius Caesar*, and *Antony and Cleopatra* into one event (presented in the 2012 season). Van Hove's longtime collaborator, the set designer Jan Versweyveld, placed the audience in the middle of the performance environment, which included a working bar right onstage. Video artist Tal Yarden placed live feeds of the actors on huge screens, even as they moved among the audience, so that the Roman amphitheater took both material and virtual form.

OPPOSITE
*Les sept planches de la ruse (The Seven Boards of Skill)*, Aurélien Bory/ Scènes de la Terre/ Compagnie 111, 2008. Photo: Richard Termine

ABOVE
*Timber*, Michael Gordon/ Mantra Percussion, 2012. Photo: Mike Benigno

**We Have An Anchor**, presented in the Harvey Theater in the 2013 season by the filmmaker Jem Cohen, also took a landscape approach. A tribute to Cape Breton, Nova Scotia, the performance combined films projected onto five large screens with poems, folkloric texts, and an original score performed live by seven indie-rock musicians (who composed it collectively). *New York Times* music critic Jon Pareles described it as "a reverie and a scrapbook, moving amid the natural and the man-made," and said the project evoked both "the sublimity of seascapes, cliffs, fields and forests, or the mundanity of a strip mall or a truck stop."

South African artist William Kentridge, best known for his drawings, prints, and animations, invigorated his chamber opera **Refuse the Hour** with expansive media elements in the 2015 festival. The production explored ideas and compared experiences of time, ruminating in lectures and in video segments about black holes, the speed of light, and the myth of Perseus,

ABOVE
*We Have An Anchor*, Jem Cohen/Wordless Music, 2013. Photo: Ed Lefkowicz

OPPOSITE
William Kentridge and Joanna Dudley in *Refuse the Hour*, William Kentridge/Philip Miller, 2015. Photo: Stephanie Berger

among other topics. Composer Philip Miller created a score making use of metronomes and clocks, among other temporal elements, while Kentridge explored anatomy and movement with objects, in lecture form, and on film. The 2015 season saw another screen-stage hybrid: **Helen Lawrence**, directed by Stan Douglas and written by Chris Haddock, made use of a downstage scrim separating the stage from the Howard Gilman Opera House. While actors onstage played this film-noir tale about the femme fatale title character, cameras captured the scenes and projected them, so that audiences took in both the live action and its filmic reproduction or computer simulation at the same time.

Another striking facet of the Next Wave's 21st-century productions: the fascination with technology, the wonder and optimism for the future expressed in the opening of *THE PHOTOGRAPHER/ Far From the Truth*, often gives way to anxieties about its dystopian implications. Artists sometimes placed machines at center stage; human behavior often revolves around objects—mechanized or not.

Man also faces off against machine in **Sans Objet**, Aurélien Bory's highly original 2012 presentation. Conceived, designed, and directed by Bory, the production was an extended, elaborate dance between two men in suits and a massive machine—a robot prototype from the 1970s.

At first it is hidden, submerged. Then, once visible, the movements of its long, telescope-shaped trunk manipulate, sliding pieces of the floor, suggesting the movements of the human performers. At times it becomes an intimate duet—sensual, beautifully acrobatic, alternately comical. At moments the men appear to be extensions of the machine, such as during an extended dance in which they take on mechanical arm and leg movements and their heads are hidden behind a large screen. Other times they adapt to the alterations to stage objects and spaces the robot makes. It is a feat of virtuosity, very likely one of the most complicated physical interactions with a machine seen onstage to date, with elements of dance and vaudeville, spectacle, curiosity. While the specter of dehumanization lies behind it, the piece ultimately demonstrates human ingenuity at the same time.

Annie Dorsen's **A Piece of Work: A machine-made Hamlet** challenged assumptions of humanists and technologists alike when it played in the 2013 season. Dorsen's "algorithmic theater" project initially put computerized chatbots center stage, asking machines that had been fed (as data) the text of Shakespeare's *Hamlet* (perhaps the greatest drama in the English language), who then generated a unique, one-time only rendering of the play at each performance, speak-

Olivier Alenda and Olivier Boyer in *Sans Objet*, Aurélien Bory/ Compagnie 111, 2012. Photo: Pavel Antonov

ing phrases and words in algorithmically determined orders. The final scene of this brilliant work involved a human element: at alternating performances, the acclaimed downtown actors Joan MacIntosh and Scott Shepherd performed the computer-generated version live, onstage as they heard it through an earpiece for the first time. Hamlet, the reflective prince who normally speaks with the eloquence of great verse, was displaced by machines; Dorsen remade the classic for a posthumanist world, finding heightened live consciousness in the actor's spontaneity.

Director, designer, and choreographer James Thierrée extended the possibilities of tanz-theater in **Tabac Rouge**, presented in the 2015 Next Wave. Based in movement—ranging from bio-mechanical to balletic to clowning—Thierrée's work is also profoundly environmental. Much of the movement responds in shape and space to the installation-like design—metal, scaffolding,

*A Piece of Work: A machine-made Hamlet*, Annie Dorsen, 2013. Photo: Rebecca Greenfield

wires, industrial lamps, and a huge suspended kinetic structure of pipes and mirrored panels. As the score ranges from nostalgic accordion music to intimate chamber music to throbbing techno bass lines conveying contemporary urgency, a series of dream-like episodes unfold—sometimes elegiac, sometimes anarchic. Highly imagistic, architectural, and dense with sensation, Thierrée's work crosses a threshold from nouveau cirque into dance-theater, exploring themes of objects, mechanization, and our creative powers. Humans act like machines; objects and technologies take on lives of their own, while at the center of it all one man, anchored in his red armchair (performed by Thierrée), apparently originates these visions in his divine, virtuosic imagination.

Additional development visible in the festival's recent years—performances melding media paid homage to earlier artists, adding another layer of meaning. Daniele Finzi Pasca and his Compagnia Finzi Pasca composed a visual homage to Anton Chekhov in the 2012

Valérie Doucet in *Tabac Rouge*, James Thierrée/ La Compagnie du Hanneton, 2015. Photo: Jack Vartoogian

Next Wave. **Donka: A Letter to Chekhov** summoned the great dramatist-author's "laughter-through-tears" Russia through a contemporary idiom of clowning, trapeze arts, hoop dancing, juggling, and song, alongside dramatic scenes, silhouetted movement sequences, and video projection. An enormous wall of reflective panels made possible farce-like entrances and exits for one sequence—all part of an idiosyncratic, free-associating whimsical response to Chekhov's ruminations on time.

Productions like these show how far the art of performance has evolved since the beginning of the Next Wave—while also coming full circle. In 1983, *THE PHOTOGRAPHER/ Far From the Truth* reached into aesthetic history for inspiration; it mused on the life and inventions of a Victorian innovator while demonstrating the power of new mixed media approaches to the stage. Today, the synthesis of genres, the fragmentation of forms and identities, and ironies of perspective are all a given, thanks to the festival's success. Today's Next Wave artists may have absorbed the freedom to cross boundaries, forged by their predecessors, but they continue to look back for inspiration as they push forward with new discoveries.

*Donka: A Letter to Chekhov*, Compagnia Finzi Pasca, 2012. Photo: Pavel Antonov

As a producer and director, my interest is in how new works are created and how we distinguish between artistic forms. What I marvel at is that BAM definitely has a BAM audience that trusts you. Certainly things sell in different ways, but you have cultivated an audience based on trust. One of the beautiful things about BAM is that you've given a home to such extraordinary, unique artists—ultimately you're curating and choosing the artists you believe are the most relevant, the most promising of our time—and your responsibility, the role you have, is to find the artists that we see on the BAM stages. People bring them to you, you find them on your own, artists approach you—but ultimately you're confronted with a choice. It's what drives you to them. And somewhere, at some point, you say to yourself: "This is an artist I will support. This is a BAM artist."

**Beth Morrison**

Theater and Opera Director

*Remains*, John Jasperse Company, 2016. Photo: Julieta Cervantes

# Scenes from the Next Wave

Susan Yung

1983

# The Gospel at Colonus

Lee Breuer, Bob Telson

*The Gospel at Colonus*, which closed out the first Next Wave Festival in 1983, was based on Sophocles' *Oedipus at Colonus*, with passages from *Oedipus Rex* and *Antigone*. It was so successful that it was recorded for *Great Performances* by PBS and was later restaged on Broadway. In retrospect, it's easy to see the broad appeal of director Lee Breuer and lyricist-composer Bob Telson's mashup of the Greek legend of Oedipus as told through a Pentecostal African American gospel service, but at first glance the premise was undeniably ambitious.

The myth's major themes of mortality, forgiveness, reckoning, and ascension are substantial topics for the many thrilling gospel and blues songs that span an emotional scale from grief to elation. These are strung together by sermons, oratory, and movement, supported by the massive sonic and visual foundation of the Brooklyn-based Institutional Radio Choir.

The production took place in the Carey Playhouse, which in 1998 was converted into the BAM Rose Cinemas. The set, by Alison Yerxa, who also co-designed the lighting and costumes—notable for blending African influences with 1980s New York style—is shaped like an amphitheater, with the chorus arrayed around the pulpit and piano on a sunken platform. The stairs—aisles for the stadium-style seating—are used effectively by the players to indicate ascent, descent, or simply the act of a journey, and the readily visible gestures and ensemble movements of the chorus kinetically underscore the drama taking place.

Morgan Freeman—then a little-known off-Broadway actor—suffused the role of "The Messenger" in *Gospel* with a firm and gentle authority, providing narration, sermons, and a benediction. He was joined in the cast by Carl Lumbly, Isabell Monk, Robert Earl Jones, Jevetta Steele, and Kevin Davis. Oedipus was played by Clarence Fountain and the Five Blind Boys of Alabama, additional musicians include J.J. Farley and the Original Soul Stirrers, the J.D. Steele Singers, and the Bob Telson Band. Telson, a musical polymath, was the organist for Five Blind Boys in addition to playing with the Philip Glass Ensemble for a spell, and writing successful pop songs. Breuer was known for his work with Mabou Mines, an experimental theater company cofounded with Ruth Maleczech, Philip Glass, JoAnne Akalaitis, and David Warrilow—providentially, each eventually presented work at BAM.

The combination of ancient mythology and modern-day evangelism in a musical theater-style revue is unorthodox, but proved to be timeless and broadly embraced by audiences. The dramatic arc's roller coaster ride wends through incest, suicide, blindings, and exile—but ultimately ends on a high note, with Oedipus facing redemption and a peaceful death. As "Lift Him Up," the penultimate number, is sung, the house itself seems to shake from its foundations to its rafters, surrounding the raucous cast and rapturous audience.

Morgan Freeman in *The Gospel at Colonus*, Lee Breuer/Bob Telson, 1983. Photo courtesy of BAM Hamm Archives

1984, 1992, 2012

# Einstein on the Beach

Philip Glass, Robert Wilson, Lucinda Childs

The 1984 Next Wave revival of *Einstein on the Beach* came together at a propitious time in the downtown New York performance art scene. Composer Philip Glass and director Robert Wilson were on the rise, experimenting but not yet established as canonical artists. The opera had premiered at the Avignon Festival in France nearly a decade prior in its incipient version, with choreography by Andy deGroat. Following a tour of Europe, it was staged in New York at the Metropolitan Opera House, but only because Glass and Wilson had scraped up enough money for two self-financed performances. For the revival at BAM, Lucinda Childs reworked the dance passages; as a dancer and choreographer, she emerged from the New York-based Judson Dance Theater collective with her own forms of rigorous conceptual and abstract dance.

The opera consists of four interconnected acts with nine scenes. The four-and-a-half hour work runs continuously; viewers are encouraged to come and go at liberty during the performance. This new version of *Einstein* was so enthusiastically received that it was performed again at BAM in 1992 and 2012. In the latter production, the lighting technology had advanced considerably, bringing to life the visual qualities that Wilson could only imagine at the time of the premiere.

As it begins, we see the title image of a shorts-clad young Einstein by the water. The scientist played the violin avocationally; his character in the opera (played by alternating virtuoso violinists) is often seated downstage, performing one line in Glass's thrilling, fluttering score for a large ensemble. Some parts advance at the glacial pace for which Wilson is known, others at a rapid clip. Set pieces—in particular a bar of light—move so slowly that their paths seem to correspond with the orbit of celestial bodies. Childs's perpetual, motivic dance phrases advance downstage and retreat as the dancers' hands scribble and flick as if compulsively. The major dance segments comprise her bold, space-eating phrases of leaps and spins punctuated with crisp arabesques. Glass's music seems tailor-made for her minimalist, serial style; in fact, she has set other iconic repertory works to his compositions.

A pair of women dressed in the style of Einstein—white shirts, grey pants, suspenders—perform what Wilson calls "knee plays," small vignettes that occur downstage during set changes. They tilt while seated on chairs, or lie on their backs with their limbs swimming in the air. At times, the set change becomes the featured attraction; the courtroom is assembled piece by piece by stagehands in an intriguing glimpse behind the scenes.

One of the most visually memorable images in the production is the "spaceship" scene, a matrix in which each square contains lightbulbs that illuminate to create lines, arcs, and circles. The structure houses the vocal quartet and a league of Einsteinites who frenetically mime the operation of control panels. To add to the mesmerizing picture, two performers with clocks float in boxes that move horizontally and vertically, steam emanates from a trap door, two strange plastic domes sit downstage left, and myriad dancers and musicians populate the apron. The rush of all of these moving elements at the climax parallels the dynamics of Glass's score—exhilarating, unrelenting, and memorable.

Lucinda Childs and Sheryl Sutton (featured) in *Einstein on the Beach*, Philip Glass/Robert Wilson/Lucinda Childs, 1984. Photo: Babette Mangolte

*Kontakthof*, Tanztheater Wuppertal Pina Bausch, 2014. Photo: Julieta Cervantes

1985, 2014

# Kontakthof

Tanztheater Wuppertal Pina Bausch

Gem-hued silk dresses, stilettos, and dark suits on the stage of the BAM Howard Gilman Opera House usually mean one thing—that Tanztheater Wuppertal Pina Bausch is in the house. One of the dances with such evocative costumes is *Kontakthof*, which the company brought to the Next Wave in 1985 and again in 2014. The title means "contact yard," and in this case, the arena resembles a generic school auditorium, complete with a curtained-off stage lining the back wall—the sets and costumes were designed by Rolf Borzik. It's a setting for one of the innovative German choreographer's most accessible works that has been performed not only by the company, but by casts composed of young and old residents of differing tour destinations. Tanztheater Wuppertal performed it both times at BAM, which has been the company's sole New York venue.

A tall window lets in the sunlight as it progresses through the theoretical day and night. One of the 23 dancers takes center stage, tugging at her face, smoothing her dress, grabbing her buttocks, and performing other obsessive gestures as if preparing to be inspected; the insecurity and vanity are at odds with the elegant formal garb. This compulsive phrase is repeated en masse to nostalgic Weimaresque recorded dance music primarily by Juan Llossas and his Tango Orchestra. The group splits in half with the women on the right, and the men with chairs at left. A frantic boogie-woogie tune begins, and the men scooch their chairs intermittently toward the women, reaching their arms and grappling hands forward in desperation. There's plenty of flirting and gaiety in this timeless mating ritual, but with bestial tendencies simmering just below the well-groomed surface.

Several hypnotic downstage crossings take place by a seemingly endless line of company members, or a group massed for maximum visual impact—an elegant stride, arms in a vee (one woman, unable to sync up, complains of her tight dress and ridiculous heels); the crossed foot hip sink; the isolated pelvic rotation; and the hilarious flappy-footed duck walk. Pull-out skits, primarily by women, dot the proceedings, as when two women in cotton candy pink behave like inseparable six-year-old pals, or one disarmingly screams "Dah-ling!" at top volume, or another is surrounded by the men, who disturbingly pinch and poke her as she remains as impassive as a puppet.

By the end of the performance, as is often the case with Bausch's pieces, we feel as if we know many of the charismatic cast members. It helps that each, in her/his native tongue, begins to tell a personal anecdote only to be cut off by the next one. In the closing sequence, the dancers walk rhythmically in a circle, repeating a chain of gestures in which the hands move about the body, busied with small tasks. The music diminishes to silence and as the curtain falls, the haunting rhythmic strides continue. It's lovely to think that these charmers and misfits will continue to pitch woo eternally.

1987

# The Mahabharata

Peter Brook, Jean-Claude Carrière

*The Mahabharata* is one of the most ambitious theatrical events to take place not only at BAM, but in the history of modern drama. Directed by Peter Brook in collaboration with Jean-Claude Carrière, the production unspools over nine hours in three plays. With 28 actors from 18 countries (including four children) and five musicians, it adapts the ancient Indian epic, an 18-volume book originally written in Sanskrit following the fortunes of, and wars between, rival family factions—the Pandavas and the Kauravas. Its timeless costumes, international cast, and modern interpretation of a historical epic would become a paradigm for many Next Wave productions to follow.

The framework for the story unfolds as the author-narrator seeks an amanuensis to transcribe his poem, and encounters a boy to whom he tells his tale. (Notably, alternating in the part of the boy, the young Akram Khan would later emerge as an independent artist in his own right whose dance-theater would also find a home at BAM.) The first play, *The Game of Dice*, lays out the many characters set against the growing discord between the two branches of the family and culminates in a round of gambling in which the leader of the Pandavas clan, succumbing to his compulsion, loses everything, including the family's birthright. The second play, *Exile in the Forest*, tells of the ensuing 12-year banishment, and the creatures, people, and pitfalls encountered along the way. *The War*, the third play, depicts the battle—inexorable, senseless, and immeasurably cruel. Many of the scenes become parables for broad themes on the human condition, such as loyalty, compassion, greed, self-sacrifice, and mortality. Natural elements—earth, water, fire—are potently visible as set pieces.

Brook already had an admirable history at BAM with his productions of *A Midsummer Night's Dream* (1971), with the Royal Shakespeare Company, and his adaptation of the 12th-century Persian epic *Conference of the Birds* (1973), and has since presented modern plays such as *The Man Who* (1995) and *The Suit* (2013). Among the most renowned contemporary directors, Brook envisions his artistic journey as a quest for meaning and purposefulness and uses theater to explore the profound conflicts of being human, such as deception and truth, harmony and discord, benevolence and evil.

*The Mahabharata* is also significant in the Academy's history as it was the inaugural production in the Majestic Theater (now the BAM Harvey Theater). It honored longtime BAM president and executive producer Harvey Lichtenstein, who, with Brook, sought a suitable space in which to present the plays. It would need to accommodate 20,000 pounds of dirt on which wars would be enacted. Intrigued by an abandoned opera and vaudeville house at 651 Fulton Street near BAM's main building, Lichtenstein became curious and together with Brook climbed through a broken window above the transom to see inside, discovering their ideal theater-in-the-rough. The amphitheater-like interior's look is patterned after the Théâtre des Bouffes du Nord in Paris, Brook's home theater, in an intentionally decaying style. The venue enables the actors and audience to engage in a mutual experience, and as noted by Brook, to develop "a closer relationship with the richest of all spectacles, which is the human being."

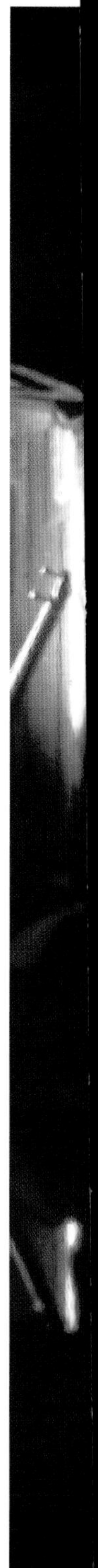

*The Mahabharata*, Peter Brook/Jean-Claude Carrière, 1987. Photo: Gilles Abegg

John Duykers and James Maddalena (featured) in *Nixon in China*, John Adams/Alice Goodman/Peter Sellars/Mark Morris, 1987. Photo: Patty Wood

1987

# Nixon in China

## John Adams, Alice Goodman, Peter Sellars, Mark Morris

After more than three decades, *Nixon in China* still resonates as revolutionary, not only within opera, but within the scope of the performing arts. The subject is the historic trip to the People's Republic of China in 1972 by then President Richard Nixon and First Lady Pat Nixon, where he ultimately met Chairman and Madame Mao, with Henry Kissinger and Chou En-lai on hand. Each of the primary elements—music by John Adams, a libretto by Alice Goodman, direction by Peter Sellars, and choreography by Mark Morris—contributed to the work's daring invention and, despite mixed reviews, what would prove to be an enduring success.

Basing an opera on a modern political event itself was radical, particularly one so politically fraught—*Nixon* was Adams's first opera; his next was the equally incendiary *The Death of Klinghoffer*, which premiered at BAM in 1991 and was revised for the 2003 Next Wave. The main character was so well known that the idea of casting anyone as Nixon, let alone an accomplished singer, must have been daunting. But Sellars succeeded with the keystone role, portrayed by James Maddalena, Carolann Page as Pat Nixon, and Sanford Sylvan as Chou En-lai in a touching and eloquent portrayal. The potential pitfall of costuming non-Asians as Chinese was handled by specifying generic dark hair, black framed glasses, and navy uniforms.

The opera is divided into six major scenes. Throughout, the point of view toggles between public spectacle and private musing. When Pat Nixon is given her own tour of a hospital, a school, and a commune, her aria reflects her thoughts about the smaller and larger implications of the trip. The memorable sets by Adrianne Lobel include the presidential couple disembarking the "Spirit of '76," a scene for many hardwired to news pictures of the actual event, and the final scene featuring a giant portrait of Mao, whose mouth is a door.

The characters' recitatives unravel personal perspectives on the portentous proceedings, supported by the chorus—primarily Mao's acolytes. The piping solo vocal repetitions and lush choral arrangements are in Adams's distinctive style. *Nixon* was the first of a number of operas that distinguish him as one of the more versatile and prolific minimalist composers working within the medium.

One of the most striking parts of the opera presents a portion of the ballet *The Red Detachment of Women*, produced by Chiang Ch'ing (Madame Mao). It's another instance of reality being folded into art, as this socialist ballet is one of modern China's best-known and time-honored dances. Segments of the original ballet—replete with warrior-like gestures—are worked into the staging as Mrs. Nixon confuses art with reality, inserting herself as an aide to the heroine by handing her a glass of juice and a rifle at strategic moments.

The opera impressively balances reality, fiction, humor, and gravity. It ends with Chou, in one of Goodman's most poetic stanzas, pondering the worthiness of the visit while resolving to persist: "To work! Outside this room the chill of grace / Lies heavily on the morning grass."

1994

# Still/Here

## Bill T. Jones/Arnie Zane Dance Company

Performed by the Bill T. Jones/Arnie Zane Dance Company, *Still/Here*—for better or worse—stands out as a milepost in the culture wars of the 1980s and 1990s, when AIDS was hitting New York with full gale force and the funding choices of the National Endowment for the Arts were coming under fire from conservatives. *Still/Here*, which was ultimately critically lauded, may be best remembered as the production that provoked dance critic Arlene Croce to pen a long essay in the *New Yorker* on how she would not be reviewing it, deeming it "victim art" and therefore unreviewable. The outcry that ensued helped to galvanize the artistic community's support of Jones's work, but the choreographer was deeply affected by the incident.

Jones, who lost his partner Arnie Zane to AIDS and was himself diagnosed with HIV, drew from 10 survivor workshops held in the months preceding the work's creation. Some of the interview footage is incorporated by Gretchen Bender into the video montage and projected onto background screens and mobile set elements.

The stage is primarily given over to the company's ferocious and individualistic dancers, who interpret handsome group phrases that crystallize into breathtaking tableaux or solos that draw on each dancer's unique strengths. Duets seem to allude to aiding a faltering friend, or rejecting alms, but none of the movement sections are overtly descriptive. Compassion and humanity prevail in the face of terrible illness.

The first act, *Still*, with its frenetic pace, features music sung by Odetta (recorded, plus a live cameo), who suffuses the material with a grounded power and solemnity. Vernon Reid provides music for the second act, *Here*, which carries a more consistently up-tempo dynamic. There are longer, flowing passages of dance, and memorable formations implying community, rather than individuals coping alone. The red costumes—constrasting with the all-white in *Still*—visually add to the act's increased dynamism and sense of resilience, and also acceptance. To wit, one person says, "Do I have hope? Yes. Do I think people will celebrate me after my death? Yes."

The finale holds joyful, unforgettable moments, many in silhouette against painted images of a heart. Dancers form a human chain while others sprint under their clasped hands, or leap ecstatically across the stage. They rush in a vortex, spinning a TV monitor that displays Jones asking, "Where are you? What does the room look like? Who's there?" as a guitar wails. The action repeats, implying the inexorable continuation of illness, the humanity entangled within, and the possibilities of death and reprieve.

*Still/Here*, Bill T. Jones/Arnie Zane Dance Company, 1994. Photo courtesy of BAM Hamm Archives

1993

# The Cave

Steve Reich, Beryl Korot

By the time Steve Reich created *The Cave* with Beryl Korot—presented in the 1993 Next Wave—he had been composing for more than three decades. But *The Cave* expanded the breadth of Reich's already impressive oeuvre by delving into subjects of biblical heritage and varying frames of identity—asking the question "Who was Abraham?" and infusing it with the differing perspectives offered by people of three nationalities. Set it amid the engaging and lively video designs by Korot in a matrix structure, plus live musicians and singers conducted by Paul Hillier, and the result was an inventive music-theater production that blurred the line to opera.

Reich and Korot amassed material for *The Cave* by interviewing a number of people in Israel, Palestine, and the United States. The titular site is said to be where Abraham's wife Sarah and his descendants were buried, as well as being the entryway to the Garden of Eden and the final resting place of Adam and Eve. In addition to the basic query about Abraham, the respondents were also asked about Sarah, Isaac and Ishmael (his sons), and Hagar (mother of Ishmael). The replies reveal geopolitical insights, and in the case of the American interviewees, some not unexpected lack of familiarity. Interspersed with video shots of selected respondents are title screens showing a hand writing in cursive or relevant images such as a map or the complex exterior of where Abraham's cave is located. Of particular interest, above the site, there has been a wall built by Herod as well as a Byzantine church and a 12th-century mosque where, uniquely, Jews and Muslims both worship.

Steve Reich Ensemble in *The Cave*, Steve Reich/ Beryl Korot, 1993. Photo: Andrew Pothecary

The score draws on the various forms for which Reich is known. It begins with a clapping section—the most basic and elemental form of percussion—and contains passages of sung recitative. Snippets of the voices of interviewees are included and often mimed by instruments, elucidating the singsong nature of verbal phrasing. Dialogue bits are separated with pensive instrumental lines, leaving space for the audience to ponder each part.

Unsurprisingly, the comments made by the American interviewees—several are artists or scientists—are humorous in that they demonstrate free association rather than obligatory biblical history. Abraham summons "Lincoln," while Ishmael summons "Moby-Dick." The pace quickens in this third and final act, with lively, harmonious four-part vocal sections for the skilled onstage singers. As the close nears, the tempo slows, the key shifts to minor, and the end note is a surprising single plinking piano note. It's a very human touch to a work that feels like a big machine of so many moving parts, in essence a catalogue of Reich's sonic inventions.

1996

# The Seven Streams of the River Ota

Robert Lepage, Ex Machina

In the years before and since 1996, when versatile Canadian theater artist Robert Lepage performed *The Seven Streams of the River Ota* at BAM, he has directed rock concerts, nouveau cirque, epic operas, and of course, more theater. And yet *Seven Streams* may best embody the alchemy of Lepage's work that has garnered him that richly varied resume. Other Next Wave productions include *Polygraph* (1990), *Needles and Opium* (1992), *Elsinore* (1997), *Geometry of Miracles* (1999), *Lipsynch* (2009), and *The Blue Dragon* (2013).

Concerning events emanating from Hiroshima, Japan, where the title river is located, *Seven Streams*—an eight-hour play, presented in two performances—flows at a steady pace, peopled by interrelated characters over generations. Its seven scenes have incisive titles—"Two Jeffreys," "The Mirror," "Words"—that reflect humor as well as the commonality of daily life, even among people from conflicting sides.

The basic set is a Japanese house with a sliding shoji screen wall separating inside (upstage) from out. With different stylized elements, it becomes a New York apartment, a monastery, a restaurant, backstage at a theater, and a Noh playhouse, among other things. An American soldier tasked with photographing the aftermath of the bombing of Hiroshima falls into an affair with the house's resident, whose physical damage he photographs as well, while registering her inner beauty. The G.I.'s sons, by different mothers but both named Jeffrey, turn out to be neighbors in New York, and the stories wend forward in such a manner, diverging from and looping back to previous characters.

There are big picture themes—war, the atomic bomb, AIDS—but the rich texture of *Seven Streams* is made up of small moments. Lepage doesn't sidestep conflict; cultural differences can be read as funny or awkward. Lepage enlists a variety of media to achieve a meditative, filmic whole. The Abbott and Costello comedy skit "Who's on First?" is seen on a video monitor, and then threaded into some later dialogue. Bunraku puppets depict scenes of an affair, and fabric banners enliven a sideshow. Shamisen music is played sparingly, dotted with chimes and percussion. There's a sense that all the elements were arrived at by subtraction rather than addition.

Hiroshima, for certain, represents death and destruction in the 20th century. We're reminded of the tawdry appetite for gore when a Zen monk is interviewed by a Hungarian reporter, and in the editing process, the producer decides to add imagery of Hiroshima to spice up the segment. In his inimitable way, Lepage acknowledges the absurdity of the times while zooming out to capture the larger picture. It's a spacious yet compact encapsulation of the horrors of warfare, subsequent rebirth, and the lives that unspool in between.

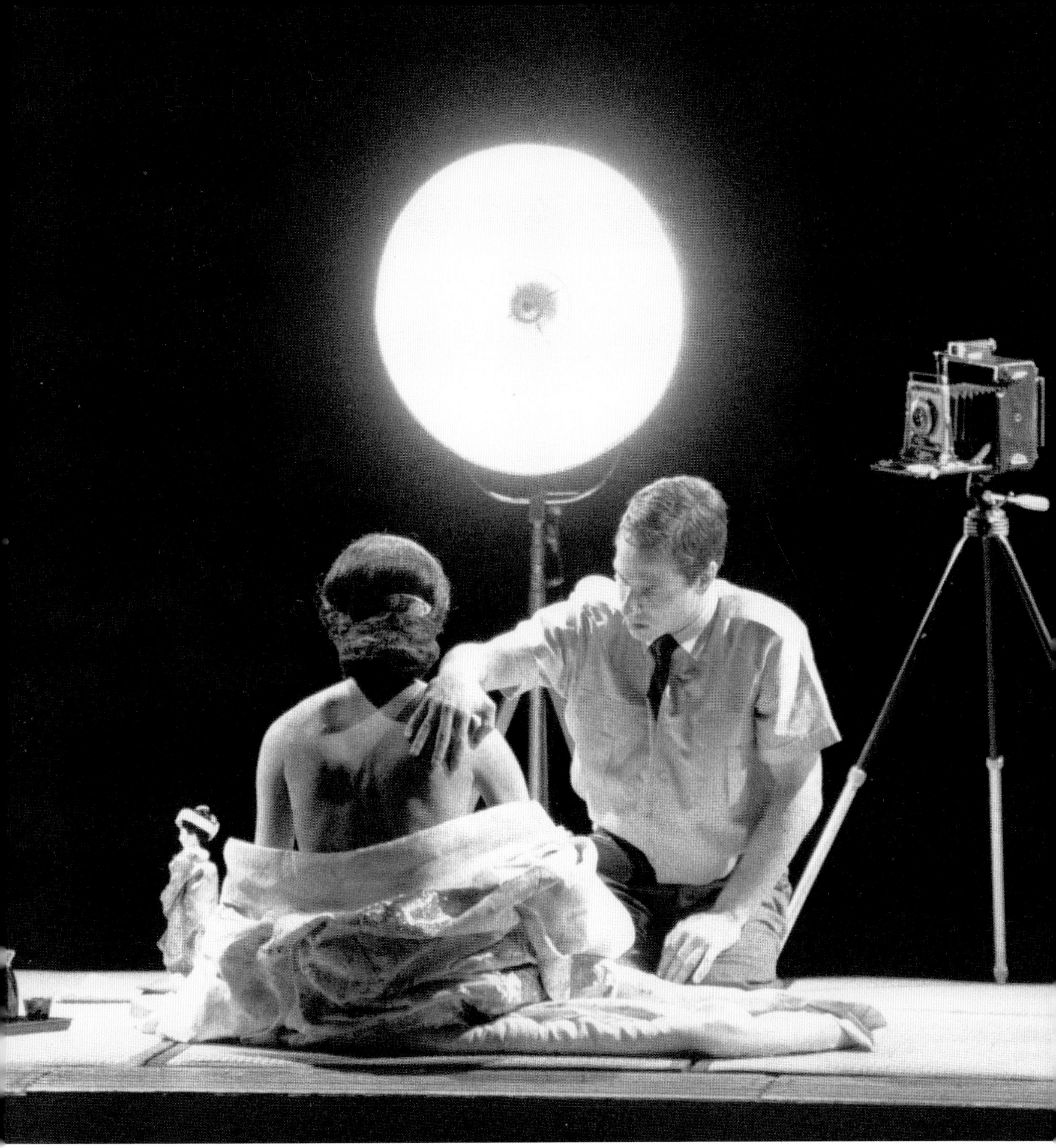

Anne-Marie Cadieux and Patrick Goyette in *The Seven Streams of the River Ota*, Robert Lepage/ Ex Machina, 1996. Photo: Dan Rest

Ralph Lemon in his *Geography*, Ralph Lemon/ Nari Ward, 1997. Photo: Tom Brazil

1997, 2000, 2004

# The Geography Trilogy

Ralph Lemon

Ralph Lemon's *The Geography Trilogy*—comprising *Geography* (1997), *Tree* (2000), and *Come home Charley Patton* (2004)—is a wide-ranging choreographic meditation on the interrelationship between disparate cultures in forming a shared history; it also represents an investigation of the creative process through experimentation and collaboration. There are recurring themes and geographical referents that provide cohesion and traction, but missing is a neat, symmetrical narrative or overt polemic to unify the parts. Rather, Lemon dares us to absorb the performances as they emerge and to assemble them as we can—if we can—into a substantive whole.

Developed over a 10-year span, the project evolved as a physical and spiritual journey of self-examination and inquiry that explores the complexities of race and the convergence of diverse elements in search of personal and artistic identity—tradition and modernity, East and West, formalism and improvisation. The focus of each part is a region—the West Coast of Africa for *Geography*; the Asian continent for *Tree*, following the path of Buddhism through India, Indonesia, China, and Japan; and returning to the United States, in particular the American South, for *Come home Charley Patton*.

Each part functions as a poetic montage of dance, music, storytelling, and media, incorporating snippets of visual/performance art that share casts and striking imagery. Sculptor Nari Ward provides sets of extraordinary visual magnitude for both *Geography* and *Tree*—respectively a curtain of bottles and a wall of wooden palettes—while in *Come home Charley Patton*, a clean, white stage—designed by Lemon—is a blank canvas upon which the swirling patterns of the dancers cavort with violet shadows, supplemented by a movable self-contained room with various unfolding and hinged components—ladders, screens—and topped by a mattress.

Dances indigenous to the varying backgrounds of the performers interweave with Lemon's postmodern movement. His fluid technique can be upper-body based, the torso spiraling and twisting on its axis, or it can increase in dynamic with abrupt stamping and darting leaps. In *Geography*, Lemon's cool, introverted style is a sharp contrast to the engaging, rhythmic phrasing of his African counterparts; whereas in *Tree*, performers create overlapping, shifting layers of action, incorporating several frustrating attempts to communicate by performers of differing nationalities that are laced with Lemon's trademark wry humor.

Sections that evoke historic, violent episodes are at once moving and disturbing. In a scene from *Come home Charley Patton*, Lemon stands on a dais while blasted with water from a firehose, overtly reminiscent of the volatile civil rights movement, while another performer reiterates a childhood story that begins humorously and then devolves into a racially tinged confrontation. It underscores the stereotyping in a society that promises equality, but repeatedly snatches it away. For Lemon, as the artistic journey continues, it is enriched by the fusion of history, myth, and tradition as a means to determine our place in the world.

1998

# EIDOS : TELOS

William Forsythe, Ballett Frankfurt

Ballett Frankfurt's *EIDOS : TELOS* served as an exhilarating initiation for Next Wave audiences to the work of American-born choreographer William Forsythe. The first act takes place in an unadorned setting of time-keeping devices—a smattering of analog clocks, a digital timer, and a metronome—plus a violinist who stands downstage playing Thom Willems's fractured score. The clocks might be a concise metaphor for the Greek title—eidos (form), telos (end; purpose)—physical manifestations of time passing, of the planet revolving around the sun, of life itself.

Varying groupings of the 33 performers in simple leotards, t-shirts, and socks are scattered around the stage, rippling and slashing through Forsythe's innovative extruded style of ballet. While an occasional virtuosic stance or move—a pointed foot extended, arms carefully arranged, or a small side leap finished by a delicately unfurling leg and hand—is drawn from classical ballet, what telegraphs the depth of the dancers' ninja technique is the sheer deftness with which they slip from one unconventional shape to the next.

The second act is dominated by dancer Dana Caspersen, whose lucidly ringing monologue while wearing only a full, swishing orange skirt alludes to the myth of Persephone as a spider woman, vividly describing digging into and emerging from the earth each year. She unfurls a length of cellophane—flamelike in color with crackling sound—which she stuffs into a klieg light fixture suspended in midair by four cables, like a spider on its web. Dancers in multihued taffeta skirts waltz onstage in an orderly sweeping flurry in a brief but unforgettably stunning scene. In sharp contrast, a man's voice is heard muttering, "I'm fuckin' dead, man," and lists threats both tame and vicious.

Two cables bisect the stage's volume at an oblique angle in the third act. As the dancers bounce off of them, they resonate, producing a muffled thunderclap. Teams pluck at the monstrous strings; the dancers play this giant instrument and become part of it, pulling, falling backward, advancing once more. In addition, they slap their torsos and chuff, creating sounds with their bodies. Brass horns crescendo to a cacophony... it feels like an explosion is imminent. Caspersen spasms, folds over onto all fours, and strips off her skirt, presumably to return back into the earth.

Since *EIDOS : TELOS*, a number of Forsythe's pieces have been performed at BAM by Ballett Frankfurt and by his subsequent troupe, the Forsythe Company, both based in Germany. His work can be as much theater and performance as dance, but we are reminded of its disciplined ballet roots in the periodic, visceral movement passages that invariably thrill audiences.

Dana Caspersen in *EIDOS : TELOS*, William Forsythe/Ballett Frankfurt, 1998. Photo: Dominik Mentzos

1999

# Songs and Stories from Moby Dick

Laurie Anderson

In *Songs and Stories from Moby Dick*, Laurie Anderson took a slightly musty subject—the 1851 Melville novel, long a staple of American literature—and frosted it in her particular brand of cool. The Opera House stage is awash in sapphire blue projections of lapping waves, maps, books in rows or opening page by fluttering page, and text in a classic serif font. When Anderson first appears, she holds an electric violin and as she plays sonorous tones, speaks in her signature soothing cadence and velvety alto. Her riveting monologues become the baseline to which the work returns—a centering ritual from which hang catchy pop songs and witty jigs.

A recurrent theme in Anderson's work—the impress of technology—is never far from the surface. At times it is front and center, as with the selection of instruments deployed in *Songs and Stories*. The talking stick (MIDI recorder/player), tape-bow violin, and vox box, which can alter emanating vocals by octaves, are used by Anderson and four other performers. These are augmented by a bass, prepared bass, and recorded samples, creating layered, dimensional sounds that fill the ear while the visuals immerse the eye.

At one point, Anderson clambers onto a giant white armchair, evoking Wonderland's Alice when she shrinks to her miniature self after drinking a potion. Anderson talks of her Bantam paperback copy of *Moby-Dick*, and about how one of the book's themes is the topic of big heads—that whales are just this huge head on top of a tail. In order for fishermen to draw the oil out of a captured whale's head, they drill a hole in its skull, and lower into it a bucket. To retrieve the last of the precious oil, a boy is sent into the cavity. Anderson describes for us the boy in the skull, the whale becoming unmoored, and without its oil for flotation, the whale carcass with the boy inside plummeting to inky depths.

Ultimately, despite jaunty dances and Abe Lincoln costumes worn by her collaborators, the heart of the piece belongs to her monologues. Her hypnotic voice and cadence smooth the way for her stories—activating the brain, producing lucid mental images that delineate the essence of the absorbing source material. They have included no less than the United States, the moon, and NASA, and most recently her beloved dog Lolabelle in the performance/film *Heart of a Dog* (2015).

Anderson had a 1981 chart-topping song with "O Superman." She folded it into the epic performance work, *United States: Parts I–IV* (1983), part of BAM's Next Wave Series, the precursor to the festival. It set an example for Anderson's performance works to follow, which have incorporated monologues, songs, video, and inventive electronic instruments. Filtered through her sensibility of cool, what are mostly familiar elements become undeniably signature Laurie Anderson.

Laurie Anderson in her *Songs and Stories from Moby Dick*, 1999. Photo courtesy of BAM Hamm Archives

1999

# Morning Song

## Jan Lauwers, Needcompany

*Morning Song*—subtitled *No beauty for me there, where human life is rare, part two*—a piece set in heaven, introduced Next Wave audiences to Needcompany, a Brussels-based performance group that daringly mixes genres in an immersive theatrical environment. A unique element is cooking, with its attendant evocations as a comforting home-as-hearth ritual and providing nutrition to survive, plus the Pavlovian sizzle and aroma of sautéing onions. Directed by Jan Lauwers, it is a companion piece to a performance of *Caligula* by Albert Camus, in which the title character says, "People die and are unhappy. This truth does not prevent people from enjoying a delicious meal." Lauwers extracted this line to use as inspiration for *Morning Song*.

A kitchen and dining table occupy the right side of the stage; the rest is occupied by a talk show style setup of chairs and microphones in front of an open area. Before any cooking takes place, the show begins with a scatological conversation among a foursome about, appropriately, how smelling food elicits hunger. While they certainly must have worked from a script, the dialogue feels ad hoc, with witty asides and digressions (an ongoing search for the cat) braided into the main conversational thread.

The bodies of two dancers pulsate, picking up a quietly building rhythm; it becomes a chant, which builds into an irrepressible rock song. Volume, dynamic, and instrumentation increase, and the dancers do a rapid stutter step and shimmy as if suddenly infused with unstoppable energy. One woman repeats a slow, introspective solo—conveying emotion rather than gesture—and retreats to a stool on which she swivels repeatedly like a self-soothing tic.

The key figure is Liliane, played by the magnetic Viviane De Muynck, who gives an overarching monologue about how the family is gathering for her daughter's wedding to a revolutionary who dies from eating radioactive snow. Each of the eight characters, who form a makeshift family, is described briefly by Liliane. Her husband wears a convincing bear suit and wanders on and off; she informs us that the taxi driver is in love with her—and at one point, they kiss passionately. A woman in pointe shoes uses them like tools, whacking their soles and stabbing her toes against the floor percussively.

Dance passages alter and give texture to the shifting mood and atmosphere rather than being stand-alone segments. The focus of the performers changes from observer to protagonist. Bad or shocking things happen: a man regurgitates; another lights flaming sparklers that he holds in his mouth; the missing cat is found, dead, tossed across the stage, and stuffed into the bear's pants.

A moody prog-rock song builds toward the finale. Two dancers move furtively in the darkness while another pair putters in the kitchen; these actions, and the music, take on equal weight. Neon letters spaced around the dark set light up, at one point forming "INFINITO," then blinking off until we read "FIN." An arc of white light descends, signaling the end of the multisensory dream.

Carlotta Sagna, Gonzalo Cunill, Viviane De Muynck, Eduardo Torroja, and Simon Versnel in *Morning Song*, Jan Lauwers/Needcompany, 1999. Photo: Stephanie Berger

2000

# Songs of the Wanderers

## Lin Hwai-min, Cloud Gate Dance Theatre of Taiwan

In *Songs of the Wanderers*, Cloud Gate Dance Theatre of Taiwan embodies the dualities of a spiritual pilgrimage and the physical muscularity of contemporary modern dance. This combination of metaphysical and corporal have been trademarks of the company's productions, all choreographed by artistic director Lin Hwai-min. Other festival appearances include *Nine Songs* (1995), *Moon Water* (2003), *Wild Cursive* (2007), *Water Stains on the Wall* (2011), and *Rice* (2015). Cloud Gate's dances are breathtakingly visual, and often incorporate or evoke natural elements, connecting us back to the earth.

In the unforgettable opening tableau of *Songs of the Wanderers*, one of the company's signature works, Wang Rong-yu—berobed with hands pressed together in prayer—stands statue-still as a stream of golden rice falls on his shaved head, pooling around his feet. His face, placidly rapt, betrays no reaction to the relentless torrent. (Audience empathy is part of the sentient experience.) Dancers enter bearing leafy fronds and tree limb staffs, on which they lean for support. The tops of two branches cross, forming a metaphorical shelter. The dancers' arms at times imitate boughs waving in the wind, sprouting upward in a surge of growth.

Haunting Georgian folk songs, alternating with silence, comprise the soundtrack. Bodies pitch down and into the rice, creating schussing sounds. A woman flips her head back, spraying grains, and a man pushes a rake very slowly while others dart about like wary hunters. A cascade of rice falls onto dancer Wang Wei-ming, nearly naked, his exposed flesh looking extremely vulnerable. He flings rice overhead in arches, thrashing, kicking, and falling into it, tossing handfuls in what could be read as ecstasy or desperation.

Dancers carry vessels of fire, introducing another life-sustaining element. As they spin ecstatically, the tinkle of bells worn on their bodies lightens the austerity of the folk songs. A mood of celebration takes over, and the performers frolic joyously as a choral song's volume increases. More rice falls in a curtain, and the dancers fling it and bound through it with glee while the standing man continues his static vigil.

In what is deemed both a "Finale" and a "Beginning," a male dancer appears midstage with a rake and very slowly begins to etch a large, perfect spiral in the rice, which endures another quarter hour. It is a reminder that a spiritual pilgrimage is never ending and requires discipline and commitment, despite blissful moments of epiphany.

*Songs of the Wanderers*, Lin Hwai-min/Cloud Gate Dance Theatre of Taiwan, 2000. Photo: Yu Hui-Hung

2003

# Rain

## Anne Teresa De Keersmaeker, Steve Reich, Rosas, Ictus

Anne Teresa De Keersmaeker's *Rain*, performed by her Brussels-based company Rosas, unites her joyous, athletic style of movement with Steve Reich's *Music for 18 Musicians*, Jan Versweyveld's shimmering set and temporally phasing lighting design, and Dries Van Noten's chic, relaxed costumes. Each element contributes effortlessly to the artistic whole, one of the most striking and transcendent dances to be performed during the history of the Next Wave Festival.

Two curved, semi-transparent curtains of hanging ropes form a passageway through which the 10 dancers enter—skipping, leaping, starting, and stopping. The movement is virtuosic, but it also looks simple enough for viewers to access. The dancers move on their own paths, seemingly at random, but at moments, fall into a line along one of the geometric shapes marked by tape on the floor. They seem impelled by the propulsive, hypnotic Reich music, which is played live by the contemporary ensemble Ictus, visible through the rope curtain upstage.

The dancers fling their arms, extend a leg, curve their torsos, and bound aloft once more. The rope curtains are at times brushed by a dancer's hand, rippling and bringing them to life. They sometimes break through this "wall," adding to the unpredictability and ambiguity. As noted by De Keersmaeker, "My choreographies often deal with the tension between the horizontal and the vertical. As a choreographer you are all the time trying to structure time and space." Repetition with modulated shifts plus duration also combine to introduce exhaustion as a factor.

As the rhythms phase and shift gradually throughout the 70-minute work, so does the coloration of the lighting—hot to cool and back again—and the hues of the costumes, which the dancers change backstage, unnoticed, on occasion. The entire work's chromatic progression may not register until a majority of the dance is over, like how sunset can take one by surprise at the end of a particularly pleasurable late-summer day, both in its rapidity and stunning beauty.

*Rain* is unmistakably sublime, but it is also challenging. Subtle shifts of rhythm, instrumentation, movement dynamics, coloration, and brightness reward attentive viewers. Like the passage of a day, the piece's progression changes temperature, if not in degrees, in evoked emotion and the effect of accumulation. The stage of the BAM Howard Gilman Opera House is transformed into an absorbing space where the creativity of an extraordinary assemblage of artists is brought together. It's a demonstration of the power of a work with no narrative, consisting solely of form and pattern and mathematics, but grounded with humanity.

*Rain*, Anne Teresa De Keersmaeker/Steve Reich/Rosas/Ictus, 2003. Photo: Stephanie Berger

Uma Ysamat in *Bright Abyss*, James Thierrée/ La Compagnie du Hanneton, 2005. Photo: Jack Vartoogian

## 2005
# Bright Abyss
### James Thierrée, La Compagnie du Hanneton

Swiss-born performance artist and director James Thierrée and his collaborators in La Compagnie du Hanneton can take everyday objects and transform them into wondrous beasts or portals into another world. In the breathtaking opening scene of *Bright Abyss*, a ladder, gardening tools, and a bellows become a makeshift cyborgian contraption by which to traverse a roiling ocean made of billowing silk. An industrial-sized wooden cable spool is used as an ad hoc conference table before the players flip it on its side and roll it like a giant wheel, with four limbs and a head popping out to form an impossibly stretched person.

The company's productions—other Next Wave ventures include *Au Revoir Parapluie* (2007), *Raoul* (2010), *Tabac Rouge* (2015), and *La grenouille avait raison (The Toad Knew)* (2017)—advance a time-honored tradition of physical theater made famous by Thierrée's grandfather, Charlie Chaplin, and the advent of moving pictures. While Thierrée does not emphasize this connection, it's hard to avoid. It would be one thing if he weren't able to measure up to the comparison, but he has taken his inherited gifts—his great-grandfather, incidentally, is playwright Eugene O'Neill—and has hammered out a unique niche in contemporary physical-theater.

While the object repurposing is dazzlingly clever, some of the finest moments in *Bright Abyss* showcase the simplicity of Thierrée's rubbery physicality and everyman persona. As he wrestles with a newspaper, its pages mysteriously stick to his hands and feet, then spill across the stage as he loses complete control of the nettlesome journal. In another scene, he fails repeatedly to sit on a chair; his legs have hilarious minds of their own and slip, cross, and slide willy-nilly. These provoke innocent, cathartic belly laughs without fail, and are reminders of the fallibility, and potential, of the human body.

One of the final set pieces in *Bright Abyss* involves a suspended metal dish shaped like a snow saucer and reminiscent of a ship's crow's nest. It's barely large enough for two, and hangs from rods high above the stage. Swinging alarmingly fast from side to side, in the manner of a pendulum, its speed is amplified by silk streamers that festoon the basket, which is formed by rope woven through the metal frame. Thierrée clambers up and down while zipping across the stage like a nightwatchman being tossed at sea, riding yet another leg on a perilous oceanic journey.

Ultimately, the distinctive Iron Age aesthetic of the many mechanical stage inventions, the all-out physical daring, and the essential humanity and humor comprising the heart of Thierrée's work unite to make *Bright Abyss* a memorable signature of an alchemist's universe in perpetual motion.

2007

# The BQE

Sufjan Stevens

The critical and popular success of composer Sufjan Stevens's *The BQE* derives in part because, or in spite of, the sheer grottiness of the subject matter: one of New York City's most wretched and crowded—but undeniably essential—highways. It weaves through the boroughs of Brooklyn and Queens and is invariably jam-packed with bombing 18-wheelers and darting commuter cars. Unexpectedly, in the eponymous first part of the work, Stevens's lush symphonic score lends a magic shimmer to the mesmerizing photographic and filmed hyper-urban imagery, while Hula-Hoopers take the stage periodically for a whimsical vaudevillean touch.

Slides and video clips comprise the visuals—cinematography by Stevens and Reuben Kleiner and projections by multimedia artist Deborah Johnson—and are projected above the large orchestra (in matching t-shirts) on a three-paneled screen. Evocative of Godfrey Reggio and Philip Glass's experimental film *Koyaanisqatsi*, released in 1983, they change quickly, approximating the speed and thrill of driving on the expressway. We virtually whiz by residential building windows situated uncomfortably close to the road—into which we might peer, should we be so inclined. Images of coursing lanes of traffic are spliced at diagonals, forming a convergent arterial network bearing the lifeblood of the city.

The infrastructure of the roadway and construction vehicles become unlikely artistic subjects lent a sense of wondrousness by the majestic score, with its ascending flute lines and bleating trumpets. Crescendos evoking Batman-like "Pows!" mix with steadily pulsing clarinet lines and twinkling celesta passages. In the finale, video of fireworks provides the background for the dancers, now rotating glow-in-the-dark Hula-Hoops. Effervescent brass flourishes worthy of Gershwin sound the work's triumphant end.

As we watch endless streams of cars and images of wheels, which resonate with the hypnotic revolutions of the Hula-Hoops, it makes sense that Stevens is from Detroit, home of the automobile. The foundation for his body of work leading up to *The BQE* included the indie albums *Michigan* (2003) and *Illinois* (2005), other celebrations of seemingly banal subject matters.

The premiere of *The BQE* included a musical supplement called "Sufjan Plays the Hits," a tongue-in-cheek nod to his pop roots. While performing a set of his incandescent songs, he dons a set of angel wings, appropriate to his soft, lilting vocals and fluent melodies. The evening proved that the composer, whose own repertory has grown in the interim to include ballet scores and a work about American rodeo, could readily contribute to both the symphonic and pop canons.

Michael Atkinson conducting *The BQE*, Sufjan Stevens (at piano), 2007. Photo: Rahav Segev

Jess Barbagallo, Sean Donovan, LaToya Lewis, and David Pence in *HOUSE/ DIVIDED*, Marianne Weems/ The Builders Association, 2012. Photo: Richard Termine

2012

# HOUSE/DIVIDED

Marianne Weems, The Builders Association

In *HOUSE/DIVIDED*, the New York-based performance-media company The Builders Association weaves episodes drawn from John Steinbeck's classic novel *The Grapes of Wrath* with those of the decade's most polarizing financial crisis catalyzed by the default on mortgage-backed securities. That may sound like unlikely fodder for a work of theater, but it exemplifies the company's focus on macro issues juxtaposed with their micro impact. Director Marianne Weems switches between the two threads—told engagingly in dialogue written by Moe Angelos and James Gibbs—at a rhythm and pace that captures our full attention.

Clips of the film version of the novel starring Henry Fonda are interspersed with live action and elements of folk music to depict the Depression-era sequences. The fiscal chaos is conveyed by live action and video (designed by Austin Switser), with chilling content taken from actual stockholder briefings given by Goldman Sachs and Lehman Brothers. Although the outcome is known, the audacity and sheer scope of the disaster still shocks.

In Steinbeck's novel, the Joad family prepares to move from Oklahoma, where they've lost their farm, to the promised land of California. They debate which precious few belongings to keep, and talk of the imagined bounty of fertile farm lands and fruit trees, whose produce they wind up picking. The focus on one family's fate enables us to empathize with the individual consequences—in this case, of a failed economy.

In contrast, the modern-day fiscal debacle is framed by the actions of unchecked corporate greed and depersonalized relationships. Locating a responsible person willing to discuss a pending foreclosure becomes an impossible nightmare as the bank that originally issued a mortgage no longer owns the debt. Various characters have specific responsibilities in the foreclosure chain—identifying properties to buy from spotting overgrown weeds, evicting squatters, auctioning off leftover possessions, removing wild animals. An entire sub-industry has grown from the irresponsible acquisition of foreclosed property, encouraged and expedited by a financial sector that considered itself immune to failure—honing in only on profits.

The Builders Association took inspiration from conceptual artist Gordon Matta-Clark—one of his repeated gestures was to slice up buildings—buying an actual foreclosed house, which is used as the primary set piece in *HOUSE/DIVIDED*. Its walls become screens for video projections; its full or empty rooms metaphors for the precarious stability of a nuclear family, handcuffed to the economics of housing. By seeing the parallel between old and new economic disasters in a format that departs from traditional scripted drama, we see how history can disastrously repeat itself, and are given a bracing look at the repercussions of unchecked capitalist greed.

2012

# Roman Tragedies

## Ivo van Hove, Toneelgroep Amsterdam

In a season that celebrated the 30th Next Wave Festival, Toneelgroep Amsterdam's *Roman Tragedies* proved there were still theatrical paradigms to shatter. Directed by Ivo van Hove, it distills three of Shakespeare's tragedies—*Coriolanus*, *Julius Caesar*, and *Antony and Cleopatra*—into a gripping five-hour exposition of politics and power, performed in Dutch with English surtitles. The bold and modern reduction of the trio of plays—and their concatenation—might have been enough of a revolution, but to boot, the audience was invited to watch seated onstage among the actors, and to change positions throughout, cued by periodic light and sound storms.

Jan Versweyveld's innovative set, with video designs by Tal Yarden, pushes the stage of the BAM Howard Gilman Opera House out to the theater's structural walls. Numerous sofas, lamps, video cameras, and monitors fill the space that surrounds a central glass hallway that serves as a makeshift morgue for dead potentates. A TV anchor desk and publicly visible make-up stations line the perimeter (the latter evocative of Théâtre du Soleil), plus a concession where viewers can buy refreshments and computer terminals available for checking email. Just above the proscenium, a red digital news zipper spews real-time headlines, tweets, and audience directives Times Square-style (for example, stating the time until Caesar's death). On the hovering projection screen, we then see Caesar's body from above, splayed as if at a crime scene in a modern, television-procedural version of lying in state.

Van Hove is a seasoned veteran of BAM—Next Wave offerings include *Opening Night* (2008), *Cries and Whispers* (2011), *Angels in America* (2014), *Antigone* (2015), *Kings of War* (2016), and *The Fountainhead* (2017)—and his productions show an acute awareness of image mediation and contextual point of view. A viewer can sit literally right next to an actor during a scene, while watching the action from a different angle on a monitor 10 feet away. The news media filters events in slightly delayed time, refracting a story's angle as time passes—spinning it, so to speak. We see Mark Antony conducting an interview in front of a bank of eight microphones, representing news outlets that will tell one story eight ways, also analogous to how audience members each see the same show differently.

The characters wear modern business attire to match the sleek, soulless furniture. But we see them apart from public appearances—lounging, getting dressed, using iPads, laughing, bickering—analogous to gawking at popular magazine coverage of modern celebrities in their sweats getting smoothies, or seeing the president golfing in shorts. Van Hove remarkably depicts these historic characters in a believable contemporary framework, infusing them (and theater) with life—sometimes banal, always electric.

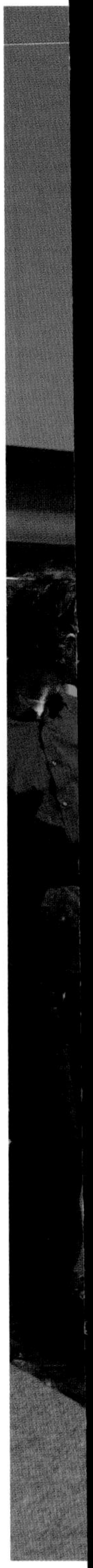

*Roman Tragedies*, Ivo van Hove/Toneelgroep Amsterdam, 2012. Photo: Richard Termine

LOWE'S

2014

# The Object Lesson

Geoff Sobelle, David Neumann

Upon entering the Fishman Space for the performance of *The Object Lesson*, audience members are greeted like old friends or new acquaintances by Geoff Sobelle, who performs solo—apart from some audience cameos. He invites them to rummage through, and sit on, one of the countless scattered cardboard boxes interspersed with old furniture and piles of books and detritus towering so high they recede into the darkness of the upper level. Sobelle, in a suit jacket but barefoot, bustles around, opening boxes and extracting a rug, side table, lamp, and Victrola playing Chopin, creating a surprisingly homey setting (designed by Steven Dufala) for this immersive performance directed by David Neumann.

Sobelle dials an old-fashioned telephone, the first of a series of clever asides that make it feel as if he is not truly alone onstage (albeit surrounded by the audience). The conversation turns to memories stirred up by objects or by association, bouncing along quickly from a youthful romance, to a trip to Germany, to a goat herder, to the cheese he made (at which point he finds, and breaks, bread to eat it with), to a blinking light observed from a hillside where he lay gazing at stars. He then clambers, goat-like, up a pile of boxes and pulls out said traffic light, which appears gigantic juxtaposed with people, rather than hanging 30 feet in the air, and repeatedly blinks, green, yellow, red.

Several viewers are pulled into the performance. He engages two people to sit at desks and take an inventory of sundry items, which elucidates the tedium of daily life. A woman receives a phone call, and then is wooed by Sobelle, who produces a bottle of wine, goblets, and a chandelier, which he enlists a man to hold above them. He chops a head of lettuce by donning ice skates and doing a charming tap routine. As he coaxes the woman into dancing, a magical packing peanut snowstorm descends from the rafters to engulf them.

In the final scene, next to a wall featuring an old library card catalogue, Sobelle rummages through bins, finding items with which to shave. One box is particularly fruitful, offering up a stream of clothing and junk, and finally a massive tangle of cords and wires that he tugs out endlessly. This engaging commentary on materialism and nostalgia exemplifies the potential of the Fishman Space—which opened in the BAM Richard B. Fisher Building in 2012—as a venue in which to realize creative visions that extend beyond a proscenium. *The Object Lesson* erases any barrier between performance and audience, further welcoming viewers by integrating them into the fabric of the production.

Geoff Sobelle in *The Object Lesson*, Geoff Sobelle/David Neumann, 2014. Photo: Max Gordon

2015

# Continu

## Sasha Waltz & Guests

*Continu* departs from German choreographer Sasha Waltz's previous Next Wave productions, where dramatic sets have featured prominently—a glass tank filled with naked bodies in *Körper* (2002), tectonically shifted wooden platforms in *Impromptus* (2005), or a room on fire, as in *Gezeiten* (2010). But *Continu*'s minimal designs direct the focus to the dance, whose two parts were originally created to inaugurate the Neues Museum and Zaha Hadid's MAXXI, in Berlin and Rome, respectively. The designs—costumes by Bernd Skodzig and lighting by Martin Hauk—hew to a black/white, negative/positive schematic that emphasizes contrast. The earthy accessibility and driving urgency of the combined dance and music bring to mind Igor Stravinsky's *The Rite of Spring*.

As the MAXXI is located in the Flaminio quarter of Rome that once housed a military compound, elements of the movement imagery in the first or "dark" act allude to the terrible consequences of war, such as fear, isolation, and mortality. In one scene, a single dancer breaks free and sprints across the stage against the lead-hued floor and backdrop, away from the huddled group. In another, except for one lone standing figure, the performers collapse to the floor. Within the expanse of the BAM Howard Gilman Opera House stage, the repeated juxtapositions of an individual to a group—massed in a wedge, or in a circle—become all the more stark.

Waltz's nonclassical choreography ranges from pedestrian to expressionistic. An emotion can be summoned by the simplest of moves—a slumped torso, defeat or surrender; a hovering balance, indecision. The primal feel is underscored by the driving percussion of composer Iannis Xenakis, performed live by Robyn Schulkowsky, and Edgard Varèse's textured, variegated soundscape punctuated by blaring horns.

In the second "light" act, Claude Vivier's slashing, sometimes atonal strings and snippets of Mozart accompany the action. The dancers have changed from dark, earth-toned costumes to beiges or, for some men, naked but for briefs. A portion of their passages are childlike, floor bound, at times sculptural, and clearly legible against the white flooring, which then becomes a canvas upon which the dancers scrawl red and black lines.

The final moment connects *Continu* to the literal upheaval of *Gezeiten*—a male dancer pulls up a corner of the marley dance floor and tears diagonally downstage with it, pulling it over his head. It is another instance of Waltz adding by subtracting, and making unexpected, imaginative use of the spartan surroundings as a means to amplify visual intrigue and drama.

*Continu*, Sasha Waltz & Guests, 2015. Photo: Julieta Cervantes

## 2016
# Battlefield
### Peter Brook, Marie-Hélène Estienne, Jean-Claude Carrière, C.I.C.T.-Théâtre des Bouffes du Nord

Nearly three decades after the Majestic Theater (now the BAM Harvey Theater) was transformed for *The Mahabharata*, Peter Brook's production of *Battlefield*—a literary coda to the ancient Indian epic—was staged by C.I.C.T.-Théâtre des Bouffes du Nord in the 2016 Next Wave Festival. The venue's dusky red walls with chipped plaster stand bare, with the backstage wings visible, just as they were in 1987 for *The Mahabharata*. And, like then, the drummer Toshi Tsuchitori sits on the stage's side, fingers suspended above the drum's surface, producing the sole music—percussion, from soft to thunderous—needed to accompany the unfolding drama.

All aspects of *Battlefield* are highly concentrated compared to *The Mahabharata*. In 2016, each actor in the trim cast of four (Carole Karemera, Jared McNeill, Ery Nzaramba, and Sean O'Callaghan) plays several roles, animals and insects included—in contrast to a cast of 28, plus five musicians for *The Mahabharata*—and its duration lasts just an hour, versus the nearly nine-hour original when epic battles were incited, fought, and won. *Battlefield* takes place in the aftermath of the Great War between rival family factions, whose few survivors lament all the wasted lives and the tragic inevitability that, despite the horrific carnage, war will be repeated ad infinitum.

With the aid of a few lengths of cloth and some elongated sticks, the actors in *Battlefield* spin engrossing parables. A snake, pigeon, mongoose, and worm become empathetic metaphors for characteristics such as righteousness, truth, and fragility. A saffron shawl draped around his head transforms Nzaramba into an old woman, and then becomes a dead man's winding sheet when the aperture is sealed shut. The forest, referred to repeatedly, represents the afterlife, and souls migrate magically between people through deep gazes. Yet among the serious topics touched upon, Brook manages to poke fun at the milieu by having an actor share "treasures" (in the form of shawls) with members of the audience he deems poor, or asking their seemingly well-off recipients to distribute them to the indigent. In the riveting closing scene, the five performers gaze toward some uncertain fate in ponderous silence until the audience's applause signals the end.

The BAM Harvey Theater was renamed in honor of legendary impresario and BAM president from 1967 to 1999, Harvey Lichtenstein, who founded the Next Wave Festival. While much remains true to the 1987 renovation—done specifically for the inaugural production of *The Mahabharata* in the style of Brook's home venue of the Théâtre des Bouffes du Nord in Paris—the benches are now comfortable theater seats, and there are two additional stage-level entrances, among other changes. But the essence of the elegantly decaying amphitheater remains, and *Battlefield* is a tribute to the timeless veracity of one of Peter Brook's essential philosophies of the theater: put two people in an empty space, and you have drama, regardless of the presence of lavish sets or production elements. Moving from *The Mahabharata* to *Battlefield* creates a full circle, in which the breadth of Brook's legendary directorial expertise is on full display.

Carole Karemera, Sean O'Callaghan, Jared McNeill, and Ery Nzaramba in *Battlefield*, Peter Brook/Marie-Hélène Estienne/Jean-Claude Carrière, 2016. Photo: Caroline Moreau

2017

# Crossing

## Matthew Aucoin, Diane Paulus, American Repertory Theater

The young and talented Matthew Aucoin wrote both the music and libretto for *Crossing*, an opera based on the journal that poet Walt Whitman kept while caring for wounded soldiers as a volunteer nurse during the Civil War. The complexity and consequences of the war are examined through three primary characters who sing Aucoin's lyrics that evoke and, at times, quote Whitman's poetry.

Whitman wanders amid hospital patients, comforting them and providing alms. A badly injured John Wormley enters, and Whitman attempts to appease his suffering. Escaped slave and now a Union soldier Freddie Stowers returns from the front, reporting a bleak picture. Wormley emerges as a dark figure—seducing Whitman, then calling him a monster, and finally unmasking himself as an enemy combatant with the mission of sending a fictional "Dear Family" letter to his Confederate cohorts to reveal the location of the hospital as a potential military target.

Directed by Diane Paulus, *Crossing* forges riveting drama from an explosive moment pivotal in America's history; from the meeting of representatives from the two opposing sides, each with his own agenda, plus the empathetic narrator Whitman; and from the horrific, ultimately allayed treachery. The vocal music shifts from soliloquies to lush group numbers for the dozen or so supporting male singers, accompanied by the chamber orchestra A Far Cry, conducted by Aucoin. At times, sung lines overlap to create rich sonic textures. The voices of the lead performers enhance their characters' traits—the clear, steady baritone of Whitman contrasts with the piercing, at times frenetic tenor of Wormley and the mellow baritone of Stowers. The only female voice is that of a woman who appears briefly as a messenger, announcing the end of the war in a clarion soprano.

Throughout, every syllable is gratifyingly audible, and Aucoin's experience as a poet is evident in the libretto's rhythm and natural flow. Jill Johnson choreographed brief but eloquent movement passages for a quartet of dancers, adding visual poetry and dynamism to the often stark setting by Tom Pye. In addition, the projections by Finn Ross transform the medical barracks into a moonlit field, augmented by Jennifer Tipton's twilight-to-dawn lighting.

*Crossing* naturally alludes to Whitman's poem "Crossing Brooklyn Ferry," but otherwise, the title's broad and unspecific meaning as both a verb and a noun allows for multiple allusions. It might be a reference to the passage between worlds (the River Styx comes to mind), or crossing moral or sexual boundaries, or the transformation of souls. It manages to focus on the micro and macro at once—on the actions of individuals, as well as huge moral, social, and political debates whose consequences still reverberate some 150 years later.

Rod Gilfry and Davóne Tines in *Crossing*, Matthew Aucoin/Diane Paulus/American Repertory Theater, 2017. Photo: Richard Termine

There are aspects of American culture that are beautiful and powerful—and often in dance there is a form of physical athleticism that enhances the role of storytelling. And with other cultures, we need to have a better understanding of each other. The Next Wave provides a window into other cultures—Sankai Juku, for example—just seeing them perform. The history of their culture informs the work, and you can't imagine their place in our culture until you see them. For me, the challenge we face in dance is to have a sense of place in relation to performance—a place that allows an artist to break more rules and be more experimental. Ultimately, what connects people to the work of Urban Bush Women is being able to feel the energy of the performer.

**Jawole Willa Jo Zollar**

Dancer and Choreographer

*"...como el musguito en la piedra, ay si, si, si..." (Like Moss on a Stone)*, Tanztheater Wuppertal Pina Bausch, 2012. Photo: Stephanie Berger

# Dance

Wendy Perron

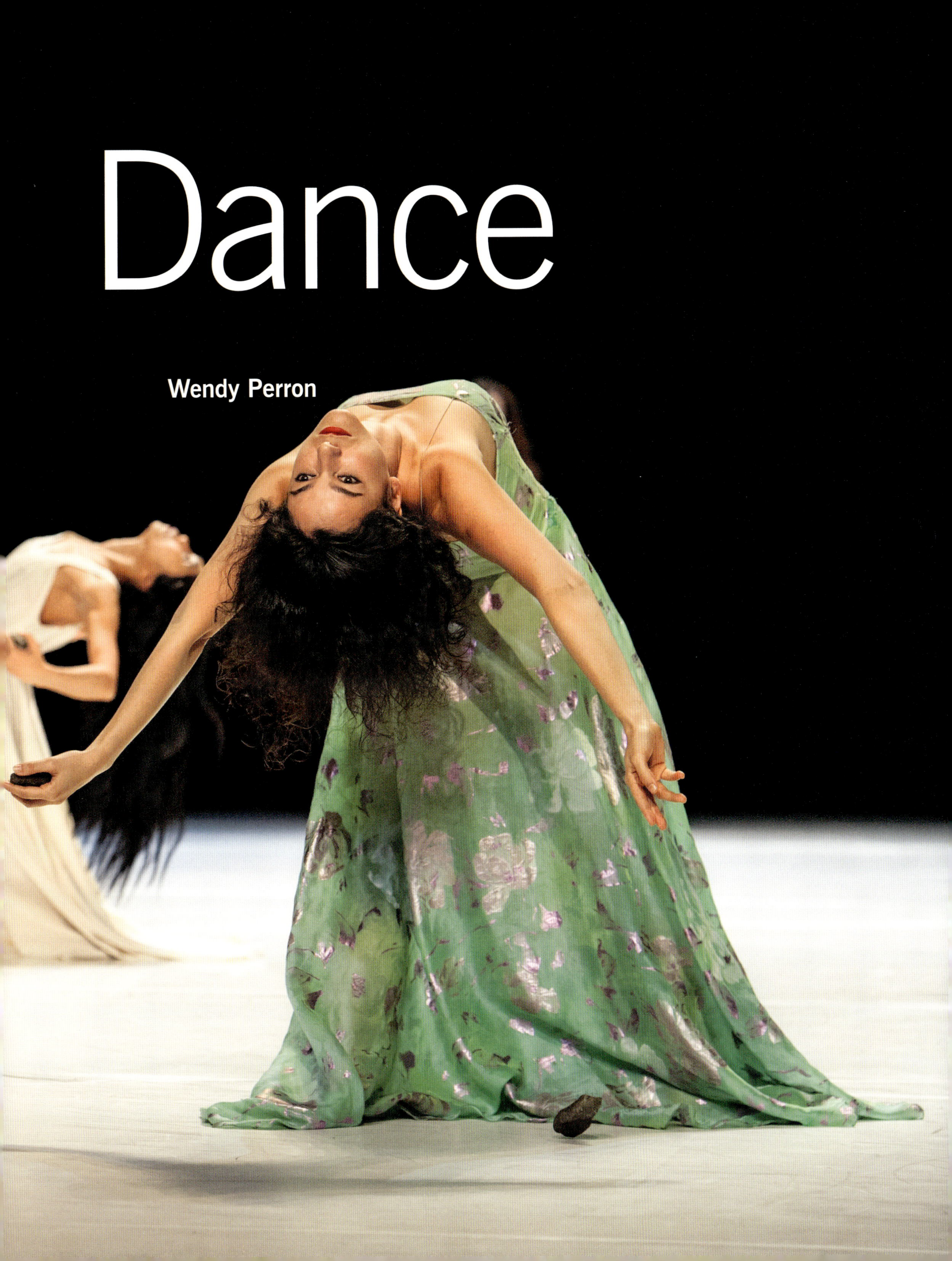

If you have followed any part of the Next Wave Festival over the course of its 35 years, you've witnessed some of the great minds of modern dance: Merce Cunningham, Trisha Brown, Bill T. Jones, Mark Morris, Pina Bausch, William Forsythe, and Ohad Naharin. These artists and many others have been nurtured and developed by legendary BAM impresario Harvey Lichtenstein and his chosen successor, executive producer Joseph V. Melillo. We have watched each of them grow and change. We have been close enough to be swept away by their beauty or staggered by their audacity. They have engaged us in the issues of our time: race, gender, the environment, the relation of art to life. Whether their aesthetic places them in the category of minimalism, tanztheater, epic narrative, or dances of cultural identity, they have all alighted in one spot: BAM. Although many new dance presenters have sprouted up in the last 35 years, the Next Wave continues to be a beacon of forward-looking dance.

These dances do the traditional work of art. They educate, edify, and entertain, but they also unleash. They unleash the individual imagination, experimental ideas, collaborative alchemy, and altered states in both performers and viewers. Some notably memorable moments: Molissa Fenley charging across the Lepercq Space, sculpting the air with her arms to the jazz music of Anthony Davis in **Hemispheres** (1983); or Bill T. Jones as a wobbly pre-verbal "fabricated" man in **Secret Pastures** (1984); or Tanztheater Wuppertal's Julie Shanahan yelling to her two suitors to throw tomatoes at her in **Palermo Palermo** (1991). You might have seen Dana Caspersen enacting a ferocious split personality, her seething body animated by the exaggerated voices of two opposite characters in William Forsythe's **I don't believe in outer space** (2011).

Not only has the Next Wave cultivated these individual artists over decades, it has also cultivated audiences. The festival has accustomed us to the unaccustomed, the unconventional, and always the unpredictable. It has raised the standards for interdisciplinary work and it has raised our curiosity for dance around the globe. It's given a home for experimental work that may or may not eventually expand into a proscenium space.

But before there was a Next Wave Festival, there was a Next Wave Series. Initiated as a pilot project by Harvey Lichtenstein for two seasons, in 1981 and 1982–83, the series gave experimental American artists an opportunity to play for a broader audience. Dance was in the forefront of the Next Wave from the beginning, guided by Lichtenstein, who had danced professionally with modern dance greats Pearl Lang and Sophie Maslow. Innovators Trisha Brown,

fueled by the illusion of spontaneity: the sense of flying high, a connection to air, decision-making on the spot, was palpable. More than any other previous work, *Set and Reset* showed how a collaboration of basically formal approaches could blossom into a fully blown opus. Anderson's music, with a tango-like beat, propelled the dance in many directions, mostly away from center stage. And Rauschenberg's set, which started as a light-filled sculptural form on the floor and then rose upward, lent a sense of liftoff. Adding to that was the riddle of the transparent wings: When the dancers were visible behind those wings, were they still performing?

For the performers, momentum of body coincided with momentum of mind. In making the dance, they had treated specific dance phrases with suggestions like "Play with being visible and invisible." For the audience, you had to sit on the edge of your seat to catch even a fraction of the interaction. When dancer Diane Madden curves over with an arm extended outward, Trisha Brown rushes in from stage left, grabs her arm and flings her across the space—to land in the arms of Stephen Petronio, who has appeared out of nowhere. Split-second timing is the name of the game. The six ready-for-anything dancers are all aiding and abetting each other's recklessness. Another time, Petronio—who would soon found his own company—slowly leans on one dancer and when he's just about to fall, a different dancer is suddenly visible underneath him. Conceal and reveal, deflect and proceed. For all of minimalism's supposed disregard for the audience, Brown captures the audience's attention with near crashes, clever escapes, and playful dares, all embedded in her dreamy fluidity and Anderson's syncopated score.

If *Set and Reset* leaned toward abstraction, *Secret Pastures* hinted at narrative. They were the two halves of the new collaborative postmodernism. In *Secret Pastures*, for which Keith Haring designed sets, Willi Smith designed costumes, and Peter Gordon's Love of Life Orchestra made the gorgeously quirky music, each element lent its own fabulousness. Gordon once commented that he as well as Jones and Zane all had "a desire for sensual answers to formal questions." Arnie Zane as "The Professor" sported a lab coat, glasses, and a Mohawk haircut. Janet Lilly sauntered in a fur coat made of white Afro wigs sewn together, and Seán Curran skipped and skittered in blue hair. As "The Fabricated Man," Jones was curious, innocent, open to learning but also vulnerable. He moved like an underwater animal, wandering and wondering despite the added lumps to his costume. Anna Kisselgoff described him in the *New York Times* as fusing "a pantherine grace with a massive power."

Arnie Zane in *Secret Pastures*, Bill T. Jones/Arnie Zane & Company, 1984. Photo: Tom Caravaglia

The most moving scene was where the Professor tries to teach the Fabricated Man how to behave. The magnetism between Zane, with his near-pantomimic sharpness, and Jones, in his feigned awkwardness was poignant. The Professor circles the Fabricated Man, who accidentally lurches at the Professor. Although the characters were cartoonish, the process consisted of solving tasks—at a wondrous level of virtuosity. Perpetually buoyant, Curran—whose own company would later perform in the Next Wave—nimbly performed an Irish jig overlaid with a series of Jones's arm gestures while also inserting ballet beats.

The giddy *Secret Pastures* astonished some, provoked others. Esteemed critic Deborah Jowitt wrote that it "may be the first dance work of any consequence to acknowledge the influence of MTV on our perception." Some critics felt the characterizations were more style than substance. Others appreciated the mashing up of aesthetics. As Kisselgoff noted in her *New York Times* review, Marcel Fieve's extreme haircuts and colors helped make the dancers look witty and chic. She felt the sensibility was "punk art domesticated, a collaboration between received intellectual influences from academe and a fashion consciousness that keeps an eye on the street." For the Jones/Zane company, *Secret Pastures* marked a pivotal moment. With its connections to the art and fashion worlds, it attracted celebrities to BAM like Andy Warhol and Madonna. Word

spread, leading to a surge of international touring. In effect, *Secret Pastures* put Bill T. Jones/ Arnie Zane & Company on the map.

## Brooklyn: Portal to Europe

The 1980s were the height of postmodern "abstract" dance in New York. Influenced by innovative choreographers like Merce Cunningham, Trisha Brown, and Lucinda Childs, American "dancemakers" were making dances about form and motion, pattern and space. At the same time, dancemakers in Europe were investigating narrative with a modernist sensibility. The Next Wave Festival was only two years old in 1985 when the Europeans started coming, beginning with German choreographer Pina Bausch and Tanztheater Wuppertal and Anne Teresa De Keersmaeker's Brussels-based group Rosas.

Bausch's work was a revelation for American audiences. And the regularity of Tanztheater Wuppertal's appearance at BAM—nearly every other year—made it an ongoing and evolving revelation. Elegance was juxtaposed with absurdity, cruelty with lavish dancing. Gender was a polarizing force; extreme stereotypes were exhibited, questioned, and mocked. Bausch excavated fantasies both dreamy and nightmarish. Flirtation devolved into abuse. A woman scrubs the floor from one side of the stage to the other while a man keeps tossing popcorn onto the floor. This kind of scene leads to questions. Are the women enjoying their abuse? Is attracting the opposite sex the main goal?

While American postmodernists like Trisha Brown and Lucinda Childs favored a "neutral" facial expression, Bausch's dancers were drenched in irony, making commentary on performance itself. They adopted a performance mask, be it sardonic, sweet, desperate, impassive, or unhinged. While Brown and Childs had an aversion to flamboyance, Bausch wrapped her women in extravagant gowns of luscious colors. The monumental set designs were possibly the prototype for the unwritten edict to "fill the stage" in Next Wave interdisciplinary collaborations. Rolf Borzik had created set and costume designs until his death in 1980; subsequently, Peter Pabst designed sets and Marion Cito the costumes. Bausch made her BAM debut in 1984 showcasing four works, and in the following year was invited to the festival for a three-week engagement. Audiences were hooked—and not just dance audiences. Her productions attracted people

*Arien*, Tanztheater Wuppertal Pina Bausch, 1985. Photo: Beatriz Schiller

of all persuasions and were often sold out. Tanztheater performers were our hostesses: smiling, unctuous, hiding naughty secrets up their sleeves. The contrast between their elegant demeanor and the absurd, sometime cruel things they did to each other was mesmerizing.

Tanztheater Wuppertal's first Next Wave Festival program—comprising **Arien**, **Kontakthof**, **Gebirge**, **The Seven Deadly Sins**, and **Don't Be Afraid**—was unsettling. At the time, the women's movement had challenged gender stereotypes, but Bausch clung to exaggerated gender roles: Men were drawn to women like catnip, and the women happily tried to please the men. Both genders poked, squeezed, and wrenched each other's body parts as an accepted ritual. In one diagonal procession, the women jammed their feet into high heels as a necessary torture. Many went to see Tanztheater Wuppertal with a combination of dread and fascination.

But one cannot deny the sheer scale of Bausch's thinking. For *Palermo Palermo*, the first thing that happened was a huge brick wall (set design by Peter Pabst) keeled over backward,

ABOVE
*Two Cigarettes in the Dark*, Tanztheater Wuppertal Pina Bausch, 1994. Photo: Dan Rest

OPPOSITE
Rainer Behr in *Vollmond*, Tanztheater Wuppertal Pina Bausch, 2010. Photo: Julieta Cervantes

scattering debris all over the stage. In **Der Fensterputzer** (1997), we encounter a red-glowing mountain of 40,000 silk flowers, also designed by Pabst, which the dancers dive into, burrow under, or slide down.

Although most of her scenes assumed an automatic heterosexuality, she expanded to other kinds of gender play. Male dancer Jan Minarik in *Palermo Palermo* strutted wearing a crown of cigarettes, bare legs, and the obligatory high heels; in contrast, Nazareth Panadero—his female counterpart—used her mannish voice to command our attention. All Bausch dancers are keenly aware of performing. Whether they are engaging in degrading or uplifting actions, they are *about* performing.

By the time of **Two Cigarettes in the Dark** (1994), the balance of brutal to benign began to tip toward the latter. It became clear that Bausch's overall theme was the absurdity of life in general rather than specifically about sexual attraction. A woman with a pot tied to her runs and smashes against a wall over and over, while a man tries to intercept her. A man wielding an ax roams ominously while a woman serenely practices yoga. Bausch's work offers the best examples of theatrical Dada in our time, with radical juxtapositions that require a double take. We get some comic relief in the person of Dominique Mercy, who periodically scampers onto the stage

as a chef/conductor, setting up a cooking table on which nothing gets made. He cavorts so recklessly that his head seems about to fling itself away from his body. Later, in a previously hidden alcove, he takes a bath—wearing flippers.

Whether her scenic collaborator was Rolf Borzik or Peter Pabst, each one of Bausch's works immersed us in a whole different world. While Americans were going minimal, she was going maximal. Gesamtwerk—the totality of parts—wins us over. In **Bamboo Blues** (2008), we are intoxicated by a world of the senses. Swatches of cloth billow; towels wrap around torsos like saris. Combativeness is gone. The elegant Shantala Shivalingappa offers segments of a long ribbon to the audience, asking sweetly, "Can you smell it? It's cardamom." Created during a residency in South India, *Bamboo Blues* nevertheless has little to do with the reality of a particular region. Hunger, poverty, stench, fires, street children—none of these things make their way into this piece. *Bamboo Blues* is all about pleasure. As Bausch has said in interviews, the real world became so full of violence that she felt compelled to create pleasure onstage, a transition notable in her later works.

The theme of water, seen previously in *Arien* and other works, reaches its peak in **Vollmond** (2010). It's as though all the glasses, buckets, and puddles of water in previous pieces poured into this great river of water on the Opera House stage. To see Rainer Behr splashing through the water, his arms and legs whipping outward, is to see a man's soul lashing out. Then, in her final work, **"...como el musguito en la piedra, ay si, si, si..." (Like Moss on a Stone)**, which came to BAM in 2012, three years after Bausch's death, we see the pleasure in a preverbal, polymorphous way. Sixteen dancers are sitting on the floor in a diagonal, alternating male and female. They are each massaging the head of the person in front of them. They are connected through touch, through care, and through the ability to take and give pleasure at once.

The BAM audience has seen Bausch's works move from harrowing to absurdist to delightful and loving. Three things draw us back—her outsized imagination, her Dadaist sense of humor, and the dancing—the dancing. Although it's not the first thing people talk about in Bausch's work, some of the best solo dancing in New York happens in Tanztheater Wuppertal. Each member of the cast is stretched, windblown, urgent yet precise, and unique. One could complain that some of the solos are long and repetitive, but the actual dancing is superb.

Hailing from Belgium, Anne Teresa De Keersmaeker's Rosas has appeared in the Next Wave Festival almost as often as Tanztheater Wuppertal. More interested in momentum and less

Pablo Aran Gimeno in *"...como el musguito en la piedra, ay si, si, si..." (Like Moss on a Stone),* Tanztheater Wuppertal Pina Bausch, 2012. Photo: Stephanie Berger

in theater, De Keersmaeker makes works that rev up minimalism into a fury of pure movement. She has partnered with Steve Reich's music many times, as they share an approach to building complexity. **Fase**, a work for two women that she performed with dancer Tale Dolven at **Steve Reich @ 70** (2006), was first developed in the early 1980s in New York at the studios of New York University's Tisch School of the Arts. She took Lucinda Childs's vocabulary of walking, twisting, and turning and imbued it with emotional intensity. The result was what *New York Times* reviewer Siobhan Burke calls "stark euphoria."

Her collaborations with Reich expanded to larger ensembles with **Drumming** (2001) and **Rain** (2003). The rhythms were tantalizing and the dancing became more forceful—impulsive, highly inflected, obsessive. De Keersmaeker's notoriety leapt forward in 2011 when Beyoncé's music video *Countdown* appropriated some of the exact moves of the choreographer's **Rosas Danst Rosas** (1986) from a YouTube clip. Charges of stealing hit social media, setting off widespread debate about the uses and abuses of appropriation.

De Keersmaeker's special brand of momentum reached an invigorating peak with **Vortex Temporum** (2016). The music ensemble Ictus played Gérard Grisey's score of the same title with its spectacularly decrescendoing notes (imagine a siren sounding backward with a myriad of textures within it) on a bare stage. Later, the musicians and dancers together created a terrific

Anne Teresa De Keersmaeker and Tale Dolven in *Fase*, included in *Steve Reich @ 70*, Anne Teresa de Keersmaeker/ Rosas/Steve Reich, 2006. Photo: Stephanie Berger

centrifugal force. Moving in concentric circles, they were so commingled—all wore dark outfits—that it was hard to discern the difference between the dancers and the musicians. That confusion added to the excitement of the gathering whirlwind of sound and motion, their orbits crashing and clashing. One dancer even shoved the pianist off his bench, and somehow the piano ended up careening around the stage while being played. It felt like the performers were veering off into a celestial system of their own.

Although Tanztheater Wuppertal and Rosas have performed at the Next Wave Festival more regularly than any other dance groups, visitors from Europe have included a wide variety of choreographers: Mechthild Grossmann, Susanne Linke, Maguy Marin, Jiří Kylián (Nederlands Dans Theater), the French-Albanian Angelin Preljocaj, and the astonishing mixed-nationality hip-hop duo Wang Ramirez. The German dance-theater practitioner Sasha Waltz mesmerized audiences with the visually stunning **Körper** (2002), followed by **Impromptus** (2005) and **Gezeiten**

*Vortex Temporum*, Anne Teresa De Keersmaeker/ Rosas/Ictus, 2016. Photo: Robert Altman

(2010). Her most recent Next Wave production, **Continu** (2015)—with its long dresses, explosive gestures, and Edgard Varèse's dissonant music—took us back to the early drama of modernism.

But the most enduring and powerful influence from Europe after Bausch and De Keersmaeker has been William Forsythe. The American-born choreographer who revolutionized ballet in our time presided over Ballett Frankfurt and later the Forsythe Company for more than 30 years. He stretched and twisted and interrogated classical ballet until it became utterly contemporary and often bizarre. He used pointe shoes not to float but to jab into the floor. Some saw the super-attenuated, aggressive bodies as distortions, but those extremes were based on classical épaulement. In 1998, **EIDOS : TELOS** jolted us with the essential wildness of Forsythe's choreography. The Ballett Frankfurt dancers thrust themselves into space, constantly interrupting their own movement as though trying to rid the body of something awful.

In 2003, the final program of Ballett Frankfurt before it transitioned into the Forsythe Company included three galvanizing works. Twenty metal tables screeched into place for **One Flat**

ABOVE
*Continu*, Sasha Waltz & Guests, 2015. Photo: Julieta Cervantes

OPPOSITE
*EIDOS : TELOS*, William Forsythe/Ballett Frankfurt, 1998. Photo: Toby Wales

**Thing, reproduced**. The dancers crawled and lunged and pounced over and under the tables, creating a swarming hive just this side of chaos. They seemed to have a terrific urge to investigate the tables, unleashing their inventiveness into a very purposeful search. In a different vein, **(N.N.N.N.)** was a cause-and-effect sequence wherein four men fit into each other's nooks and crannies like a puzzle. The most pristine piece was **Duo**, a duet mostly in unison, danced by two women in sheer black tops. With a spare soundscape by longtime Forsythe composer Thom Willems, it lays bare the powerful legs, destabilized pelvis, and extreme torquing of the upper body that characterize the Forsythe style.

Forsythe considers the stage a laboratory, and he's experimented with radical new ways of generating and organizing material. In **Decreation** (2009), he used a device to "conduct" the dancers from backstage, thus varying their timing on the spot. It was Forsythe's of-the-moment attention to the performance/audience relationship that determined how he conducted. Similarly, in **Sider** (2013), the dancers were listening to scenes from *Hamlet* through earpieces, and

Forsythe's voice would interrupt the Elizabethan cadence to guide them in speed and structural options. Just as Bausch was a leader in dance-theater, Forsythe exerted similar influence over post-classical ballet, which continues to be felt here and in Europe.

## Epic Narrative

In the 1990s, African American choreographers felt a pull toward narrative as a means to tell their stories, which some have argued was a natural rebound from formalism. Dance scholar Ann Cooper Albright has called this direction "epic narrative" and points to four choreographers, all of whom have visited the Next Wave Festival, working in this vein: Jawole Willa Jo Zollar, Garth Fagan, David Roussève, and Bill T. Jones.

Zollar's **Praise House,** performed by her group Urban Bush Women in 1991, was based on the life of visionary black painter Minnie Evans, but the larger story was the profound black experience of turning suffering into joy. *Praise House* drew upon African American cultural traditions, including shouts and field hollers, to tell the story of an artist alienated from the church.

Carl Riley's gospel music infused it with a sense of place and time.

Zollar embarked on a more complex project in the 2008 Next Wave with **Les écailles de la mémoire (The Scales of Memory)**, a collaboration between the all-female, Brooklyn-based Urban Bush Women and Senegal's all-male Compagnie Jant-Bi. A major effort to understand Africa diasporan cultures, the collaboration itself was epic. The men don't just dance, they *go* at dancing. Yet Urban Bush Women dancer Nora Chipaumire—who returned to the Next Wave in 2012 and 2016 with her own special brand of gender chutzpah—gives them a run for their money. She taunts, yells, and out-dances them.

Other images refer to slavery: Men struggling with their hands clasped behind them as though trying to free themselves from shackles, heads bowed in supplication; women and men standing on a bench as though being sold at auction. The lighter moments see women strutting their stuff for the benefit of the men. One man does an amazing ass shimmy. The common ground between the male Africans and the female African Americans is well earned, gradually arrived at, and full of humor.

Garth Fagan's **Griot New York,** which premiered in 1991 and returned in 2012, explores a remarkable range of tones and moods. Fagan merged the Caribbean tradition

OPPOSITE
*Praise House*, Urban Bush Women, 1991. Photo: William H. Struhs

RIGHT
Nora Chipaumire in *Les écailles de la mémoire (The Scales of Memory)*, Compagnie Jant-Bi/Urban Bush Women, 2008. Photo: Jack Vartoogian

of storytelling with the American sculptor Martin Puryear and jazz great Wynton Marsalis. Fagan spices the techniques of Merce Cunningham, choreographer Lester Horton, and ballet with a sensual twistiness and mischievous pelvis. In a dance that's a cross between a funeral dance and vaudeville, Natalie Rogers sashays and skitters onto the stage, does a slow and viscous solo with stretched classical lines, and then breaks it up with angular elbows, flexed feet, and jittery twitches: a seamless amalgam of cultural tropes.

*Griot New York* also contains one of the most casually tragic scenes in memory. It portrays homeless people either running around frantic or lounging around stoned. During the long section, one dancer inches slowly along the floor. A limp figure sprawls across his lap. Is he sleeping; is he dead? They stay together as they make their way from one side of the stage to the other, surrounded and sometimes hidden by the general commotion. Eventually, we see that the prone figure has some kind of palsy—his hand is shaking. Fagan, who also created the dances

ABOVE
Valentina Alexander and Norwood Pennewell in *Griot New York*, Garth Fagan/Wynton Marsalis/Martin Puryear, 1991. Photo courtesy of BAM Hamm Archives

OPPOSITE
David Roussève (featured) in his *The Whispers of Angels*, David Roussève/REALITY, 1995. Photo: Dan Rest

for *The Lion King* on Broadway, is a choreographic griot telling a story that doesn't shy away from suffering.

Another seasoned storyteller, David Roussève, choreographed three epic narratives for the festival, all in the BAM Harvey Theater (formerly the Majestic Theater): **Urban Scenes/Creole Dreams** (1992), **The Whispers of Angels** (1995), and **Love Songs** (1999). Each one has a hard edge—nothing goes down easy with Roussève. He can catch you in the middle of a heart-warming tale and dip it in acid. In *Whispers of Angels*, he teamed up with jazz queen Meshell Ndegeocello, gospel singer B.J. Crosby, and filmmaker Ayoka Chenzira to tell stories of black folk from previous centuries. He splices an annoying account of auditioning for a soap opera with painful stories of plantation life. Not one to simply celebrate black culture, Roussève, as the narrator, says lines like, "I stopped believing in everything black because everything black stopped believing in me." His stage is populated with different generations and types. Funny can be brutal and brutal can be surreal. Angels, ancient people, eccentric characters, innocent children—all are subject to the harshness born of slavery, but the ultimate message is one of hard-earned hope.

Bill T. Jones's **Still/Here** (1994) was an epic narrative, followed by an epic debate. The piece paid tribute to those who died or were dying of AIDS or other terminal illnesses. Gravitas had replaced chic in his work. With **Last Supper at Uncle Tom's Cabin/The Promised Land** (1990), Jones emerged as a leader of the multicultural side of the so-called culture wars. Deeply affected by Zane's death from AIDS, and infected with the virus himself, Jones planned *Still/Here* to include material from his survival workshops, in which people with terminal illnesses articulated their fears and hopes. These participants would be seen in projections, and their words would provide text for the professional dancers to speak. He wanted to learn from what they were going through. Like his Fabricated Man in *Secret Pastures*, he was open, absorbent, and vulnerable.

When the press release went out saying that there would be videos and text taken from people with terminal illnesses, dance critic Arlene Croce had a fit. Her attack on *Still/Here*, published in the *New Yorker* under the title "Discussing the Undiscussable," turned the piece into a cause célèbre. She refused to attend the performance, not wanting to see "dancers I'm *forced* to feel sorry for because of the way they present themselves: as dissed blacks, abused women, or

disenfranchised homosexuals—as performers, in short, who make out of victimhood victim art." Letters poured in to the magazine, some defending her choice and others defending Jones's right to make art out of whatever was preoccupying him.

This debate reverberated around the country and has become required reading to understand the culture wars of the 1990s. Croce was railing against the oncoming inevitability of multiculturalism and inclusion in the arts. But beyond the debate, *Still/Here* became known as a cri de coeur in the age of the AIDS crisis. With his small group of diverse dancers, Jones managed to project hope, wisdom, and humor. The dancers recite phrases taken from the survival workshops, each time announcing the name of the participant first. *Still/Here* is epic in that it plumbs the mysteries of life and death in a poetic way. The quotes and gestures transcend the deadly circumstances to attain a kind of universality. *Still/Here* is a requiem, which, of course, is a time-honored form in music, theater, and dance.

## Modern Takes Root and Branches Out

Ever since 1952, when Harvey Lichtenstein studied dance with Merce Cunningham at Black Mountain College, he was convinced that Cunningham was the future of modern dance. In 1954, when most of the dance establishment was dismissive of Cunningham, Lichtenstein offered him his first full evening of performance in New York City. Later, in 1968, he named the group a resident company at BAM. Longtime Cunningham dancer Carolyn Brown says the opportunity gave the choreographer "a kind of security that Merce had never known." The company performed there many times, the last being **The Legacy Tour** at the 2011 festival.

Cunningham and avant-garde composer John Cage had blasted open the relationship of music and dance. They created the two parts independently, bringing them together only for performance. The two men, who were partners in their personal lives as well as their artistic lives, never aimed to impart a single meaning or message, but were open to various interpretations. The Cunningham style of clean, unmannered, multidirectional movement was paired with experimental, sometimes cacophonous music by Cage or one of his colleagues. Not only was there no clear narrative, but the structure shunned the typical A-B-A format that was so reliably legible in most ballet and modern dance.

Odile Reine-Adelaide in *Still/Here*, Bill T. Jones/Arnie Zane Dance Company, 1994. Photo: Dan Rest

True to form, each of Cunningham's Next Wave outings contained some sort of unorthodoxy. The soundscape of **Roaratorio: An Irish Circus on Finnegans Wake** (1986) mixed Cage's compositions based on pages from James Joyce's epic novel *Finnegans Wake* with sounds of laughter, seagulls, water pouring, a dog barking. A cluster of onstage chairs provided a resting spot for the dancers, most often used by Cunningham himself, who was already showing signs of debilitating arthritis. In the program **Forward & Reverse**, staged in the 1997 festival, video artist Elliot Caplan embedded video monitors into surrounding walls in **Installations.** They formed such an unusual décor that Anna Kisselgoff called them "opaque windows." The series also included the New York premiere of **Rondo** and **Scenario,** whose grotesquely lumpy costumes by Comme des Garçons designer Rei Kawakubo tested our faith in Cunningham's open-mindedness.

ABOVE
*Roaratorio*, included in *The Legacy Tour*, Merce Cunningham Dance Company, 2011. Photo: Julieta Cervantes

OPPOSITE
*Second Hand*, included in *The Legacy Tour*, Merce Cunningham Dance Company, 2011. Photo: Stephanie Berger

**Split Sides,** which premiered at BAM in 2003 as part of the 50th anniversary of the Cunningham company, embraced chance in a very visible way. Each night before the show someone rolled the dice—onstage in view of the audience—to determine which half of the choreography would be first. They rolled again to decide the sequence of the music (either Sigur Rós or Radiohead), and again for the backdrop (by either Robert Heishman or Catherine Yass). We were watching chance in action. On opening night, Robert Rauschenberg and Carolyn Brown rolled the dice. We were watching history in action. *The Legacy Tour*, which crisscrossed the country for two years after Cunningham's death, reprised *Split Sides* with old favorites such as *Roaratorio*, *RainForest*, and **Second Hand**, first performed in 1970, and later works including **Pond Way** (1998) and **BIPED** (1999).

## The Poetry of Motion and Objects

No young dancemaker was untouched by the Cunningham/Cage influence. New Yorkers like John Jasperse, Wally Cardona, and Kate Weare have continued in the spirit of experimentation with a keen focus on the specificity of movement. They tend to have less interest in chance methods and more interest in creating a visual field that triggers certain tasks. Each of the cho-

reographers deploys everyday materials to arrive at a poetry of motion and objects. All have the uncanny ability to create something out of basically nothing.

In **Misuse liable to prosecution** (2007), John Jasperse filled the stage of the BAM Harvey with hundreds of coat hangers and water bottles, creating a kind of homemade, random beauty. He applied a methodical approach to functional movement. In **Giant Empty** (2001) that approach had rendered his nude duet with Miguel Gutierrez fascinating. The small adjustments of hands, feet, butt cheeks, and back of head formed interlocking parts of a two-person puzzle. *Giant Empty* placed the body in a liminal space between the sculptural and the sexual. Gutierrez, in his own work, has taken the absurdist edge that Jasperse plays with and magnified it. His Next Wave debut, **And lose the name of action** (2012), is a kind of oddball contemplation of aging. The cast, including "older dancers" like Ismael Houston-Jones and K.J. Holmes, sometimes sits among the audience and guides us through a mock séance. The sound and light create a disorienting waywardness, and all performers are resolutely unpolished.

In **Everywhere** (2005), Wally Cardona, took on a workmanlike demeanor as he placed wooden beams vertically in rows. When he started adding a beam horizontally on top of each stanchion to make T-shapes, the configuration multiplied and changed the space. The banging, thudding sounds of beams added to Phil Kline's sound score. Eventually the beams were reshaped into a staircase that a female dancer perched on, in contemplation. A male dancer hovered over the first step, arms holding a beam high overhead. Then he put the beam down and—lest you thought Cardona would get sentimental on us—he sat on a step and turned away from her.

Kate Weare, impulsive and fierce, premiered **Dark Lark**, a series of solos, duets, and trios, in 2013. There is something mythic about these encounters but it's still intimate enough for the Fishman Space. The mood ranges from a private sense of wonder to a primal urge to fight. The contenders seem locked in a needy/belligerent love/hate battle with each other.

Jonah Bokaer, who danced in the Cunningham company and choreographed opera for Robert Wilson, was commissioned to be the inaugural dance artist for the smaller, flexible Fishman

OPPOSITE
Miguel Gutierrez and John Jasperse in *Giant Empty*, John Jasperse Company, 2001. Photo: Maria Anguera De Sojo

ABOVE
Kathryn Sanders and Joanna Kotze in *Everywhere*, Wally Cardona Quartet/Ethel, 2005. Photo: Stephanie Berger

Space at the BAM Fisher Building in 2012. Melillo encouraged him to create a different kind of viewing experience than in the Opera House or the Harvey Theater. For **ECLIPSE**, Bokaer and architect Anthony McCall placed the audience on four sides and filled the room with 36 lightbulbs arranged in neat descending rows of six. The first row of spectators was seated inside that grid. The choreography and the installation were meticulously timed, and when Bokaer passed his hand in front of a bulb, he seemed to magically bring on a mini-eclipse. Four years later, Bokaer created **Rules Of The Game**, with stunningly ominous film projections by his longtime visual collaborator Daniel Arsham and music by Grammy Award-winning composer, Pharrell Williams.

Others, like Tere O'Connor and Jodi Melnick, both of whom also performed in the BAM Fisher, lend an elliptical quality to the postmodern sensibility. You really don't know what's going on until something big and dramatic hits you. In O'Connor's **BLEED** (2013), we get fragments

ABOVE
*Rules Of The Game*, Jonah Bokaer/Daniel Arsham/Pharrell Williams/David Campbell, 2016. Photo: Stephanie Berger

OPPOSITE
Cynthia Oliver (featured) in *BLEED*, Tere O'Connor Dance, 2013. Photo: Ian Douglas

of ambiguous, whimsical behavior. Heather Olson kneels over a prone man, playing some sort of patty-cake game. She could be a nurse, a sister, a mother, a playmate. He could be dead or alive. Suddenly everyone's running in a circle, looking upward as though expecting lightning, gathering force until Olson leads them into a diagonal where they seem to be fighting an earthquake. They are shaking as though electrified, as though they themselves *are* the lightning and the thunder, all connected to each other like the old tale of the golden goose. People drop to the floor one at a time—an apocalypse.

In a calmer, less agitated vein, Jodi Melnick—who danced at the Next Wave Festival with Nina Wiener in 1987—premiered **Moment Marigold** (2014)**,** a trio for women. Deadpan but glamorous, Melnick moves with a kind of gliding femininity that is a mystery in itself. In this piece, the three women conjure a private world of crystalline gesture, with the help of Joe Levasseur's ingenious lighting. But in the end there's a chilling tenderness to the way they arrange each other on the ground, fanning each other's hair out. Are they preparing to bury their best friends?

Other Next Wave artists like Susan Marshall and David Dorfman have taken postmodernism into psychological realms. Marshall first came to the Next Wave Festival in the Lepercq Space with a very physical piece: **Interior with Seven Figures** (1988). It depicts the struggle of

relationships with a certain toughness. One man is bent over, holding a woman roughly, grappling with her changing position, trying to keep control over her, possibly to kiss her. She climbs him like a tree. It's an arduous, unwinnable partnership—the awkwardness of human need.

David Dorfman, who performed in Marshall's *Interior*, used some of that same grappling energy in **underground** (2006) at the BAM Harvey, but it's between the central figure (a beleaguered Dorfman) versus the group rather than between partners. With his defiant stance and shouted questions, he veers toward the political, reliving questions prompted by the revolutionary Weather Underground when he was a teenager: Are you a pacifist? In a violent world, can you fight for peace? Is violence ever justified? Is your country worth killing for?

## Mark Morris: Merging Dance with Musicality

In some ways, choreographer Mark Morris is a throwback to pre-Cunningham times. Devoted to the idea of music and dance "going" together, he tends to choose classical music—played live—and relies on its classical structure. This occasionally appears predictable, but in his best work—and he is fantastically prolific—the music and dance together gather force. We experience the wholeness of the work immediately and thoroughly.

By 1984, the year of Morris's festival debut in the Lepercq Space, he was, according to Jennifer Dunning in the *New York Times*, "being talked of as the most solidly promising heir to the mantle of the modern dance greats." His solo **O Rangasayee,** danced to an Indian raga, awed critics by the sheer chutzpah of taking on the role of an Indian classical dancer, as well as by the freedom of his dancing and the richness of his choreography. The conventional theme-and-variations format works for him and his inventiveness and humor keep tumbling out. He also gave us luxurious movement at a time when the postmodernists were keeping it simple. As Jeff Seroy wrote in the *Paris Review*, "Part of the genius of *O Rangasayee* is that it returns one of the oldest and hoariest of modern dance tropes—the exotic Eastern solo of Denishawn days—to its primal roots in the ecstatic."

OPPOSITE
*underground*, David Dorfman Dance, 2006. Photo: Jack Vartoogian

ABOVE
Donald Mouton and Michael Gallo in *L'Allegro, il Penseroso ed il Moderato*, Monnaie Dance Group/ Mark Morris, 1990. Photo: Klaus Lefebvre

In 1990, Morris presented the New York premiere of **L'Allegro, il Penseroso ed il Moderato** at the BAM Opera House; the choreography breathes with Handel's oratorio and yet allows Morris's goofiness to creep in. Only Morris could get away with having people stand there with arms extended as tree branches, and three men being pulled by dancers as hound dogs. The big rounded arcs of the body hark back to Doris Humphrey and the free-flowing skips are pure Isadora Duncan. *L'Allegro* was brought back to BAM in 2001; when it was broadcast on PBS *Great Performances* in 2015, critic Alastair Macaulay referred in the *New York Times* to its "miraculous beauty."

Morris is not afraid to be entertaining. The motifs, messages, and jokes are easy to follow. He presents a community in every piece, and it's a community of fallible human beings, not the super virtuosic dancers we see on the ballet stage. The performers' enjoyment is contagious, easily crossing the footlights.

*The Hard Nut*, Mark Morris Dance Group, 2016. Photo: Julieta Cervantes

The Mark Morris Dance Company is something of a fixture at BAM, and the work produced most often in the festival is **The Hard Nut.** Popular as a holiday tradition with both art audiences and families, it's fun for the kids, and the adults chuckle every time they catch one character humping another in the first act. All the peaks and valleys, dangers and harmonies of the majestic Tchaikovsky score find their counterpart in Morris's choreography. The bold black and white sets by Adrianne Lobel contrast nicely with Martin Pakledinaz's riotously colorful costumes; both are inspired by a comic artist with a dark side, Charles Burns. Some characters, for instance the happy black maid, are a bit off key, but everyone gets the jokes. *The Hard Nut* is a relief for those who find other Next Wave offerings puzzling.

The gender play in *The Hard Nut* has more than entertainment value; it is part of an ongoing interest of Morris's. In works like *O Rangasayee*, *L'Allegro*, and **Championship Wrestling after Roland Barthes** (1984), he rejects the obvious gender divide that is natural to ballet and modern dance and instead concocts an upbeat androgyny. In *The Hard Nut,* the corps of snowflakes—all-female in most other Nutcrackers—is co-ed, and they all wear two-pieces: tops and tutus.

The emotional center of this *Nutcracker,* however, is still the shy and tender Marie, a child full of wonder and idealism. All manner of jokey things happen to her, but in the final pas de deux she is swept up into young adulthood by love—with the help of all the crazy characters who return to usher her into her dream of romance. Morris wins us over with a sincere core surrounded by comical edges.

## A Growing Hybridization

One of the unique aspects of Next Wave Festival is the prominence of collaboration wherein dance is just one element in the mix, illustrated by the influence of BAM "regulars" David Gordon and Big Dance Theater as well as intriguing hybrid productions such as Sarah Michelson's **DOGS** (2006), Akram Khan and Juliette Binoche's **In-I** (2009), and David Michalek's **Hagoromo** (2015).

David Gordon, as much a playwright as a choreographer, has devised four "dancing-and-talking" productions for the festival—all with Gordon's special brand of inquisitive irreverence. His grand opus, **United States** (1988), was co-commissioned by BAM and 26 presenters

around the country. Gordon gathered written bits of local color from these presenters, to which he added movement material recycled from previous works. Included in this mélange was "Slaughter on Tenth Avenue" from *On Your Toes*, based on the 1948 Hollywood movie danced by Gene Kelly and Vera-Ellen. Naturally, former Cunningham dancer Valda Setterfield, Gordon's wife and muse, played the Vera-Ellen character while Gordon approximated Gene Kelly. His character gets shot, setting off a corps of policemen—his own version of the Keystone Cops—who console the now widowed and veiled Valda. Like Trisha Brown and Lucinda Childs, Gordon was a founding member of the groundbreaking Judson Dance Theater of the 1960s. He is not beholden to any particular method but always engages his audience with a sense of play.

The tiny Big Dance Theater, a true hybrid of dance and theater, presents vivid characters in a collision of genres and narratives. The directors, Annie-B Parson (dance) and Paul Lazar (theater), create a collage of images that intersect each other. In 2014's **Alan Smithee Directed This Play: Triple Feature** (a reference to Hollywood directors who didn't want to claim a show they felt wasn't up to snuff), the added component of film enlarged, foreshadowed, or echoed events onstage. The Dadaist landscape of *Alan Smithee*, complete with fur coats, long telephone calls, and cigarettes, could change from combative to docile on a dime. Shards of text from the movies *Terms of Endearment* and *Doctor Zhivago* interrupt other narratives, in the same sense that, as mentioned previously, William Forsythe's dancers interrupt themselves physically. This kind of interruption, according to postmodern theory, wakes the brain up, even if the overall gist remains an enigma.

Next Wave hybrids have included three other intriguing productions at the Harvey. In Sarah Michelson's absurdist *DOGS*, four dancers navigate huge spiraling sculptures and tree-sized sprouts of lighting instruments while engaging in a kind of mad hatter's tea party; roast chicken was served to audiences at intermission. Akram Khan's duet collaboration with actor Juliette Binoche titled *In-I* infused questions of intimacy that touched on racist tropes with visceral struggles. The elegance and force of Binoche as a mover matched Khan's vulnerability as a storyteller. And in *Hagoromo*, David Michalek's enchanting vision for telling a Japanese Noh drama in music, puppetry, and dance, David Neumann's choreography for ballet star Wendy Whelan distilled her essence to slowed down, otherworldly gliding.

Jennifer Howard and Sarah Michelson in *DOGS*, Sarah Michelson/Parker Lutz, 2006. Photo: Julieta Cervantes

## Going Global

In the 1990s, Lichtenstein and Melillo started looking for Next Wave programming beyond Europe and embraced an international artistic perspective. They imported the calligraphic beauty of Taiwan's Cloud Gate Dance Theatre, the intense ritual of the Paris-based Japanese butoh group Sankai Juku, and the cryptic imagery of Saburo Teshigawara from Japan. They also brought in the steady beat of Brazil's Grupo Corpo and the rawness of Bangarra, the Aboriginal group from Australia. Each of these groups transported us to a different geographical and mental landscape.

Another force that has taken the dance world by storm is Ohad Naharin and his Tel Aviv-based Batsheva Dance Company. Just as Forsythe has redefined ballet, Naharin has turned modern dance inside out, giving us a staggering vitality barely contained by a sophisticated sense of form. Although precisely choreographed, his dances plunge us into an experience of humanity

ABOVE
*Mamootot*, Ohad Naharin/ Batsheva Dance Company, 2005. Photo: Julieta Cervantes

OPPOSITE
*Three*, Ohad Naharin/ Batsheva Dance Company, 2007. Photo: Richard Termine

in a raw state. Gaga, his improvisational method or "movement language," enables Naharin and his dancers to make wild, unpredictable movement that is true to their nature. Younger choreographers all over the world have been influenced by his unflinching investigations, and Gaga workshops are in demand as a training method that energizes all corners of the body.

In 2005, Naharin brought the disarming **Mamootot** to the Next Wave, performing in the intimacy of a dance studio at the nearby Mark Morris Dance Center. In the brightly lit space, the Batsheva dancers, looking somehow caught off guard, are wearing something like tie-died long underwear. Nothing about these dancers is conventionally beautiful, but one sometimes finds oneself gasping at the emotional beauty of the interactions. At one point a woman is lying down, while a nude man dances quietly near and over her. He kisses his own hand, then his knee, then the other knee but never touches her. Finally, she crawls up into his arms and he walks off with her slowly, her limbs dangling down. The mix of wonder and eroticism in *Mamootot* was called "pretty thrilling" by *New York Times* critic John Rockwell.

A sly sense of humor permeates the three sections of **Three** (2007). The penultimate scene has three sets of dancers lining up to take turns exposing different parts of their bodies.

It's a somber-to-silly depiction of the extreme vulnerability that's essential to Naharin's work. And then, to change the mood, they stride low to the Beach Boys song "Welcome." As the lights fade, they are all still striding, threading through each other with purpose and direction, filling the space with a kind of rhythmic communal bliss.

In 2014, Naharin presented the bracing **Sadeh21**. A string of solos that expands to duets and trios, it can ricochet from tender to disturbing to soothing. One woman treads around the stage, hiking each hip up in a ridiculously distorted walk—for so long that it becomes second nature. One dancer tries desperately to latch onto another's legs until she gives up hope. Just as your heart can contract watching these dancers, it can also expand. A small group of three people opens up to let another person into the circle, then another and another until the circle looks too big for the stage. Meanwhile, the hip-hiker is now treading in place.

Naharin was neither the first nor the last Israeli dance artist to come to the Next Wave. In 1983, the festival invited Rina Schenfeld, a celebrated dancer/choreographer who danced with Batsheva before Naharin took the helm as director. London-based choreographer Hofesh

Shechter, who had also danced in Naharin's Batsheva, brought his driving, tribal **Political Mother** in 2012; he returned in 2017 with a bleak, darkly beautiful vision of survival in **Grand Finale**. And in 2016, Zvi Gotheiner, who came to New York from northern Israel in 1978, presented a travelogue of sorts, **On The Road**, based on the Beat generation novel by Jack Kerouac.

Many choreographers have incorporated high technology into their work, but Gideon Obarzanek devised an especially spooky world in his **Mortal Engine** (2009). This piece from the Australian group Chunky Move started with digital animations of roving circles and ovals that somehow morphed into humans. Obarzanek and his team created the illusion that the dancing body generated light and shadow. Whenever the bodies moved, they seemed to be burning the space around them. Inky, smudgy shadows threatened to envelop the six dancers. With mesmerizing effects, *Mortal Engine* was a precise vision of gloom.

Possibly the most global Next Wave participant, in the sense of far off as well as the sense of planetary precariousness, was Lemi Ponifasio's **Birds With Skymirrors** (2014). The Samoan-born, New Zealand-based Ponifasio sent monk-like men scurrying while making hieroglyphic

OPPOSITE
*Political Mother*, Hofesh Shechter Company, 2012. Photo: Julieta Cervantes

ABOVE
*Birds With Skymirrors*, Lemi Ponifasio/MAU, 2014. Photo: Jack Vartoogian

gestures. A nude woman shouted warnings of impending doom. On film, a pelican rose up, straining to flap its wings in an oil spill. Although parts of the performance were inscrutable (or literally too dark to see), the message about an impending ecological apocalypse was clear. In the program notes, Ponifasio pointed out that in the Pacific Islands, climate change is "already here."

## Ralph Lemon: The Geography Trilogy

Unique among Next Wave offerings was Ralph Lemon's monumental **Geography Trilogy**, spanning ten years. Lemon had danced with Meredith Monk but his early work was more formalist than imagistic. However, Monk's interdisciplinary approach and her connection to the deep past had sunk in, and in going forward he was also going back. He decided to explore his own racial background by traveling far and wide. The trilogy comprises three different explorations into his artistic, ethnic, and spiritual history. For **Geography** (1997), the first installment of the trilogy, he

*Come home Charley Patton: Part 3 of The Geography Trilogy*, Ralph Lemon, 2004. Photo: Jack Vartoogian

traveled to his ancestral home of Africa; for **Tree** (2000), to his spiritual home of Asia; and for **Come home Charley Patton** (2004), to the racist United States South.

In an era when many artists were giving a mere nod to other cultures, Lemon was immersing himself geographically, physically, and artistically. His research produced three poetic evocations of time and place, each with its own balance of peace and turmoil. For the first part of the trilogy, he gathered four dancers and two drummers from West Africa and a Guinean storyteller living in Brooklyn. He had entered new territory and felt, he told me, "profoundly discombobulated." The search for new materials and performers catapulted him way beyond his comfort zone. He ripped away stereotypes by giving the men cream-colored linen suits instead of either traditional African regalia or the bare-chested muscular look of, say, the Alvin Ailey company. Nari Ward's curtain of recycled bottles and box springs transported us to a village of huts and dirt roads. Although Lemon cast himself as an exile from Africa (the structure was loosely based on the *Oresteia*), he often moved among his diasporic cast. While the West African performers did a stomping dance, torsos twisting, arms windmilling, knees flying up, Lemon himself was more swoopy, fluid, stretched. He danced with less of a beat, aloof from the pounding of the drums. He retained his postmodern self while still being one of the men.

But his postmodern "self" got interrogated and pelted. As Ann Daly wrote in the *New York Times*, "He has put postmodern dance on trial, and race is the grand inquisitor." Sitting in a circle, the men argued with each other. A stylized fight broke out between two of them: head-butting, gripping, hurtling, and falling. Again and again. Lemon did not shy away from violence. Nor did he shy away from beauty. Ward's gorgeous set, the rhythms of the drums, and the beguiling movement qualities came together to create a visual and cultural richness.

*Tree*, the second part of the trilogy, traced the route of Buddhism through Asia. The production was a collage of different cultures, languages, dances, and musics. Performers included men and women from Ivory Coast, China, India, Japan, Taiwan, and the United States. Costume designer Anita Yavich's extended their backpacks upwards with bicycle wheels that Lemon called "mandala vehicles." We heard two simultaneous stories in two languages in two different parts of the stage. As a choreographer, he nearly crossed the line of disrespect: smoking on the same stage as classical Indian dance. *Tree* was more peaceful than *Geography* but also had moments of perverse cultural collision. A classical Odissi dancer was accompanied by African drumming.

Two Asian men in blackface played traditional instruments similar to a harmonica and a banjo. Again, Lemon is pelted with stones. Was he making himself the target as atonement for transgressing against traditions?

The final part, *Come home Charley Patton*, brought video into the mix. We saw Lemon, wading in water up to his waist while reading from a book. We saw the 99-year-old Walter Carter of Yazoo, Mississippi, get up and do a dance rooted in Africa. The cast was smaller—just four men and two women, all of them American except for the Ivorian dancer Djédjé Djédjé Gervais, a constant throughout all three parts. The sound score traveled through various blues songs and other music while the dancers shuffled with precise footwork in a forerunner of the "buck dance."

There were odd, jarring juxtapositions. Okwui Okpokwasili sang Jacques Brel but then put iron horseshoes around her neck, harking back to captured slaves. She told a searing story about how in the fourth grade she and a white girl kept yelling the N-word at each other until

the teacher informed Okwui that the other girl *"can't* be a nigger." A small screen placed high up showed an animation of James Baldwin's face speaking in his real recorded voice. It was as though Baldwin were overseeing the proceedings.

While in the previous two pieces Lemon was pelted with stones, here he was assaulted by a fire hose, an echo of the famously brutal police response toward civil rights marchers in the early 1960s. It was viscerally shocking to see a blast of water trained on Lemon while he continued dancing, slipping, and staggering under the force of the blast—dancing for survival.

The *Geography Trilogy* was more than one dance artist's exploration into the past. It investigated the nature of what it is to be a global citizen, to not flinch at the painful contradictions that quest might involve. It also integrated the Next Wave audience racially. As Lemon said recently, "For the first time in my work, I was getting black people to my shows." Obviously there was a personal satisfaction in this. But it reflects a larger accomplishment that BAM in general has been able to effect: integrating the audience.

OPPOSITE
Megumi Eda in *Itutu*, Armitage Gone! Dance, 2009. Photo: Julieta Cervantes

ABOVE
*Dream'd in a Dream*, Seán Curran Company/ Ustatshakirt Plus, 2015. Photo: Julieta Cervantes

## Crossing Cultures

While not as long-term a commitment as Lemon's *Geography Trilogy*, other cross-cultural forays include Karole Armitage's **Itutu** (2009), Reggie Wilson's **Moses(es)** (2013), and Seán Curran's **Dream'd in a Dream** (2015).

Armitage collaborated with Burkina Electric, an African pop band led by composer Lukas Ligeti. Visual artist Philip Taaffe channeled the pop African blend into a series of backdrops depicting fauna with an almost predatory look. At times, with Peter Speliopolous's kicky tutu-reverse costumes, the piece looked like a quirky fashion parade. The choreography sets African chest contractions against balletic leaps. The spirit of melding reached a poignant peak in a duet between the exquisite Megumi Eda and Zoko Zoko, a West African dancer who was part of Burkina Electric: a tender, patient, seductive sharing of styles and sensations.

For *Dream'd in a Dream*, instead of inviting other cultural traditions into his own craft, Seán Curran went toward them. Through the BAM-produced DanceMotion USA℠, a program of the U.S. Department of State, the Seán Curran Company traveled to Bishkek, Kyrgyz Republic, in Central Asia. There they encountered a traditional music ensemble called Ustatshakirt Plus. A former folk dancer himself (a champion Irish step dancer) as well as a former member of the Bill T. Jones/Arnie Zane Dance Company, Curran devised folk steps to mesh with the traditional mountain music. With nine benches onstage the dancers reclined and rested, danced and dreamed. When the musicians stepped downstage, we could see that their instruments were variations on banjos and recorders.

In a recent conversation, Curran said that when he was invited to make a piece for the Harvey Theater, he was thrilled. He thought back to 1987, when Peter Brook inaugurated the Majestic Theater (now the Harvey) with his legendary production of **The Mahabharata**, and he knew he had to "fill the space" visually. Mark Randall, Curran's longtime visual collaborator, hung a magnificent carpet of reds and purples to transport us to the region. The choreography was simple, nothing fancy, but fostered a warm feeling among the cast. While *Itutu* was bold and chic, *Dream'd in a Dream* evoked a sweetness from its dancers and musicians.

Like Lemon and Curran, Reggie Wilson gathers ideas as he travels. For *Moses(es)*, which focused on the overlap between various Moses myths—including Zora Neale Hurston's *Moses,*

*Man of the Mountain*—and the African diaspora, he spent time in Israel, Egypt, and Turkey. Wilson's Fist & Heel Performance Group includes both dancers and singers, and, as in the African tradition, there's a fluidity between singing and dancing. Sometimes Wilson sits on a chair stamping and clapping while the dancers follow along in what he calls his "post-African/ neo-HooDoo" style. The music, as eclectic as Wilson's influences, ranges from Louis Armstrong's "Go Down Moses" to gospel, Egyptian, and Hebraic songs.

## Altered States

When a choreographer thrusts her or his dancers into the outer reaches of the imagination, they can plunge into extreme psychological states. Witnessing this kind of unmooring from the roots of sanity is partly what pulls us back to the Next Wave again and again.

Josephine Ann Endicott cut a sordid, messy, over-the-top figure in Pina Bausch's original *Kontakthof*. Excessive in every action and self-mocking to the hilt, she threw decorum to the

Eiko & Koma in their *Night Tide*, included in *New Moon Stories*, 1986. Photo: Beatriz Schiller

winds. She was more than on the verge; she had tipped over the edge into a kind of insanity. The result was riveting, even alarming.

The duo Eiko & Koma enter into another kind of extreme state. When they perform, they seem to be caught in a post-human apocalypse. Either the human world has self-destructed, or they are victims of a vast natural disaster. They have a visceral kind of need that stretches out time, and yet they command our attention. They create their own environment and then become part of it. For **Night Tide**, included in **New Moon Stories** (1986), Eiko & Koma's inverted nude torsos resemble randomly placed boulders. In their production **Tree** (1988) (not to be confused with the Ralph Lemon production), they seem to be made of leaves. Collaborating with Native American musician Robert

Djédjé Djédjé Gervais, David Thomson, and Darrell Jones in *How Can You Stay In The House All Day And Not Go Anywhere?*, Ralph Lemon, 2010. Photo: Stephanie Berger

Mirabal for **Land** (1991), they thrash on parched earth; Koma pushes a bear carcass. Perhaps they are drowning in **River** (1997), one desperately trying to rescue the other. You can barely distinguish them as human: they are part of the driftwood. We, as audience, have to tap into our own powers of concentration in order to fully experience their super slow dive into the primal imagination.

Culturally, their work is related to butoh, the form that was developed in Japan during the United States occupation there in the 1950s. The New York-based Eiko & Koma studied with Kazuo Ohno, one of the two founders of the form, and were devoted to him until he died. Extreme states, super slow pace, and a connection to nature are all characteristics of butoh. But they feel their work is independent, so they do not label it butoh.

In 2000, Eiko & Koma devised a cave-like environment for **When Nights Were Dark**. With the celestial sounds of a live praise choir and their typical slow motion, they could either be being born or dying. Sunlight seeps thru the stalactites as the whole "cave" makes one full rotation during the 75-minute performance. The two sink lower into the cave and rise up to come together, though an age seems to pass before they actually touch each other.

In William Forsythe's *Decreation*, which is based on poet Anne Carson's essay and opera of the same title, each member of his cast locates a center of madness within themselves. Toward the end, dancer Georg Reischl seems to break down before our eyes. He's shifting on his feet and lamenting that his "spiel," his story, is gone. As he expresses his torment at not being able to retrieve it, he cannot stop moving. In a talk after the performance, Forsythe explained that the idea of extreme states came from Carson's view of mystics. He said of his dancers: "They are also contemplating the idea of these mystics in these extreme states. Carson calls it extasis. Georg's misery is a kind of ecstasy at the same time."

The second half of Ralph Lemon's **How Can You Stay In The House All Day And Not Go Anywhere?** (2010) includes a 20-minute process of going past exhaustion. The five improvising dancers lose their bearings and their energy, yet they keep going because they can't seem to remember how to stop. The flesh comfort among them—touching, leaning, supporting—provides a kind of harboring. In this case, the extreme state of the performers had its roots in Lemon's real life. When he made this piece, he had just ended a long vigil over his lover, the Odissi dancer Asako Takami, watching life ebbing away from her. He recently told me, "I didn't have the opportunity to think about anything other than this moment of dealing with a sick and then dying body.

That became the work. I was watching this incredible genius dancer body falling apart, daily. In a weird way, a perverse way, I got to see that falling apart violently, horribly, and beautifully." His state of mind seeped through the entire piece. The dancers, staggering and falling, weren't "performing" anymore, they were just surviving. And we were there to witness it. One could call it anti-choreography, as Lemon had witnessed anti-life overcome his partner.

But Lemon wasn't done with grief yet. After this section, Okwui Okpokwasili was onstage alone, sobbing honestly, ferociously, heartbreakingly for ten minutes. Lemon has said that she prepared for this ordeal by exposing herself to images of people suffering—and that she was a surrogate for his own mourning. Her crying jag was a tour de force that had a few people leaving the theater—but the rest of us glued to our seats.

## The New Wave: Transgressive, Gritty, Interactive

As Next Wave favorites wind down—the Cunningham company folded two years after his death; Trisha Brown's company rarely performs on proscenium stages; Pina Bausch's Tanztheater Wuppertal is in flux; and the Forsythe Company has disbanded—a new crop of choreographers has sprung up. Among them are Kyle Abraham, Faye Driscoll, and Nora Chipaumire. These three have shown the kind of stark originality the festival is known for. In the 2016 festival, they all made excellent use of the flexible Fishman Space, while also tackling difficult subjects.

**Pavement** is Kyle Abraham's poignant take on the 1991 John Singleton movie *Boyz N the Hood***,** transposed to the Hill District of Pittsburgh, where he grew up. Abraham is bent on "investigating the state of Black America and a history therein." The eight dancers of Abraham.In.Motion combine his mellifluous amalgam of hip-hop and postmodern improvisation with gently devastating images of police brutality. By the end, you feel familiar with the streets of the Hill District. The chilling "normalizing" of police profiling is met with a camaraderie born of survival instincts, all against a backdrop of music that ranges from Bach and Vivaldi to Sam Cooke and Donny Hathaway—an operatic array for a history of survival.

Faye Driscoll unleashes a kind of 360-degree zaniness in **Thank You for Coming: Play**. Audience members are asked to write words on slips of paper that are later incorporated in a lament: "Ohhhh X, Ohhh Y," uttered in wonder and mock despair by Driscoll herself. In a section of astounding virtuosity, words and gesture are dislodged from each other and repeated with slightly different changes until finally the words and gesture match up. Driscoll, who has been influenced by both Tere O'Connor and Big Dance Theater, specializes in destabilizing whatever you thought was certain. The dancers change their costume and their tone in madcap succession. Talking about extreme states: Brandon Washington taps into his own lament, chanting over and over, "Where is my mom?" As he flails and bounces off the walls, it is somehow funny too, possibly because of the playful context. But like Georg Reischl in *Decreation*, he is caught in an ecstatic lament.

In **portrait of myself as my ~~father~~,** which was part of BAM's Brooklyn–Paris Exchange with Théâtre de la Ville, Nora Chipaumire thrashed against ropes that restrained her in a makeshift boxing ring. Head covered with a towel, midriff bared, wielding boxing gloves, she was chomping at the bit to break out of the box of one gender or another. She accosted the audience with growls, grunts, and accusations in French. We heard humiliating disses on black masculinity that her father, who was largely absent from her childhood, undoubtedly endured as a black man in Zimbabwe.

Kyle Abraham in his *Pavement*, Abraham. In.Motion, 2016. Photo: Ian Douglas

She imagined herself teaching him how to get his swagger on. Senegalese dancer Pape Ibrahima Ndiaye leapt in and out of the boxing ring. Finally, Chipaumire bent over and lifted Ndiaye onto her back, saying, "I carry the carcass of my father." Like Driscoll, Chipaumire excels at destabilizing, ejecting us from our center of comfort.

This tradition of discomfort continued in the 2017 festival with Germaine Acogny, known as the mother of contemporary African dance, who performed a solo choreographed for her by Olivier Dubois of Ballet du Nord that nearly unhinges her. A guest at the annual DanceAfrica festival of African dance at BAM, Acogny brought her all-male Compagnie Jant-Bi to the 2008 Next Wave to collaborate with Urban Bush Women on *Les écailles de la mémoire (The Scales of Memory)*. Nine years later, she performed **Mon élue noire (My Black Chosen One): Sacre #2,** a driven solo to a recording of Igor Stravinsky's *Sacre du Printemps,* in which she runs in place, pipe clutched in teeth, at a pace that would exhaust any other 73-year-old. Even if you were not French-speaking, you could catch on to the fury of her monologue about colonization.

Making her Next Wave debut as a choreographer, Cynthia Oliver—who performed in Tere O'Connor's *BLEED*—asked her cast to dig beneath the stereotypes of black masculinity in **Virago-Man Dem.** She sometimes put them in situations that made them squirm but ultimately expanded their range of emotions and textures.

Another kind of boundary-pushing is the collaboration between video wizard Charles Atlas and former Cunningham dancers Rashaun Mitchell and Silas Riener. **Tesseract** extends Cunningham's embrace of technology with 3D film and live video-mixing that ensures a heaping dose of chance. The six dancers were filmed, edited, and projected by Atlas in real time, making for some ghostly effects. Mitchell and Riener are Next Wave alums as dancers—both appeared in the Cunningham company's **Nearly Ninety** program in 2009 and again in the *Legacy Tour* in 2011—but *Tesseract* was their Next Wave debut as choreographers.

To complete a full circle, Tanztheater Wuppertal Pina Bausch's double bill that first wowed New York in 1984 returned to the festival. Bausch's powerfully bleak **Café Müller** and her raging **Rite of Spring** shook New Yorkers and alerted the BAM audience that complacency had no place at the festival. In 2017, it again met with an astonished and appreciative audience.

The waves of the Next Wave Festival will continue to bring stimulating artists to our shores, to reveal the depth and diversity of dance from near and far. Some of these artists con-

sciously risk failure—and, admittedly, it's exciting to see how close they come to the precipice. But more than that, the Next Wave also reveals our own reactions, the varieties of method and madness within ourselves. While we return to the festival again and again because of our curiosity, we do not sit outside it, judging it from a distance. We are inevitably pulled into the arena—mentally and sometimes physically—whether it's the Howard Gilman Opera House, the BAM Harvey Theater, or the BAM Fisher. When we go to a Next Wave performance, we honor the curiosity within ourselves.

Shamar Watt and Nora Chipaumire in *portrait of myself as my ~~father~~*, Nora Chipaumire, 2016. Photo: Julieta Cervantes

OPPOSITE
Ushio Amagatsu in his *Umusuna: Memories Before History*, Sankai Juku, 2015. Photo: Jack Vartoogian

ABOVE
*17c*, Annie-B Parson/Paul Lazar/Big Dance Theater, 2017. Photo: Rebecca Greenfield.

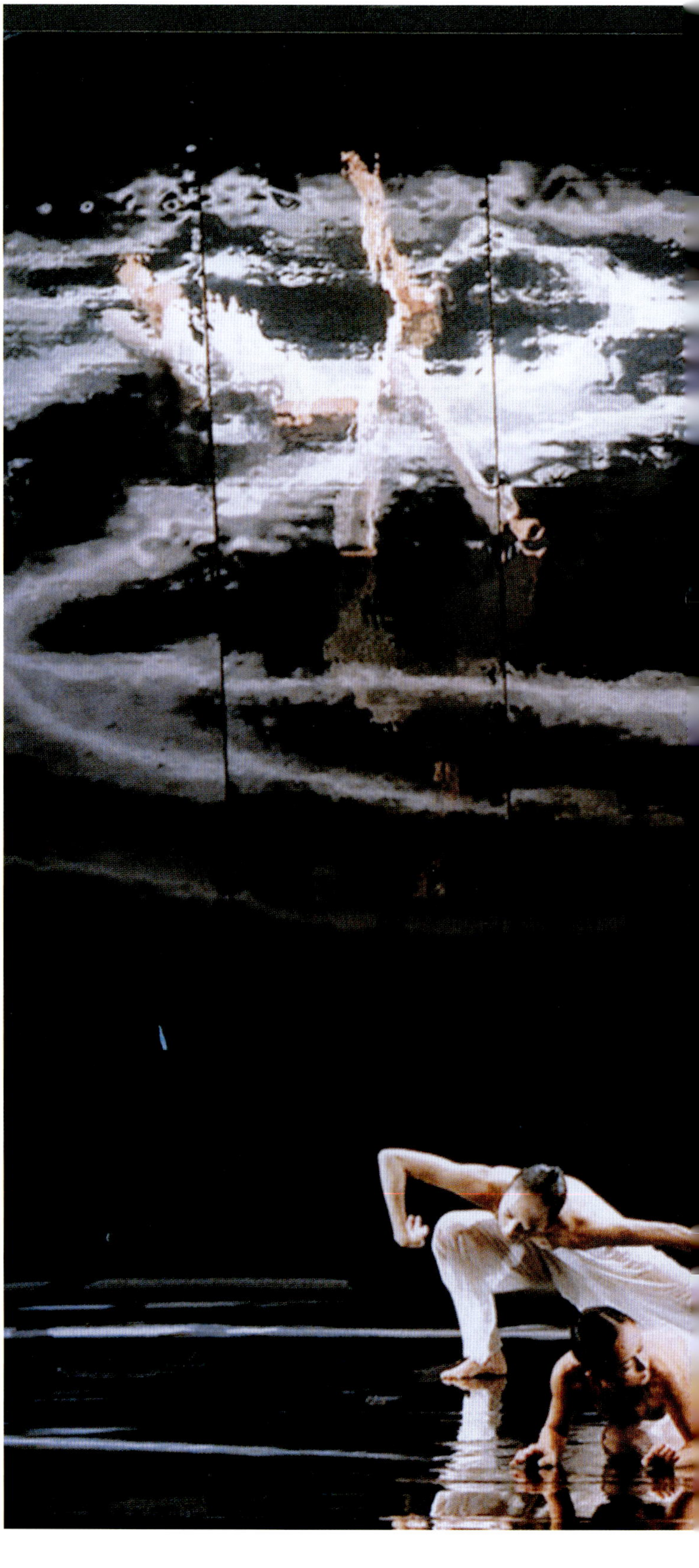

*Moon Water*, Lin Hwai-min/ Cloud Gate Dance Theatre of Taiwan, 2003. Photo: Teng Hui-En

ABOVE
*On the Road*, ZviDance, 2016. Photo: Ian Douglas

OPPOSITE
Mikhail Baryshnikov and Trisha Brown in *You Can See Us*, included in *Trisha Brown at 25: Post Modern and Beyond*, Trisha Brown Company, 1996. Photo: Dan Rest

ABOVE
*Continu*, Sasha Waltz & Guests, 2015. Photo: Julieta Cervantes

OPPOSITE
Pape Ibrahima Ndiaye in *Les écailles de la mémoire (The Scales of Memory)*, Compagnie Jant-Bi/Urban Bush Women, 2008. Photo: Jack Vartoogian

*Moses(es)*, Reggie Wilson/ Fist & Heel Performance Group, 2013. Photo: Julieta Cervantes

*Decreation*, The Forsythe Company, 2009. Photo: Julieta Cervantes

*The Rite of Spring*,
Tanztheater Wuppertal
Pina Bausch, 2017. Photo:
Stephanie Berger

As a professional curator and artistic director of the Next Wave Festival, you have traveled the globe; you have a community of people around the world who are friends, people you care about, and people you have influenced and who have influenced you. And this speaks to your ability as a strategist, and it raises the question about taste—meaning the attraction you have to a particular work that you decide to bring to BAM. What you've done with the Next Wave is to create something that feels necessary, has impact, and matters in people's lives. The camaraderie between individuals is a significant element in our lives, and I think it's ultimately the subject matter of theater.

**Anne Bogart**

Theater and Opera Director

*Six Characters in Search of an Author*, Emmanuel Demarcy-Mota/Théâtre de la Ville, Paris, 2014. Photo: Richard Termine

# Theater

Roger Oliver

Harvey Lichtenstein began his career as a dancer, and his first love was dance. So not surprisingly, it was his concentration on modern dance that paved the way in transforming the moribund Brooklyn Academy of Music into a world-renowned performance venue. In his early tenure as executive producer, Lichtenstein focused on presenting such modern dance masters as Martha Graham, José Limón, Anna Sokolow, Merce Cunningham, Paul Taylor, and Alwin Nikolais, and seemingly overnight, as touted in the *New Yorker*, "the somnolent Academy became the country's leading dance center." In the late 1960s and early 1970s, however, Lichtenstein began to present the work of two contrasting but equally visionary directors, Robert Wilson and Peter Brook, and theater evolved as an increasingly central aspect of BAM programming. For Lichtenstein, theater became a deep-seated passion, and as a result he envisioned BAM with a renewed sense of purpose as a showcase for the multidisciplinary arts.

The emergence of the director as a major creative and interpretive force in theater is a fairly recent phenomenon. Until the late 19th century, playwrights, actors, and sometimes designers dominated what appeared onstage. But once seminal early 20th-century theater practitioners like André Antoine and Konstantin Stanislavsky demonstrated how an individual's point of view could both unify and electrify the theatrical experience, the central place of the director as a kind of collaborator-in-chief had been established. The importance of the director's place in theatrical collaboration has only grown and intensified from the mid-20th century to the present. Thus, it seems appropriate that from the inception of the Next Wave Festival its theatrical offerings have been distinguished by the work of major directors from both the United States and the international theater community.

Robert Wilson initiated a long-standing relationship with BAM beginning in 1969 with the production of *The Life and Times of Sigmund Freud*, followed in the next decade by works such as *Deafman Glance* (1971), *The Life and Times of Joseph Stalin* (1973), and *The $ Value of Man* (1975), establishing him as a creator of non-narrative visually arresting theater where he often served as writer and designer as well as director. One critic characterizes his approach to theater as "alchemy of the eye," and Wilson characterizes himself as a "visual artist" who has "no sense of direction until I have a sense of space."

Wilson's landmark collaboration with Philip Glass on the opera **Einstein on the Beach** marked a new chapter in his work, where the music of major composers accompanied his stun-

Sheryl Sutton and Lucinda Childs in *Einstein on the Beach*, Philip Glass/ Robert Wilson/Lucinda Childs, 1984. Photo: Babette Mangolte

ning stage pictures. Originally staged at the Avignon Festival in France, *Einstein* was given two sold-out performances in 1976 at the Metropolitan Opera House—self-financed by Wilson and Glass—but it was not seen again in New York until its major remounting in the 1984 Next Wave and then brought back for return engagements in the 1992 and 2012 festivals. In the latter incarnation of *Einstein*, theater technology had caught up to Wilson's conception of the work, allowing him to realize it more fully than had previously been possible.

Following the success of *Einstein*, Wilson collaborated with Glass on the 1986 Next Wave production of **Act V—the Rome Section**, the fifth of Wilson's six-part contemporary epic **the CIVIL WarS: a tree is best measured when it is down**, followed by a myriad of collaborative offerings: with David Byrne, **The Forest** (1988); with Tom Waits, **The Black Rider: The Casting of the Magic Bullets** (1993); with Waits and Kathleen Brennan, **Alice** (1995) and **Woyzeck** (2002); with

Lou Reed, **Time Rocker** (1997) and **POEtry** (2001); and with Rufus Wainwright, **Shakespeare's Sonnets** (2014). In addition, the festival has hosted such original works by Wilson as **The Golden Windows** (1985) and **Letter to a Man** (2016), starring Mikhail Baryshnikov, as well as productions of modern classics like August Strindberg's **A Dream Play** (2000) and the Brecht/Weill masterpiece **The Threepenny Opera** (2011). In the first 35 years of the Next Wave Festival, Wilson's work has continued to illuminate both past and present with his incandescent theatrical imagination.

While Wilson eschews narrative for an abstracted, often dreamlike set of images that invite the spectator's substantial attention, British-born director Peter Brook is a master story-teller who finds ways of infusing old tales with new theatrical meaning. He first came to BAM in 1971 with his historic reimagining of *A Midsummer Night's Dream* for the Royal Shakespeare

*The Forest*, Robert Wilson/David Byrne, 1988. Photo: Martha Swope

Company. In 1973, he returned with a company of actors from his newly formed International Centre for Theatre Research in Paris for a one-month residency that culminated in Lepercq Space performances of *Conference of the Birds*, a dramatization of a 12th-century Persian poem that follows a community of mythical birds through the trials and tribulations of their journey in search of truth and the essence of life.

In 1987, Brook would make his debut Next Wave appearance with his acclaimed production of Jean-Claude Carrière's nine-hour theatrical adaptation of the ancient Indian Sanskrit epic **The Mahabharata,** which marked a turning point that signified the emergence of BAM—and specifically the Next Wave Festival—as an international artistic entity known for innovative and ground-breaking performance. BAM subsequently became one of the co-producers of Brook's six-hour television adaptation of his work that then became a three-hour feature film shown at the New York Film Festival. It also led to a major expansion of the BAM campus.

Brook had insisted that *The Mahabharata,* which had been performed at his Théâtre des Bouffes du Nord in Paris and at the Avignon Festival in an open-air performance, could not work in the BAM Opera House. When their search for an appropriate theater space for *The Mahabharata* led Lichtenstein to show him a dilapidated theater-turned-movie-house called the Majestic (now the BAM Harvey Theater), a few blocks from the Opera

Gerhard Hoberstorfer, Jessica Liedberg, and Kajsa Reingardt in *A Dream Play*, Robert Wilson/Stockholm's Stadsteater, 2000. Photo: Stephanie Berger

House, Brook immediately saw that it could be the perfect "empty space" for his production—the New York equivalent of the Théâtre des Bouffes du Nord, down to its intentionally decaying look.

The success of *The Mahabharata* solidified Brook's reputation as an innovative and ambitious theater practitioner, and the renamed Harvey would be home to an aesthetic range of experimental works that followed: *The Cherry Orchard* (1988), *The Man Who* (1995), *The Tragedy of Hamlet* (2001), and *The Suit* (2013). In 2016, after a 30-year hiatus, Brook and his collaborator, Marie-Hélène Estienne, returned to the material of the Indian epic for the Next Wave production of **Battlefield**, a coda of sorts to *The Mahabharata*. While the original production brought to the stage the titanic battle between members of rival family factions, *Battlefield* dealt with the aftermath of war and a leader's attempt at healing and reconciliation. A chamber work with four actors, *Battlefield* showed that whether working on the grandest of scales or more intimately, Brook was one of the great theater magicians of our time.

## Early Collaborations

From its inception, the Next Wave Festival had two overarching goals. One was to foster interdisciplinary collaboration featuring artists from theater, music, dance, and the visual arts. The other was to offer cutting-edge artists the opportunity to work on a larger scale than had been possible before. For theater artists from around the globe, the festival also became a major venue where they could show work that reexamined the past, either through reinterpretations of classic works or viewing historical eras, events, and individuals in radical new ways.

Launched in the fall of 1983, the inaugural season of the Next Wave Festival opened with a work that embodied all three of these distinctions. **THE PHOTOGRAPHER/Far From the Truth** examined the work and life of the pioneering 19th-century British-born photographer Eadweard Muybridge through the tripartite structure of play/mixed media presentation/dance. An earlier version of the work, featuring the music of Philip Glass, had been performed at the Holland Festival, but for its American premiere Glass's collaborators—director JoAnne Akalaitis, writer Robert Coe, choreographer David Gordon, and designers Wendall K. Harrington, Santo Loquasto, and Jennifer Tipton—created a new work marked not only by Muybridge's photographic innovation but such diverse sources as Victorian melodrama and the work of German surrealist artist

Bruce Myers in *The Mahabharata*, Peter Brook/ Jean-Claude Carrière, 1987. Photo: Giles Abegg

Max Ernst. For Akalaitis, a founding member of the avant-garde theater company Mabou Mines, *THE PHOTOGRAPHER/Far From the Truth* allowed her to create a new kind of work that was not "a semi-opera or an operetta or a musical comedy or anything like that."

Another mainstay of Mabou Mines, Lee Breuer went much farther back in history as his inspiration for **The Gospel at Colonus,** a revisioning of Sophocles' 5th-century BCE masterwork *Oedipus at Colonus* through the lens of a contemporary Pentecostal gospel service. With music by Bob Telson and led by actor Morgan Freeman as "The Messenger," the cast included four authentic gospel units, Clarence Fountain and the Five Blind Boys of Alabama, J.J. Farley and the Original Soul Stirrers, the J.D. Steele Singers, and Brooklyn's own Institutional Radio Choir, which was the congregation of the gospel service and the equivalent of the Greek tragedy chorus. After its BAM performances, this acclaimed production toured extensively throughout the United States, performed in Paris, and ultimately had a Broadway run as well. Public television's *Great Performances* taped a live performance and CD and DVD recordings followed.

Breuer and Telson returned for the 1988 festival with an even bolder experiment in cross-cultural collaboration, **The Warrior Ant,** based on Breuer's own mock epic poem about the lives and loves of a Samurai ant. Conceived as a 12-part, 12-hour extravaganza, the BAM performances encompassed Parts I–IV and the epilogue, Part XII. Each episode had its own musical and theatrical style, ranging from Trinidadian Carnivale to reggae and from Arabic music to bunraku and other puppet sequences. As with *The Gospel at Colonus*, Breuer collaborated with designers Alison Yerxa, Ghretta Hynd, and Julie Archer on the production.

The second season of the festival opened with a different kind of collaboration, this time between Meredith Monk and Ping Chong, two multimedia artists usually solely responsible for the style and content of their work. Chong had been a member of Monk's company, The House, and thus had collaborated with her previously, but **The Games** (1984) marked a reunion of sorts after a long period of working independently. Monk characterized *The Games* as "a futuristic parable set on another planet in the far future" and while both directors shared in the conception text and staging of *The Games*, each took primary responsibility for an area that marked their individual work: audio-visual design for Chong and choreography and music for Monk, who has subsequently made regular appearances in the festival with her musical ensemble performing her compositions.

Next Wave Festival poster for *The Gospel at Colonus*, Lee Breuer/Bob Telson, 1983. Courtesy of BAM Hamm Archives

2 WEEKS ONLY
DECEMBER 15 THRU 31
"REACHES TOWARD ECSTASY.
As a work of musical theater, the evening is triply blessed in its adaptor-director, composer and cast. . .The stage threatens to lift off its moorings, joining the show in an evangelical musical flight."
— Mel Gussow, New York Times
"LIVING, DAZZLING, EXHILARATING.
The best white man's capturings of the essence of black music since Gershwin's Porgy and Bess. HALLELUJAH!"
— Alan Rich, Newsweek
"WONDERFUL, HYPNOTIC, EXHILARATING.
Quite conceivably a turning point for the theater as a whole. Don't walk, run; on the way home you'll probably feel like flying."
— Michael Feingold, Village Voice
"TERRIFIC, DAZZLING.
Pierces the heart of myth and moves the audience to a divine frenzy. SEE IT!"
— Clive Barnes, New York Post
THE GOSPEL AT COLONUS
"HURRY TO BAM TO SEE IT!
This production is the most satisfying presentation so far in BAM's Next Wave series, and that's saying a lot."
— Peter Goodman, Newsday
Conceived, Adapted and Directed by LEE BREUER
Music Composed, Arranged and Directed by BOB TELSON
BAM
Brooklyn Academy of Music
30 Lafayette Avenue, Brooklyn, N.Y. 11217
Information (212) 636-4100
Produced by the Brooklyn Academy of Music in association with Liza Lorwin and the Walker Art Center
Chargit (212) 944-9300

Three of Ping Chong's own theatrical creations, on the other hand, have been part of Next Wave festivals to follow. **The Angels of Swedenborg** (1986), performed by Chong's Fiji Theater Company, was inspired by the work of 18th-century Swedish scientist/philosopher Emanuel Swedenborg and Argentinian writer Jorge Luis Borges. In 1995, he returned with **Chinoiserie,** the second part of a trilogy on East-West relations that spanned from the 17th century into the future and drew on sources including Cantonese opera and Chong's childhood in New York's Chinatown. Then in 2010, he brought to the Next Wave **Throne of Blood,** his stage adaptation of Akira Kurosawa's acclaimed 1957 Samurai film version of Shakespeare's *Macbeth*. Like Kurosawa, Chong also drew on the Japanese Noh theatrical tradition for his production.

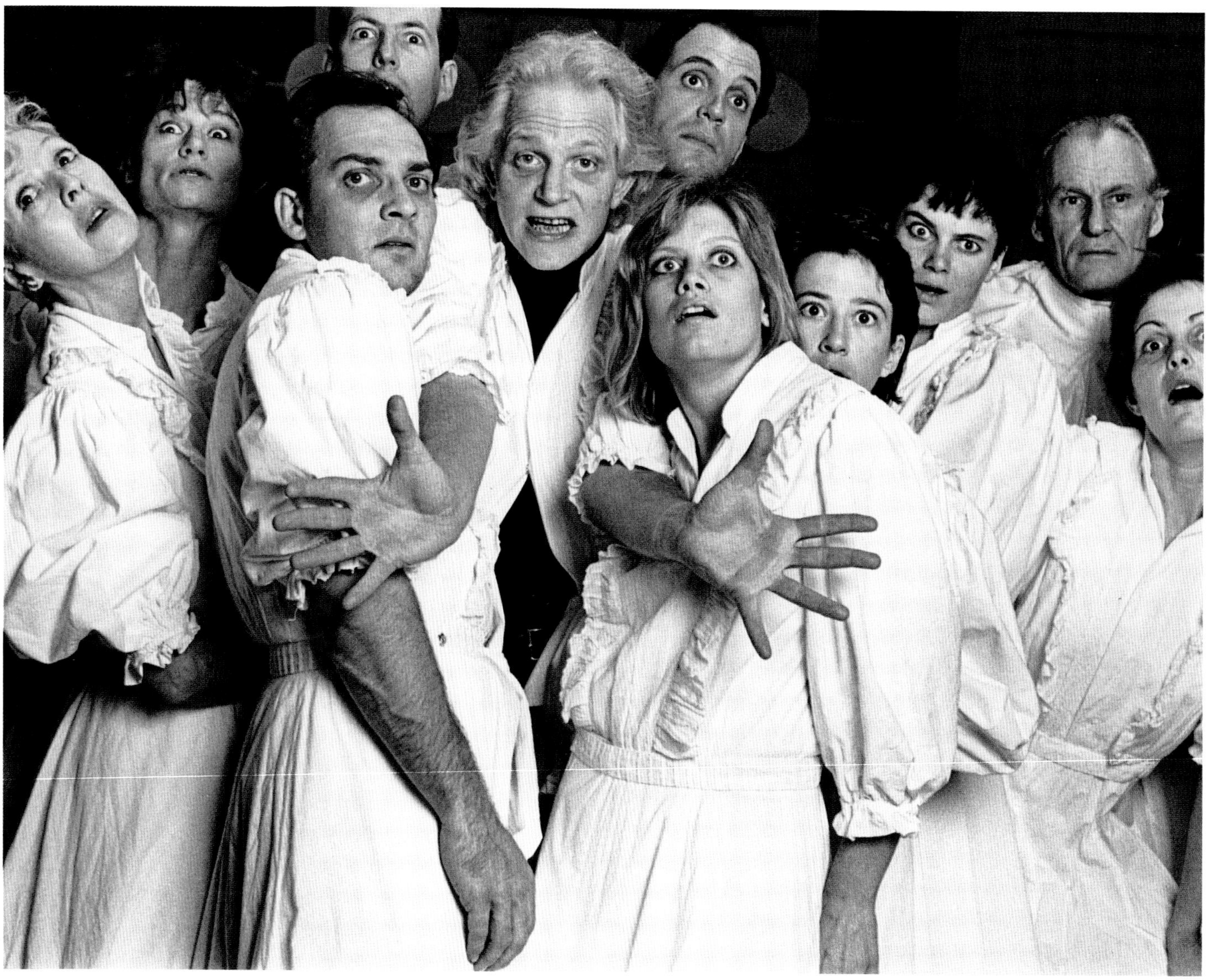

Other notable theatrical experimental directors invited to BAM to be part of collaborations or to present large-scale works included Richard Foreman, Stephan Balint, Peter Sellars, and Martha Clarke. Known for the "downtown" theater works of his Ontological-Hysteric Theater, which he wrote, directed, designed, and performed in, Foreman collaborated with writer Kathy Acker, composer Peter Gordon, and painter David Salle on **The Birth of the Poet** (1985), a work that centered on a phantasmagoric journey that ranged from the Roman Empire to contemporary Iran and the New York City of the near future.

Another mainstay of the downtown theater scene, Squat Theatre, known for its productions in a storefront theater where the audience inside the theater could see passersby on the sidewalk and vice-versa, presented **"L" Train to Eldorado** in the 1987 festival. Written and directed by Stephan Balint, this multimedia work featured both live actors and film projections of faces on sculptural figures. The 1987 festival also saw two productions by internationally acclaimed director Peter Sellars, highlighting his versatility as both theater and opera director. His theater work, **Zangezi,** subtitled **A Supersaga in Twenty Planes,** was based on a 1922 Futurist drama by Russian writer Velimir Khlebnikov, who wouldn't live to see it performed. *Zangezi* was actually the Next Wave Festival's second Russian Futurist or Cubo-Futurist work, as a reconstruction of the 1913 **Victory Over the Sun** was part of the inaugural festival. Sellars's production of the John Adams/Alice Goodman opera **Nixon in China,** with choreography by Mark Morris, closed the 1987 festival. Although Martha Clarke began her career as a dancer with Pilobolus, she achieved greater prominence as a director of music-theater works. Her 1990 work **Endangered Species** used the words of Walt Whitman as well as animal (including the elephant Flora and Dickie the giraffe) and human performers to explore environmental issues and our relationship with nature. *Endangered Species* continued Clarke's collaboration with composer Richard Peaslee and designers Robert Israel and Paul Gallo as well as the Music-Theatre Group, which co-commissioned the work with BAM.

## SITI Company/The Builders Association

While the early years of the Next Wave Festival focused on bringing together individuals from different disciplines, collaborative companies took center stage as the festival developed, often

*The Birth of the Poet*, Richard Foreman/Kathy Acker/Peter Gordon/David Salle, 1985. Photo: Beatriz Schiller

under the direction of an artistic visionary. Many of these companies came from abroad, making the Next Wave a truly international festival. American artists continued, however, to be important contributors to BAM's theatrical offerings.

One of these artists, Anne Bogart—the 2012 recipient of BAM's Richard B. Fisher Next Wave Award, which recognizes one outstanding Next Wave production per festival—is co-artistic director of SITI Company, which she cofounded in 1992 with Japanese theater icon Tadashi Suzuki. An actor-oriented company "built on the bedrock of ensemble," SITI combines the rigorous physical discipline of Suzuki's actor training with Bogart's improvisatory techniques known as Viewpoints. The company first appeared at BAM in 2000 with their production of **War of the Worlds,** coauthored by Bogart and playwright Naomi Iizuka.

Although an actor-oriented company, SITI has had a long collaboration with resident playwright Charles L. Mee, also a Fisher Award winner, and performed two productions from Mee's "Lives of the Artist" series in the Next Wave, **bobrauschenbergamerica** (2003) and **Hotel Cassiopeia** (2007). The former is described as "a wild road trip through an American landscape,"

*bobrauschenbergamerica*, Charles L. Mee/Anne Bogart/SITI Company, 2003. Photo: Richard Termine

which multimedia artist Robert Rauschenberg might have assembled if he were a playwright. The latter is based on the work of American artist Joseph Cornell and questions what it would be like if Cornell's boxes could speak. In addition to his collaborations with SITI, Mee's play **Big Love,** a contemporary adaptation of Aeschylus' play *The Suppliants* directed by long-time collaborator Les Waters, was part of the 2001 Next Wave Festival.

The eclectic nature of Bogart's work with SITI can be seen in her more recent Next Wave offerings. In 2012, she directed **Trojan Women (After Euripides),** described as a "highly modernized adaptation of Euripides' anti-war drama." She then collaborated with the Bill T. Jones/Arnie Zane Dance Company in **A Rite** (2013), an exploration of Igor Stravinsky's *Rite of Spring*. Presented in the 2015 Next Wave, **Steel Hammer** brought her together with composer Julia Wolfe, a founding member of Bang on a Can, for a music-theater piece.

While SITI Company ranges from Greek tragedy to modern artists for its inspiration, The Builders Association, founded in 1994 by artistic director Marianne Weems, describes itself as a "performance and media company that creates original productions based on stories drawn from contemporary life." **Alladeen,** seen at BAM in 2003, a collaboration with the London-based company motiroti, dramatized the work of international call centers where Indian operators were trained to "pass" as Americans. **Super Vision** (2005), a collaboration with dbox,

Carolyn Baeumler and K.J. Sanchez in *Big Love*, Charles L. Mee/Les Waters/Goodman Theatre, 2001. Photo: Richard Trigg

a multidisciplinary studio specializing in 3D digital media, focused on surveillance and data collection in the 21st century while **Continuous City** (2008) explored how technological advances have allowed individuals to "simultaneously occupy multiple locations."

In 2012, The Builders Association explored the contemporary crisis of home foreclosures and the resultant dislocation of families juxtaposed with America's great novel of internal migration, John Steinbeck's *The Grapes of Wrath*. Dominating the stage in **HOUSE/DIVIDED** was an actual foreclosed house from Columbus, Ohio, dismantled and reassembled to physically embody the reality of foreclosure. As with previous Builders Association productions, projections and video images were an integral part of the performance's storytelling.

Tanya Selvaratnam, Rizwan Mirza, Jeff Webster, and Jasmine Simhalan in *Alladeen*, Marianne Weems/Keith Khan/Ali Zaidi/The Builders Association/motiroti, 2003. Photo: Richard Termine

## Global Perspectives

The most active and engaging participant in the Next Wave is Tanztheater Wuppertal, the company founded and led by Pina Bausch until her death in 2009. Bausch is identified primarily as a choreographer, but her oeuvre included many pieces that were just as, if not more, concerned about creating a new form that gave equal importance to choreographic and theatrical elements. Early in the life of the company, she articulated her philosophy about her performers: "I pick my dancers as people. I don't pick them for nice bodies, for having the same height, or things like that. I look for the *person* . . . the personality." As her work evolved, those personalities were given greater prominence—company members would walk downstage and speak directly to the audience, and sometimes leave the stage to interact with them.

The theatricality of Bausch's work came through not only when she staged her versions of early works like **Arien**, **Kontakthof**, and **The Seven Deadly Sins**, performed in the company's first Next Wave residency in 1985, but in the strong, sometimes startling settings of many of her later works. Working with scene designers Rolf Borzik, and from the 1980s onward Peter Pabst, Bausch placed her performers in such memorable environments as a pool of water overseen by a hippopotamus, a mountain comprising two tons of dirt, a stage full of carnations, a fish tank, and a collapsing brick wall.

The Next Wave Festival not only became the sole New York home of Bausch's Tanztheater Wuppertal but the venue for the next generation of German tanztheater creators. These included Reinhild Hoffmann's Tanztheater Bremen, which performed **Callas** (1985) and **Machandel** (1989), based on Grimm's fairy tales, and in more recent years, Sasha Waltz & Guests, performing such dance-theater works as **Körper** (2002) and **Gezeiten** (2010) in addition to more pure-dance pieces like **Impromptus** (2005) and **Continu** (2015).

Another long-running relationship between BAM and an artist has been with Canadian director, actor, writer, designer, and filmmaker Robert Lepage. He first appeared in the Next Wave with **Polygraph** (1990), which he coauthored and directed (and later filmed). One critic has characterized Lepage's work as "a visual laboratory," conducting experiments "attuned to the synergistic possibilities that emerge when art encounters science and technology." In addition to his

extensive theater work, Lepage created *KÀ* for Cirque du Soleil and directed numerous opera productions, including *Bluebeard's Castle/Erwartung* and *The Nightingale and Other Short Fables* for the Canadian Opera Company, performed at BAM in 1993 and 2011, respectively, and Wagner's *Ring* cycle, *La Damnation de Faust*, and *L'Amour de Loin* for the Metropolitan Opera.

His work has embraced such subjects as the addictions of Jean Cocteau and Miles Davis in **Needles and Opium** (1992); the aftermath of the atomic bomb blast on Hiroshima in **The Seven Streams of the River Ota** (1996); and the reenactment of *Hamlet* with all the roles performed by a single actor in **Elsinore** (1997). In 1999, he brought his exploration of the relationship between the iconic architect Frank Lloyd Wright and the spiritual teachings of George Gurdjieff to the Harvey with **Geometry of Miracles** and nearly a decade later a nine-hour exploration of the human voice with **Lipsynch** (2009).

In recent years, Russian director Lev Dodin and his Maly Drama Theatre of St. Petersburg have performed at BAM three revelatory productions of Anton Chekhov masterpieces: *Uncle*

ABOVE
*Callas*, Reinhild Hoffmann/Tanztheater Bremen, 1985. Photo: Klaus Lefebvre

OPPOSITE
*Geometry of Miracles*, Robert Lepage/Ex Machina, 1999. Photo: Emmanuel Valette

*Vanya* (2010), *Three Sisters* (2012), and *The Cherry Orchard* (2016). The first appearance of the company, however, was during the 1994 Next Wave Festival with a contemporary work, **Gaudeamus.** Adapted by Dodin and his directing students from the St. Petersburg Theatre Institute and members of the Maly company from the 1988 novel *Construction Battalion (Stroibat)* by Sergei Kaledin, *Gaudeamus* dramatized the lives of Red Army conscripts drawn from the margins of Soviet society. In his production, Dodin made extensive use of music and dance to, in his own works, "speak not only to the lowest level, the depth men can sink, but also of the possibilities inherent, the potential, the positive essence of man."

The same festival that introduced the Maly Drama Theatre to Next Wave audiences also marked the debut of another company that has been a frequent visitor to BAM, Cheek by Jowl. Formed in 1981 by director Declan Donnellan and designer Nick Ormerod, the London-based company tours internationally and produces or co-produces plays in English, Russian, and French. For its initial Next Wave appearance in 1994, the company startled audiences and critics with

an all-male production of Shakespeare's **As You Like It** led by an incandescent performance of Rosalind by Adrian Lester. In 2006, Donnellan and Ormerod returned to the festival with another all-male production of Shakespeare's **Twelfth Night,** this time with Russian actors from the Chekhov International Theatre Festival; relying on imagination rather than elaborate production values, other Cheek by Jowl productions for the Next Wave include John Webster's **The Duchess of Malfi** (1995), **Othello** (2004), and **The Winter's Tale** (2016).

In addition to productions of the Bard in their original language, BAM has a long history of hosting companies from throughout the world presenting Shakespeare in their native tongues. One of these, a landmark production of **Macbeth** directed by famed Japanese Yukio Ninagawa, was part of the 1990 festival and made a return appearance in 2002. Like Kurosawa's *Throne of Blood*, Ninagawa used aspects of Noh theater in his productions but added the beauty of Japanese visual art through a *mise-en-scène* dominated by the cherry blossoms that symbolize Japanese history and culture.

Alexey Dadonov and Sergey Mukhin in *Twelfth Night*. Declan Donnellan/ Nick Ormerod/Chekhov International Theatre Festival, 2006. Photo: Richard Termine

## Age of Wonder

In recent seasons, BAM has presented four great actors—Ian McKellen, Frank Langella, Derek Jacobi, and Antony Sher—as King Lear. As part of the 2001 Next Wave, however, a very different production of Shakespeare's tragedy was offered by Belgian-Flemish director Jan Lauwers and his Brussels-based Needcompany. Performed with minimal sets and costumes, Lauwers emphasized what he saw as the negative and hopeless qualities of the play. Even though Needcompany is known primarily for original works, Lauwers believes, "It's good for an ensemble to do Shakespeare every so often, just to recharge the batteries."

Three of Needcompany's original works have been seen at BAM under the umbrella of the Next Wave. The first, **Morning Song** (1999), is a companion piece to the company's earlier production of Albert Camus's *Caligula* and, according to Lauwers, is a burlesque taking place in heaven—which includes a working kitchen—with all the characters dead. The second, **Isabella's room** (2004), dramatizes the memories of a 94-year-old blind woman who can visualize her memories due to a camera that has been implanted in her brain. In 2010, the company presented **The Deer House,** where a group of actors is forced to confront the world

Toshiaki Karasawa in *Ninagawa Macbeth*, The Ninagawa Company, 2002. Photo: Richard Termine

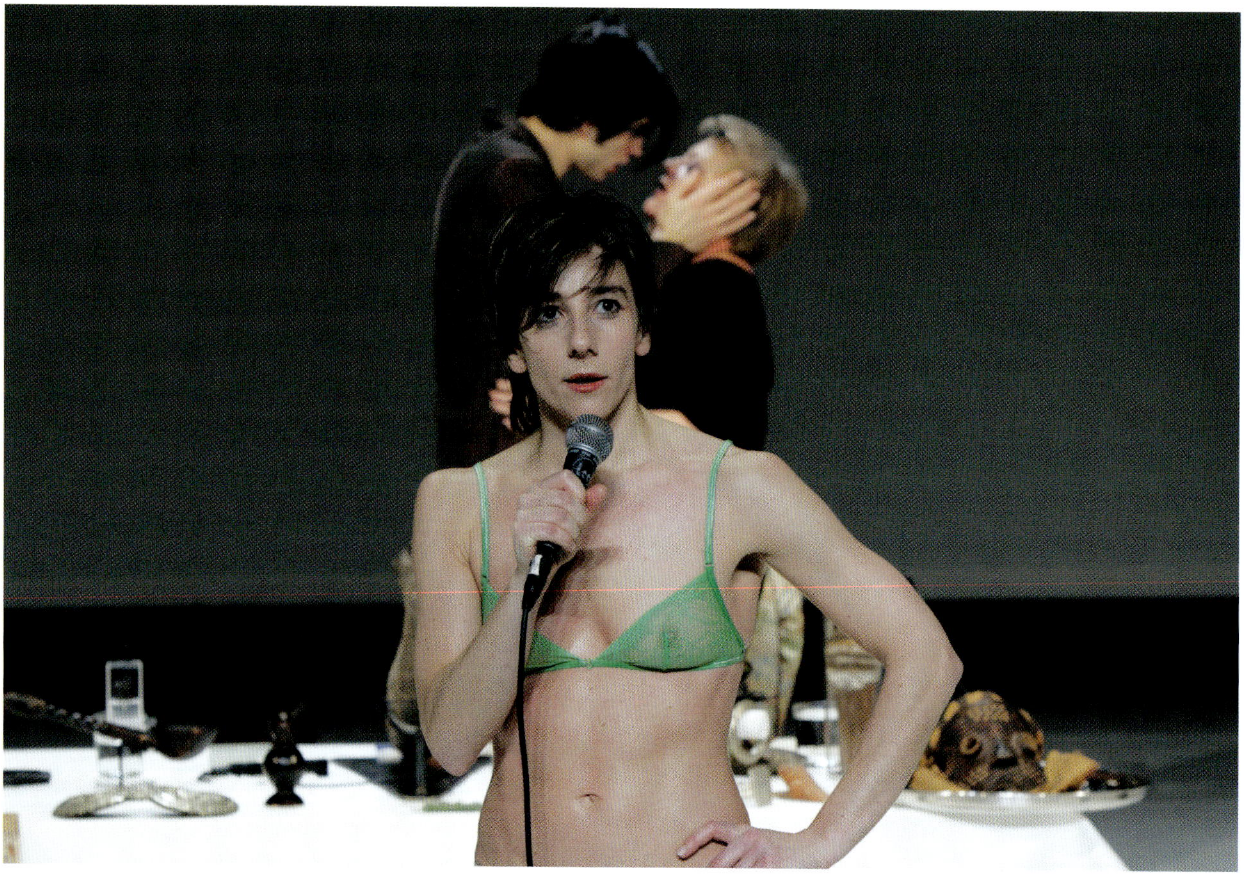

they live and perform in. All three plays were written by Lauwers in collaboration with his company and used extensive live rock music and dance in association with the texts.

Another Belgian-born director, Ivo van Hove, also incorporates both Shakespeare and contemporary plays in the repertory of his Amsterdam-based Toneelgroep company, which made its debut in the 2008 festival with **Opening Night**. Van Hove has directed many English-language works, including **Antigone** with Juliette Binoche, seen in the 2015 festival, and won a 2016 Tony Award for his Broadway production of Arthur Miller's *A View from the Bridge*. Van Hove's two Shakespeare productions for Toneelgroep at BAM—**Roman Tragedies** (2012) and **Kings of War** (2016)—condensed several plays into one evening to show how texts dealing with Roman or English history can comment upon each other and our contemporary world. *Roman Tragedies* placed *Coriolanus*, *Julius Caesar*, and *Antony and Cleopatra* into a multimedia world of video cameras and TV screens and invited the audience to go onstage during the performance,

ABOVE
Tijen Lawton, Maarten Seghers, and Viviane De Muynck in *Isabella's room*, Jan Lauwers/ Needcompany, 2004. Photo: Richard Termine

OPPOSITE
Elsie de Brauw in *Opening Night*, Ivo van Hove/ Toneelgroep Amsterdam/ NTGent, 2008. Photo: Richard Termine

becoming, in the words of one critic, "the nameless citizens of Rome... implicated in the action." With *Kings of War*, van Hove created a four-hour cycle of English plays that combined *Henry V*, *Henry VI, Parts 1–3*, and *Richard III*, once again placing the plays in a modern context to deal with, in the director's words, "the theme of leadership."

The eclectic nature of van Hove's Dutch-language work with Toneelgroep can be found in the contemporary texts he staged for the Next Wave. Two of these, *Opening Night* and **Cries and Whispers** (2011), were stage adaptations of screenplays by John Cassavetes and Ingmar Bergman, respectively, and were given multimedia productions that both acknowledged and expanded upon their origins. His 2014 production of Tony Kushner's **Angels in America** showed another side of van Hove's artistry. In collaboration with his longtime designer Jan Versweyveld, they stripped Kushner's epic of much of the realistic detail that had characterized previous productions. In 2017, van Hove and his Toneelgroep collaborators set their sights on a very different work, Ayn Rand's controversial 1943 novel **The Fountainhead.** In updating his stage adaptation to a contemporary architect's loft-office, van Hove once again used projected video images of the stage action as an integral part of his vision.

The Next Wave Festival has increasingly played host to a series of continental European directors who have interpreted early modern and modern plays in exciting and sometimes startling new ways. One is Thomas Ostermeier, who since 1999 has been resident director and member of the artistic direction of the Schaubühne in Berlin. In addition to a stage adaptation of Rainer Werner Fassbinder's screenplay for **The Marriage of Maria Braun** (2010), Next Wave audiences have seen his versions of three Henrik Ibsen plays: **Nora (A Doll's House)** (2004), **Hedda Gabler** (2006), and **An Enemy of the People** (2013). In these productions, Ostermeier stripped away the Victorian trappings often associated with the Norwegian playwright and confronted his audiences with visceral contemporary accounts of Ibsen's dramatizations of the struggles between men and women and between individuals and society. In 2017, Ostermeier turned to one of Shakespeare's greatest villains, Richard III, in a startling modern update complete with a persistent drumbeat and soliloquies captured by an overhead microphone.

Another German director known for his stark and emotionally explosive productions of classic plays, Michael Thalheimer, brought productions from two different companies to the Next

Wave. His first production, Gotthold Lessing's 1772 tragedy **Emilia Galotti,** was performed by the Deutsches Theater Berlin in 2005, followed two years later in 2007 by his staging of Frank Wedekind's **Lulu** for the Thalia Theater. According to Thalheimer, "The main point of my work is to completely focus, to boil down to the minimum, to the intensity, to the core of the piece, to get rid of everything that is superfluous."

The Next Wave production of another staple of the German repertory, Georg Büchner's **Woyzeck** (2008), perfectly illustrates the rich diversity of contemporary European theater. Director Gísli Örn Gardarsson of Iceland's Vesturport Theatre reset the play in a factory dominated by a water tank in which much of the action took place. A score by Nick Cave and Warren Ellis that ranges from rock to waltzes emphasized Gardarsson's "maximalist" approach to the play, including a violinist playing while on a trapeze. In 2010, the company returned in a joint production with London's Lyric Hammersmith of a physically dazzling stage adaptation of Franz Kafka's **Metamorphosis,** which Gardarsson co-adapted, co-directed, and starred in as Gregor Samsa. Two years later, Vesturport teamed with another company, Reykjavík City Theatre, for its circus-inspired version of the Faust legend, **Faust: A Love Story.** Described as "loud, fast, explosive, poetic and acrobatic," the production once again featured a score by Cave and Ellis.

OPPOSITE
Brigitte Hobmeier and Bernd Moss in *The Marriage of Maria Braun*, Thomas Ostermeier/Schaubühne am Lehniner Platz, 2010. Photo: Julieta Cervantes

ABOVE
Fritzi Haberlandt and Felix Knopp in *Lulu*, Michael Thalheimer/Thalia Theater, 2007. Photo: Richard Termine

While many companies include stage adaptations of works of fiction—like Vesturport's *Metamorphosis*—in their repertories, the London-based Shared Experience has specialized in such work since its founding. Its first appearance in the Next Wave in 1998 featured Nancy Meckler's production of Leo Tolstoy's **Anna Karenina**. In 2004, Meckler, co-artistic director of Shared Experience with Polly Teale, directed a production of E.M. Forster's **A Passage to India** adapted by Martin Sherman and co-produced by the Nottingham Playhouse. In the company's own words, their work "celebrates the union of physical and text-based theater."

## Embracing the Past and Present

In addition to innovative productions of Shakespeare, classics from the world repertory, and theatrical adaptations of great fiction, the Next Wave Festival has afforded its audiences the opportunity to experience exciting productions of 20th-century masterworks as well. Two of these plays, Eugène Ionesco's **Rhinoceros** (2012) and Luigi Pirandello's **Six Characters in Search of an Author** (2014), came in thought-provoking and deeply felt productions by Emmanuel Demarcy-Mota and the Théâtre de la Ville, Paris. Known for evolving his pro-

Gísli Örn Gardarsson in *Metamorphosis*, Vesturport Theatre/Lyric Hammersmith, 2010. Photo: Richard Termine

ductions over long periods of time, he first directed the Pirandello play in 2001 and the Ionesco in 2004. In 2017, Demarcy-Mota brought to life a much lesser known work, Albert Camus's **State of Siege,** written in 1948 as a response to 20th-century totalitarian dictatorships and the manipulation of their populaces.

While many of the Next Wave theater presentations in recent years have shown how multimedia approaches can illuminate classic plays, a wide variety of other sources have also inspired contemporary artists. A stunning example was **BASETRACK Live** (2014), from En Garde Arts, created by Edward Bilous, adapted by Jason Grote, and directed by Seth Bockley, with music by Michelle DiBucci. Drawn from video testimonials, photography, and a website, *BASETRACK Live* allowed audiences insight into the experience of U.S. Marines in Afghanistan and their families back home. A totally different world was evoked in the 2015 festival by **Helen Lawrence.**

*Rhinoceros*, Emmanuel Demarcy-Mota/Théâtre de la Ville, Paris, 2012. Photo: Pavel Antonov

Conceived and directed by photographer/filmmaker Stan Douglas and written by television and film producer/director/writer Chris Haddock and produced by Canadian Stage, it brought to life post–World War II Vancouver in a *film noir*-tinged revenge story that was simultaneously stage action and live film.

Even though the director has been the focal point of many Next Wave productions, great actors in the BAM tradition dating back to Edwin Booth and Sarah Bernhardt have made their mark as well. Fiona Shaw devastated audiences with her no-holds-barred **Medea** (2002) in a production directed by Deborah Warner for the Abbey Theatre that transferred to Broadway. She then made Coleridge's poem **The Rime of the Ancient Mariner** (2013) come to theatrical life under the guidance of Phyllida Lloyd. In 2008, she also brought Winnie, the eternal optimist of Samuel Beckett's *Happy Days*, to BAM, and another Beckett protagonist, the eponymous (and

Lisa Ryder and Allan Louis in *Helen Lawrence*, Stan Douglas/Chris Haddock/Canadian Stage, 2015. Photo: Richard Termine

only) character in **Krapp's Last Tape** (2011), was memorably portrayed by John Hurt in Michael Colgan's Gate Theatre production.

The French actress Isabelle Huppert has made three appearances in the Next Wave Festival. In 2005, she gave a searing portrayal in her American stage debut of Sarah Kane's troubled protagonist in **4.48 Psychose** and then returned in 2009 in Robert Wilson's version of Heiner Müller's **Quartett.** Most recently, she appeared in **Phaedra(s)**, multiple approaches to Euripides' and Racine's tragic queen, in a 2016 production directed by Krzysztof Warlikowski—no stranger to the Next Wave, having directed productions of **The Dybbuk** (2004) and **Krum** (2007) for the TR Warszawa company.

When Lichtenstein brought Brook's *A Midsummer Night's Dream* to BAM in 1971, he began an ongoing association with the Royal Shakespeare Company that has enabled the BAM audience to experience some of the most extraordinary theater of our times. From revelatory productions of *Richard II*, *Henry V*, *Love's Labour's Lost*, and Maxim Gorky's *Summerfolk* in the 1970s to Trevor Nunn's staging of *King Lear* and Chekhov's *The Seagull* and Gregory Doran's offering of the complete second Henriad, King and Country, comprising *Richard III*, *Henry IV, Parts 1–3, and Henry V*, BAM has been the principal New York venue for this acclaimed company.

BAM also forged a major relationship with the Royal Dramatic Theatre of Sweden, presenting famed director Ingmar Bergman's productions of plays ranging from Shakespeare to Schiller, Ibsen,

Fiona Shaw in *Medea*, Deborah Warner/Abbey Theatre, 2002. Photo: Stephanie Berger

Strindberg, O'Neill, and Yukio Mishima. Traveling the world over for the best in international theater, executive producer Joseph V. Melillo programmed an extraordinary range of innovative performance from the Cape Town-based Handspring Puppet Company in South Africa to the Abbey Theatre in Dublin, U-Theatre from Taiwan to the Berliner Ensemble, the Prague National Theatre to the Chorus Repertory Theatre of Manipur—essentially bringing the world to Brooklyn.

## Physical Theater

From its beginnings, the Next Wave Festival also embraced a different style of theater, one tracing its roots back to *commedia dell'arte* that was oriented toward performers rather than texts, emphasizing physical skills and entertainment. Some of these performers were grouped under the rubric of "new vaudevillians" because they revisited and updated such traditional forms as juggling, clowning, and mime. In 1985, juggler Michael Moschen and clown/mime Bob Berky, in collaboration with sculptor John Kahn and composer David Van Tieghem, created **The Alchemedians,** a work that attempted to integrate their individual skills into a larger theatrical context. Three years later, they returned with separate works. Moschen resumed his collaboration with Kahn and Van Tieghem in a solo show, **Michael Moschen in Motion**, which extended his exploration into combining juggling and dance. Berky's **The Power Project (Antic Variations),** in collaboration with writer/director Mark Harrison, presented him as a politician who at times left the stage to interact with the audience, "gauging opinions, finding support, bolstering his constituency and teaching the masses how to recognize the truth."

Bob Berky in his *The Power Project (Antic Variations)*, 1988. Photo courtesy of BAM Hamm Archives

One of the earliest groups identified as "new vaudevillians," the Flying Karamazov Brothers brought a contemporary version of Igor Stravinsky's 1918 music-theater work **The Soldier's Tale (L'Histoire du Soldat)** to the 1986 festival. Directed by Robert Woodruff with a new libretto by playwright Len Jenkin and company member Paul Magid, the production enlivened this fable about a soldier's encounter with the devil by the customary Karamazov blend of juggling, music, and comedy.

The most unusual company to participate in the Next Wave has to be Zingaro, a French equestrian troupe of 26 horses and their riders led by artistic director Bartabas. None of BAM's theater spaces would accommodate the company's ring and stable needs, so a tent was constructed in Battery Park City for the engagements of **Chimère** (1996) and **Eclipse** (1998). While the former drew on the Indian music from Rajasthan for inspiration (visually and aurally), the

*La grenouille avait raison (The Toad Knew)*, James Thierrée/La Compagnie du Hanneton, 2017. Photo: Max Gordon

latter included a seven-member Korean folk music ensemble that accompanied the spectacular exploits of the horses and their riders.

More recently, the Next Wave has become the New York home of one of Europe's most exciting performing artists, James Thierrée. The son of circus performers Victoria Chaplin and Jean-Baptiste Thierrée and the grandson of Charlie Chaplin and the great grandson of Eugene O'Neill, Thierrée and his La Compagnie du Hanneton made their first Next Wave appearance in 2005 with the mesmerizing **Bright Abyss**, followed in 2007 with **Au Revoir Parapluie,** a work dominated by magical ropes on which myriad physical feats were performed. He returned in 2010 with **Raoul,** where Thierrée encountered a series of magical creatures on his journey, and **Tabac Rouge** (2015) filled the stage of the Howard Gilman Opera House with a variety of performers who helped Thierrée bring to life his vision of a Lear-like king dealing with mortality. In 2017, BAM presented Thierrée's

ABOVE
*Les sept planches de la ruse (The Seven Boards of Skill)*, Aurélien Bory/ Scènes de la Terre/ Compagnia 111, 2008. Photo: Richard Termine

OPPOSITE
David Menes, Félix Salas, Catherine Girard, and Rolando Tarquini in *Donka: A Letter to Chekhov*, Compagnia Finzi Pasca, 2012. Photo: Pavel Antonov

latest exploration of fantasy and feats of physical virtuosity, **La grenouille avait raison (The Toad Knew)** where a brother and sister were held captive underground by the title amphibian.

As a means to program the newest generation of "new vaudeville" performers, BAM executive producer Melillo introduced productions that fell under the tent (metaphorically speaking) of *nouveau cirque* ("new circus"). Performed in the 2008 festival, **Les sept planches de la ruse (The Seven Boards of Skill),** conceived and directed by Aurélien Bory, brought together his Compagnie 111 and Scènes de la Terre with acrobats and Peking opera performers from Dalian, China, to transform the ancient Chinese game of tangram into a work that was described as "poised at the intersection of physical-theater, modern dance and waking dreams."

Once again the truly international nature of the Next Wave Festival can be seen in some of the other *nouveau cirque* performances. In the 2009 festival, for example, Cirkus Cirkör from Sweden, under the direction of founder Tilde Björfors, brought **Inside Out,** with actors and acrobats taking audiences on a tour of human anatomy accompanied by the "dub-punk-new wave-electro-inspired" band Irya's Playground. Switzerland was represented by two very different artists, Daniele Finzi Pasca and Martin Zimmermann. Finzi Pasca, creator of Cirque du Soleil's *Corteo*,

used acrobatics, juggling, clowning, and music to present Anton Chekhov's characters as they had never been seen before in **Donka: A Letter to Chekhov** (2012). In 2013, director/choreographer Zimmermann collaborated with composer Dimitri de Perrot in **Hans was Heiri**, described by its creators as built "from little things that happen when a person feels unobserved." Zimmermann returned two years later with **Hallo,** a solo work where he showed his clown skills maneuvering through a shifting architectural landscape.

From another continent came the Australian company Circa in a collaboration unusual even for BAM with **Opus** (2015), featuring the acrobats of Yaron Lifschitz's company performing amid the blindfolded musicians of the Debussy String Quartet while they played three of Dmitri Shostakovich's string quartets.

## New Voices

In addition to providing a platform for major cutting-edge artists to create large-scale works and introducing major international artists to New York audiences, the Next Wave Festival also sought to give younger artists the opportunity to gain wider exposure and recognition. During the first decade of the festival, the Lepercq Space, located on the second floor of the Opera House building, served that purpose. A flexible theater that could

*Hans was Heiri*, Zimmermann & de Perrot, 2013. Photo: Pavel Antonov

accommodate several hundred audience members, the Lepercq Space—originally the Academy's ballroom—returned to its origins as an event space that later became home to the BAMcafé.

The young American artists who presented work in the Lepercq Space often used various performance and multimedia techniques to explore social and historical issues. In **Democracy in America**, performed in 1984, Tim Miller, inspired by the 19th-century travels of Alexis de Tocqueville, crossed the country with a video crew taping interviews about America and our political system and values. These interviews were then shaped into a multi-channel installation that formed the background of Miller's performances. In the following year, Chris Hardman and the Antenna Theater production of **Russia** also used taped interviews to create a work that was less about the actual Soviet Union and more about paranoia and intolerance. And in the 1986 Next Wave, the production of **Social Amnesia...a live movie**—a collaboration between the Baltimore-based Impossible Theater and John Schneider of Milwaukee's Theatre X—looked at America's complex relationship with technology before the era of smart phones and social media.

The proximity to the audience in the Lepercq Space also allowed cutting-edge artists to incorporate traditional theater forms into their storytelling. For the 1989 production of **Stuff**

**As Dreams Are Made On**, his solo version of Shakespeare's *The Tempest*, Fred Curchack used masks, dolls, and shadow puppets, as well as acrobatics and mime, to bring the Bard's late romance to life in a completely new way. Two years later, Eric Bass/Sandglass Theater used puppets to present a collaboration with director Richard Edelman and composer Alan Bern, **Invitations to Heaven (Questions of a Jewish Child)** that was based on Bass's own family story.

With the opening of the flexible, 250-seat Fishman Space in the BAM Fisher Building in 2012, Next Wave executive producer Melillo was once again able to program the kind of intimate works by young artists previously performed in the Lepercq Space. In the inaugural season, for example, a new generation of cutting-edge performers was represented by spoken word/hip-hop theater artist Marc Bamuthi Joseph, who presented **red, black & GREEN: a blues,** a multimedia work on environmental justice and social ecology created in conjunction with singer and visual artist Theaster Gates.

OPPOSITE
Tim Miller in his *Democracy in America*, 1984. Photo: Dona McAdams

ABOVE
Theaster Gates, Marc Bamuthi Joseph, Tommy Shepherd, and Traci Tolmaire in *red, black & GREEN: a blues*, Marc Bamuthi Joseph/Michael Garcés/ Living Word Project, 2012. Photo: Richard Termine

The intimacy of the Fishman Space made it the perfect venue for solo (or virtually solo) pieces that embodied the wide range of performance being practiced today. Presented in the 2013 festival, Suzanne Bocanegra's **Bodycast: An Artist Lecture by Suzanne Bocanegra Starring Frances McDormand** was inspired by the two years visual artist Bocanegra spent in a bodycast while a teen. As Bocanegra, barely visible and audible to the audience, read her text about her life and art, her words were related through an earpiece to Tony- and Academy Award-winning actor Frances McDormand, who then delivered those words as if they were an artist's talk, complete with slides. In 2017, Bocanegra presented **Farmhouse/Whorehouse: An Artist Lecture by Suzanne Bocanegra Starring Lili Taylor**, which brings to life Bocanegra's evocation of her grandparents' life across the street from the famed Chicken Ranch, "the best little whorehouse in Texas." Thaddeus Phillips, head of the Philadelphia-based Lucidity Suitcase Intercontinental, created, designed, and performed **17 Border Crossings** (2015), an examination of the complex-

ABOVE
Thaddeus Phillips in his *17 Border Crossings*, 2015. Photo: Ed Lefkowicz

OPPOSITE
Danuta Stenka in *Request Concert*, Yana Ross/Łaźnia Nowa Theater/TR Warszawa, 2016. Photo: Richard Termine

ities of international travel. For his return engagement in the 2017 festival, Phillips collaborated with installation artist Steven Dufala in **A Billion Nights on Earth,** an exploration of a father-son relationship drawing on inspirations as diverse as pop-up books and Kabuki theater with a score by Juan Gabriel Turbay.

Yana Ross's production of Franz Xaver Kroetz's 1973 play **Request Concert** (2016) presented its actor, Danuta Stenka, with the opposite challenge. There is no dialogue in Kroetz's play about a woman's life in her apartment complete with bath and kitchen, with only a disembodied voice on the radio. Ross's production updated the script's scenario, replacing the character's knitting in the original with an online game. The play was performed surrounded by the audience, who stood throughout the production.

Two other Fishman Space presentations went even farther in involving the audience in the action of the play, which in both cases were performed by the authors. In Geoff Sobelle's **The Object Lesson** (2014), directed by David Neumann, the audience was invited to explore

the set, described as an "epic storage facility of gargantuan proportions," while Sobelle presented what he called "a meditation on our relationship to things." In **HOME,** performed in the 2017 festival, Sobelle expanded his exploration of theatrical space by leading an ensemble of dancers and designers in constructing and then inhabiting a house onstage in the Harvey Theater. Miranda July's **New Society** (2015), on the other hand, required the audience to fully participate in creating a community from the ground up that spanned 20 years. The award-winning writer, filmmaker, and visual artist was described as "risking all" in "testing the limits of what is possible with two hours and a room full of strangers."

In a way though, it's what the Next Wave Festival has done throughout its history—Provide a home for artists willing to take risks in order to expand what is possible when an audience enters a theater.

OPPOSITE
Miranda July in her *New Society*, 2015. Photo: Rebecca Greenfield

ABOVE
Geoff Sobelle in *The Object Lesson*, Geoff Sobelle/David Neumann, 2014. Photo: Max Gordon

*Kings of War*, Ivo van Hove/Toneelgroep Amsterdam, 2016. Photo: Richard Termine

ABOVE
Ingo Hülsmann in *Emilia Galotti*, Michael Thalheimer/Deutsches Theater Berlin, 2005. Photo: Richard Termine

OPPOSITE
Lars Eidinger in *Richard III*, Thomas Ostermeier/Schaubühne Berlin, 2017. Photo: Richard Termine

OPPOSITE
Eric Berryman (featured) in *Steel Hammer*, Anne Bogart/Julia Wolfe/SITI Company/Bang on a Can All-Stars, 2015. Photo: Richard Termine

ABOVE
Juliette Binoche and Patrick O'Kane in *Antigone*, Ivo van Hove/Barbican/Les Théâtres de la Ville de Luxembourg, 2015. Photo: Stephanie Berger

*All That Fall*, Gavin Quinn/Pan Pan Theatre, 2012. Photo: Ed Lefkowicz

Before there was a Next Wave, contemporary music was limited in many ways, and at BAM it was essentially set free. This is where people like Philip Glass and Steve Reich—and other BAM artists like Meredith Monk—found a steady partner who would believe in them over the years. BAM became a home for revolutionary American productions that could previously only happen in Europe, and the Next Wave gave new composers the opportunity to show they were capable of having a powerful impact on contemporary music. It was music that served as a proposition to a theater artist or a choreographer to add something and change its content. The reason BAM played such a major role in the imagination of young musicians is that at the time the visual and performing arts were open to new composers, and the music world was closed to them.

**David Lang**

Composer

Rod Gilfry (featured) in *the loser*, David Lang, 2016. Photo: Richard Termine

# Music and Opera

Mark Swed

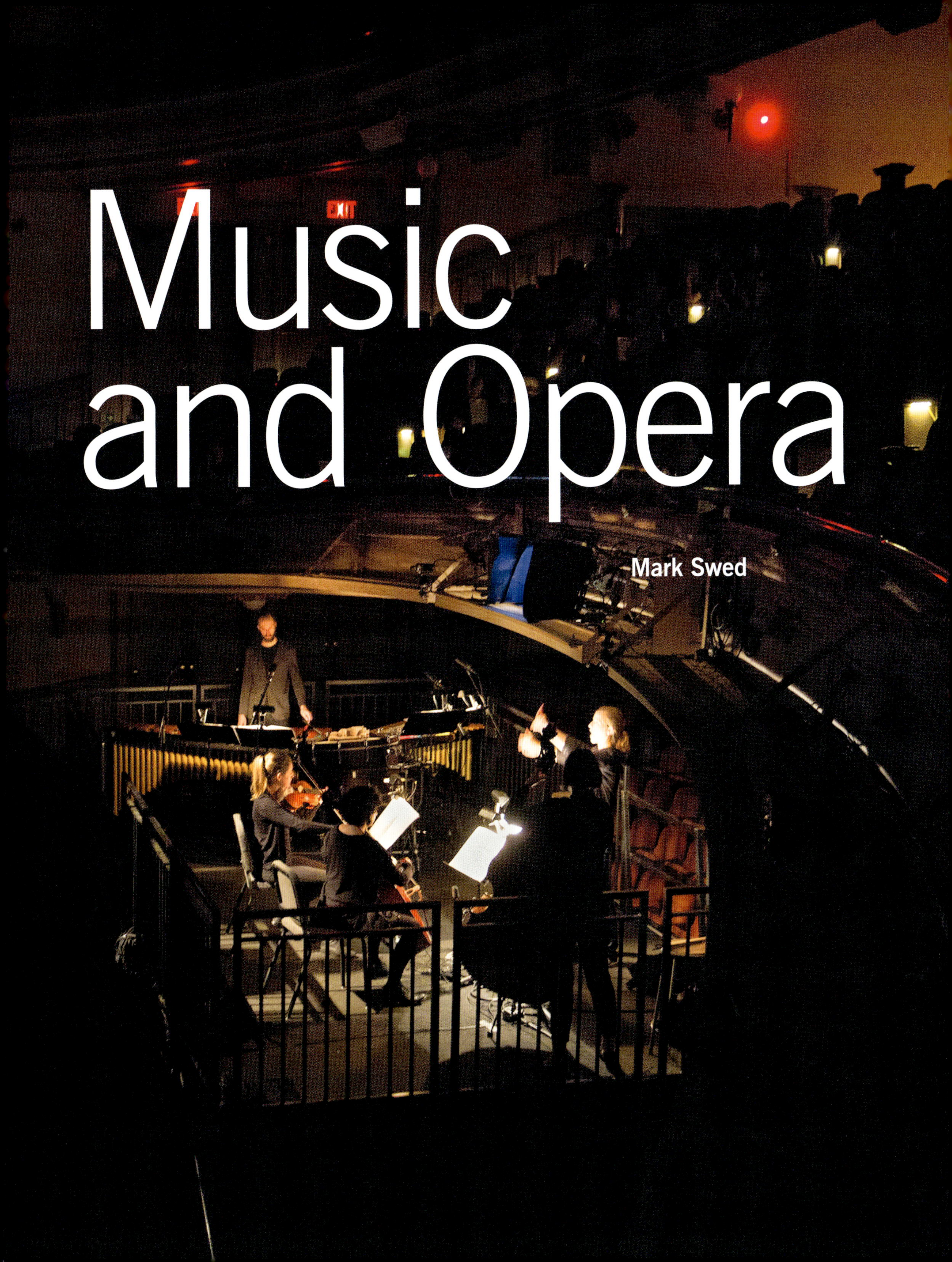

The Next Wave began wave-free. Without sound waves, that is—when the Trisha Brown Company inaugurated the opening season in the fall of 1981 of what was deemed the Next Wave Series at the Brooklyn Academy of Music with the choreographer's **Glacial Decoy**, which has no accompaniment. Accustomed to working in silence, Brown liked to say that she didn't want music to dominate the dance.

But music soon prevailed. Brown's next work in the program was the premiere of **Son of Gone Fishin'**, her first dance with a score. Robert Ashley played bits from his revolutionary opera-in-progress, **Atalanta (Acts of God)**. No one appears to have paid much attention to the composer's noodling on the organ; the music was barely acknowledged in the reviews. But Ashley's droning was background for an original and uniquely American kind of opera. He and a handful of other reformist American avant-garde composers were initiating what would become a central premise of the Next Wave Festival: to make modern music useful again.

ABOVE
Douglas Perry (featured) in *Satyagraha*, Philip Glass, 1981. Photo: Harry M De Ban

OPPOSITE
*Now Eleanor's Idea*, Robert Ashley, 1994. Photo: Dan Rest

Opera heralded the transformation, but as Ashley explained, "America didn't come to opera through evolution . . . around 1970, all of a sudden, people said let's do opera." Of particular relevance, the subject matter of *Atalanta*—the second part of a vast 20-hour opera cycle that included *Perfect Lives* and **Now Eleanor's Idea**—would turn out to be immigration, as noted by the composer, "where we came from and the ideas we brought with us."

Exactly three weeks after the premiere of *Son of Gone Fishin'*, the first season of the series and forerunner of the festival presented its first major attraction: a production of Philip Glass's **Satyagraha**. Where the opera came from was the minimalist style Glass pioneered in loft, club, and gallery concerts with his Philip Glass Ensemble and also by accompanying experimental theater productions. With *Satyagraha*, Glass took the major step of tailoring his repetitive style to the conventional resources of an opera company. His earlier **Einstein on the Beach**, the groundbreaking 1976 music-theater collaboration with Robert Wilson, had required only the physical resources of an opera house, not its musical ones. The premiere of *Satyagraha* in Rotterdam the year before it reached New York City opened the door for "minimalism" in opera.

The music coefficient in the Next Wave equation was, of course, hardly limited to opera. But neither was a "put on a show!" attitude limited to opera, and it was the promise of a newly functional music that became a distinguishing element of the Next Wave and the mission of BAM's then president and executive producer, Harvey Lichtenstein. As a student at Black Mountain College, he had been formed by the experimental college's culture clash that pitted the insistence of European émigré artists on artistic order as being necessary for maintaining cohesion against the attempts of John Cage to overthrow nostalgia and open the mind to new discoveries.

When Cage famously enlisted choreographer Merce Cunningham, painter Robert Rauschenberg, poet Charles Olson, writer M.C. Richards, and pianist David Tudor to make a formless theater event that became known as the first "happening" in 1952, each artist merely did something personally meaningful. The untitled event, which was never documented and, aided by the mystique, went on to have an enduring influence on American performance including no small one on the Next Wave. It not only made "let's do opera" a mantra two decades later, but it also formed the template for what became the characteristic Next Wave attribute of bringing artists from different disciplines together on their own equal terms.

First, though, Lichtenstein's objective when he came to BAM in 1967 had to be the revitalizing of the waning institution, which he did in significant part by transforming it into a home for progressive dance—with a particular sympathy for Cunningham and his influence—and experimental theater. Doing so included somehow exciting Manhattan audiences to venture into a dodgy part of Brooklyn. Marketing mattered.

The inaugural season of the Next Wave Series consisted of what seemed an unlikely if not ill-conceived union of three dance companies and the opera *Satyagraha*. Presenting the programming under the brand of the "Next Wave," however, emphasized a shared sensibility. If as an audience member you were interested in *Glacial Decoy* or *Son of Gone Fishin'* or choreographer Lucinda Childs's **Relative Calm**, which concluded the season, perhaps you would also like *Satyagraha*. After all, the composer for *Relative Calm* was Jon Gibson, a founding member of the Philip Glass Ensemble, and Robert Wilson had designed the décor.

It soon became clear that, amid a dizzying variety of Next Wave events, music is what embodied, however loosely, that shared sensibility, impossible as it might seem to pin down amid

OPPOSITE
Robert Spano and James Maddalena in *Die Winterreise*, Christian Boltanski, 1998. Photo: Toby Wales

ABOVE
Kronos Quartet in their *Awakening: A Musical Meditation on the Anniversary of 9/11*, 2011. Photo: Stephanie Berger

the extreme eclecticism that characterized the 35 succeeding Next Wave seasons. It was all here: jazz, pop, classical music, traditional and new musics from New York, San Francisco, Europe, the Balkans, Asia, the Middle East, Africa, South America. But whether baritone James Maddalena sang Schubert's **Die Winterreise** (1998) accompanied by Robert Spano on piano or served as the captain of the *Achille Lauro* in John Adams's **The Death of Klinghoffer**, performed at BAM in 1991, whether Wynton Marsalis revived jazz standards or John Zorn feistily dismantled them, whether pop tribute was paid to Nico or operatic tribute to Anna Nicole, each kind of music, and use of music, arrived in distinctive fashion. From Rufus Wainwright's versions of Shakespeare sonnets to Fela Kuti's Afrobeat, song was reinvented. From Kronos to ETHEL, the string quartet went where no string quartet had ever gone before.

## Next Wave Minimalism

In the end, the shared sensibility turned out to be as much in the sharing as the sensibility, with the expectation that

Nmon Ford and James Maddalena in *The Death of Klinghoffer*, John Adams/ Alice Goodman, 2003. Photo: Stephanie Berger

however new or unexpected the musical thinking, in some way it related to life as it was at the moment being led, to the social fabric of the time. But this also meant the overthrow of restrictions avowed by a post–World War II European avant-garde that sought to overcome history by replacing unfettered musical expression and its associations with mathematical logic, electronic manipulation of sound, and a comforting complexity as a means of forging a new sonic landscape in service of an unsentimental musical future. However amazing the results could be, a general audience found little personal connection and felt left behind.

The solution came from a trio of young American composers who advocated that rhythmic repetition, tonality, and melody be reintroduced into new music, by no means an easy task. Rejecting a European avant-garde orthodoxy with little relevance to American life or music in the 1960s, Terry Riley's iconic *In C*, composed in 1964, inspired Glass and Steve Reich to go one step farther and explore the return to conventional harmony and rhythm with the young composers' radically unconventional early experiments in mind-bending patterning. Everything the old avant-garde outlawed would be what minimalism first allowed.

Minimalism, of course, could hardly remain minimal for long. Step by step, Riley, Glass, and Reich, each with his own concerns, filled in their new style's blank slate by reaching out to musics of various genres, eras, and cultures, from 14th-century polyphony to psychedelic rock, from African drumming to Indonesian gamelan, from Stravinsky to Ravi Shankar. By the 1980s, a mature minimalism was ready for the big stage, and both Glass and Reich inevitably found themselves BAM's informal house composers. Malleable minimalism, moreover, appealed to BAM's community of visual artists, poets, theater directors, lighting designers, and postmodern choreographers, making it an ideal foundation for combining arts.

Being the model of a collaborative composer, Glass proved a perfect poster boy for the Next Wave idea. Perhaps ironically, given Glass's recognizably distinctive sound, one piece sometimes sounding much like the next, his music has also proved the most adaptable to diversely innovative multimedia and theatrical contexts. That was evident from the start, with Glass's improbable early encounters with the world of opera staged over the first four years of the Next Wave.

Despite being a mix of dance, film, theater, and visual art with practically no singing, **THE PHOTOGRAPHER/Far From the Truth**, which inaugurated the Next Wave Festival in 1983, was called by Glass an opera (only much later re-categorized as a work of music-theater). The highlight the following year was the first revival and revision of *Einstein on the Beach*, revealing, in retrospect, the DNA of an incipient Glass opera. Together these three disparate works became known as portrait operas of revolutionary historical figures—the young Gandhi developing non-violent principles in South Africa, Eadweard Muybridge examining the plasticity of time through stop-motion photography, and Einstein quantifying the plasticity of time.

Glass's music had a different fluid narrative purpose for each score, depending on resources and/or collaborators. *Einstein* is an opera of images that vaguely, if at all, suggested Einstein. *Satyagraha* is more specific in its scenes, but obscure in its Sanskrit sung libretto. *THE PHOTOGRAPHER/Far From the Truth* returns to the *Einstein* way, relying on the Philip Glass Ensemble but now with film and David Gordon's choreography.

By the time the *Einstein on the Beach* revival occupied the BAM Opera House in 1984, the Next Wave had produced some 30 programs that already covered a vast musical landscape. Minimalism prevailed but in different guises and in most cases with different theatrical and programmatic intent. The bulk of the examples, though, revealed a style uniquely suited for any and all things theatrical or programmatic.

Even Reich had begun letting his painstaking absolute-music counterpoint take on extra-musical implications. Steve Reich and Musicians opened the second Next Wave Series with a program that included the world premiere of **Vermont Counterpoint**. It required

Next Wave Festival poster for *The Way of How*, George Coates Performance Works, 1983. Courtesy of BAM Hamm Archives

flutist Ransom Wilson to perform live along with a recorded track of him playing several other interlocking flute lines moving in and out of phase with each other. In so doing, an exercise in chaste counterpoint is turned into a compelling spectacle of musician against machine, where the machine is that musician. The program also featured Reich's joyous **Tehillim**, adding a specific spiritual dimension to his work for the first time by setting Psalm texts for four soprano soloists and ensemble.

Two years later, the Brooklyn Philharmonic, conducted by Michael Tilson Thomas, gave the American premiere of Reich's **The Desert Music**, a pulsating large-scale 50-minute work for chorus and orchestra that sets texts by poet William Carlos Williams. Delighted to have Williams's validation of his style, Reich based the central section on a Williams stanza with the lines: "it is a principle of music / to repeat the theme. Repeat / and repeat again, / as the pace mounts. The / theme is difficult / but no more difficult / than the facts to be / resolved."

*The Gospel at Colonus*, Lee Breuer/Bob Telson, 1983. Photo: Martha Swope

The pace quickened as minimalism abounded, and so did the volume. But the context always changed. In Glenn Branca's dense, deafening **Symphony No. 3 ("Gloria")**, part of the second season of the Next Wave Series, electrified harpsichords played with guitar pickups created a cosmic drone over an earsplitting driving beat. Paul Dresher's electric guitar score to George Coates's surreal theater piece, **The Way of How** (1983), borrowed from Reich's early use of tape loops while at the same time satirizing elements of popular American music. Peter Gordon threw in all but the kitchen sink in his zany score for the Bill T. Jones/Arnie Zane & Company dance piece **Secret Pastures** (1984), with a set design by Keith Haring. John Adams created an electronic backdrop of Romantic-era lushness and contemporary beat for his contribution to **Available Light** in the 1983 festival, a dance work by Lucinda Childs with a chain-link set by architect Frank Gehry originally made for the opening of a new Gehry-designed addition to the Los Angeles Museum of Contemporary Art. With Meredith Monk's deceptively simple vocal music in her dance-theater piece **The Games** (1984), voice and body movement were in illuminating parallel.

## Next Wave Spectacle

Clearly, not everything could be minimalist. In the 1983 festival, there was the progressive jazz of the Art Ensemble of Chicago in concert, as there was the agreeably pop-flavored jazz of the Penguin Cafe Orchestra. Bob Telson's score to **The Gospel at Colonus** incorporated the gospel music of Clarence Fountain and the Five Blind Boys of Alabama in Lee Breuer's contemporary reinterpretation of Sophocles' Oedipus story. The jazz language of pianist Anthony Davis's accompaniment to the Molissa Fenley and Dancers premiere of **Hemispheres**, with designs by Francesco Clemente, alluded to Africa, Asia, and formal aspects of an older avant-garde. But even here, Davis's repetitive energy made a knowing bow to Glass and Reich. In the Next Wave context, a rare staging of the Russian Futurist opera **Victory Over the Sun**, with its original collage-like music by Mikhail Matiushin (from the same year, 1913, as, but eclectically decades ahead of, Stravinsky's *Rite of Spring*) and visual designs by Kazimir Malevich showed that the roots of what was happening in revolutionary music-theater could be found in the artistic roots of the Russian Revolution.

But it took two epic works that had evolved over several years to more fully imply the possibilities music now provided for a revolution in the art of performance. The first was the premiere of Laurie Anderson's eight-hour **United States: Parts I–IV** and the revival of *Einstein on the Beach*, in 1983 and 1984, respectively.

Anderson's one-woman show—in which she was author, composer, designer, videographer, musician, and performer (along with a small host of backup musicians and technicians)—provided broad and wry perspective on how the technology in the early '80s affected American society. By relating unusual observations of what she saw around her through halting speech and dry song against drones coming from her electric violin or keyboard, all underscored by quirky video and projections, Anderson could make it hard to tell whether the curious was somehow obvious or the obvious, curious. The delivery, sometimes lowering her voice to baritone through a vocoder, linked together the 88 thematically or musically unconnected numbers. The musical language fell somewhere between classic minimalism and pop, exemplified by her hit single, "O

Superman," which just happened to be a sweeping performance-art rewrite of a well-known opera aria: French composer Jules Massenet's "Ô Souverain, ô juge, ô père," in which "sovereign, judge, father" are now "superman, judge, mom and dad."

There is also a judge in *Einstein on the Beach*—and a violin, Einstein's instrument. There are Robert Wilson's glowing stage pictures. *Einstein* is likely the first opera where imagery—relativity suggested by steam engine or spaceship, a light bar slowly ascending to an ecstatically swirling organ solo that is neither the experience nor explanation of relativity, but an emotional response to it—takes the place of story. A small chorus counts out Glass's rhythms in numbers and sings pitches in solfeggio syllables. What there is of actual text, which is spoken, is an enlightened autistic stream-of-consciousness from Wilson protégé Christopher Knowles or from other performers who recite their own lines, including choreographer, dancer, and reciter Lucinda Childs's cyclic supermarket speech.

Much about the first production, which had its premiere in Avignon in 1976 and that year traveled to the Metropolitan Opera for two self-financed performances, had been makeshift. But new choreography from Childs for the BAM revival added a sophistication that helped illuminate the score. Mainly, though, Glass's ensemble had reached a level of refinement that brought out both musical subtleties and theatrical flourish that made the initial *Einstein* seem more like a workshop and the revival a finished masterpiece.

Furthermore, *Einstein* returned just in time to greatly bolster a growing appetite for immensity in the arts, helping the 1980s to be a golden age for dance/theater/opera/symphonic events grand in scope, ambition, and daring. Composers were widely enticed to work on large operatic, quasi-operatic, mock-operatic, and self-styled operatic palates for the first time in more than half a century. Just as the operatic language of Monteverdi, Handel, Mozart, and Wagner had once been a music of the future that claimed the greatest public excitement, so could contemporary composers once again reclaim the "next wave." BAM got big.

The 1986 festival opened with the most ambitious joint project John Cage and Merce Cunningham were ever able to fully realize. For four decades, they had, individually and together, caused the greatest transformations of their respective disciplines in their lifetimes. While **Roaratorio** was featured at BAM as an event by the Merce Cunningham Dance Company with music by Cage, the impetus for the work had all along come from an electronic tape score that Cage made on com-

Laurie Anderson in her *United States: Parts I-IV*, 1983. Photo: Perry Hoberman

mission by Pierre Boulez's Paris computer music studio, IRCAM. Fixated on James Joyce's experimental novel *Finnegans Wake*, Cage traveled throughout Ireland with a tape recorder to capture all the sounds he could identify in the novel. Spliced together at IRCAM, using the chance procedures Cage had pioneered, they became the atmospheric soundscape for the live performance, to which Cage added groups of Irish folk musicians spread around the Opera House. The composer himself sat at a table and read, for chance-determined intervals, his own poetic transformations of the *Wake*. Cunningham's abstract choreography was, as was his habit, made apart from the music, but not apart from the joyous celebration of the work.

For his part, Boulez regretted *Roaratorio*, finding its earthiness an insult to the experiments in acoustical properties he oversaw at IRCAM. Cage had briefly been an inspiration to Boulez decades earlier when both were exploring methods of indeterminacy as a means to discover sonic combinations they never would have thought of otherwise. But Cage went too far in rejecting convention for Boulez, who would eventually become the prime boogeyman of the minimalists. *Roaratorio* was the last straw for Boulez. But for New York's downtown artists who made up the core of the Next Wave, Boulezian disapproval only confirmed Cage as their indispensably permissive father figure.

That went to the extent of including even William Bolcom, whose

Next Wave Festival poster for *Roaratorio: An Irish Circus on Finnegans Wake*, Merce Cunningham Dance Company/John Cage, 1986. Courtesy of BAM Hamm Archives

**Songs of Innocence and of Experience** was the other massive masterpiece of the 1986 Next Wave. On the surface, this was about as far from Cage's innocence or experience as could be encountered. One of the most extravagant works in contemporary symphonic or song literature, this three-hour setting of William Blake's illustrated books of poems on the nature of good and evil requires no less than a large symphony orchestra, enhanced by rock guitarist, country fiddler, jazz saxophonist, and whatnot. Also needed are a variety of choruses and vocal soloists adept at a remarkable range capable of Wagnerian grandeur or reggae.

Bolcom conceived it 30 years earlier while a music student in Seattle, an eclectic so distraught by the academic 12-tone strictures of the 1950s he was ready to give up composing. But a happenstance encounter with Cage made him feel he somehow had authorization to go his own way, which in *Songs of Innocence and of Experience* is every way. Although the piece begins with an orchestral explosion, as loud and dissonant as the feistiest '50s orchestral experiments, the crashing chord's purpose here is to blast out of that European alternative universe into our own of rhythm-and-blues, music hall songs, and all the rest, in the Cagean belief

Claudia Cummings and Harlan Foss in *the CIVIL warS: a tree is best measured when it is down: Act V–the Rome Section*, Robert Wilson/Philip Glass, 1986. Photo: Tom Brazil

that neither innocence nor experience can be separated from the world that we inhabit and how we inhabit it. Like *Roaratorio*, Bolcom's song cycle is held together not by cause and effect but by exuberant incident in an environment that invites inclusivity.

As these two works along with Glass's portrait operas and Anderson's *United States: Parts I–IV* suggested, the extravagant 1980s had become a period for spectacle in which anything was possible. And the spectacles only got grander with Robert Wilson's **the CIVIL warS: a tree is best measured when it is down**, Peter Brook's **The Mahabharata**, and Robert Ashley's huge opera trilogy renamed under the collective title *Now Eleanor's Idea*.

The 12-hour *CIVIL warS* was to have been Wilson's magnum opus with the possible exception of his 168-hour *KA MOUNTAIN AND GUARDenia TERRACE*, an unrepeatable event held on an Iranian mountaintop. Commissioned for the 1984 Los Angeles Olympics Arts Festival, *CIVIL warS* was meant to include sections—some operatic, some not, and involving several composers—produced in different countries. Although the L.A. project had to be scrapped for lack of funding, many sections, such as the one for Rome with a score by Glass, did receive their initial overseas premieres and this Roman next operatic step for Glass ended the 1986 Next Wave.

Composed at the same time as *Akhnaten*, the last of Glass's portrait operas, the "Rome Section" proved delirious mishmash. The main characters include Italian nationalist Giuseppe Garibaldi, Hercules (who gets a magnificent Handelian bass aria sung in Latin), Abraham Lincoln on stilts, Mrs. Lincoln not on stilts, Robert E. Lee in a spaceship, a Snow Owl, an Eagle, and the Sun. The exceptional challenge for Glass was writing his gracious score to fit Wilson's already completed staging, working like a film composer might, making this perhaps the most serviceable opera score ever written until Glass did himself one better at the 1994 Next Wave by composing a new opera to be performed live to Cocteau's film *La Belle et la Bête*, with the original soundtrack turned off and the singers lip-syncing to the movie.

The grandeur of Brook's nine-hour *The Mahabharata* began with its classic source, the Indian epic being the longest book ever written and encompassing much of what makes humanity tick. Among Brook's many remarkable aspects was his use of a multinational cast and the opulent multinational music devised by Japanese percussionist Toshi Tsuchitori, who employed dozens of Asian, African, and Middle Eastern instruments. Five musicians improvised in a controlled theatrical situation that lent the production far more than its special atmosphere. Under

*My Lai*, Jonathan Berger/ Kronos Quartet, 2017. Photo: Richard Termine

Tsuchitori's lead, the musicians gently controlled the pulse of the actors' performance, while simultaneously appearing to take their cues from the actors' breathing.

Larger than all of these was Ashley's opera trilogy, *Now Eleanor's Idea*. Trisha Brown's opening Next Wave program gave only the barest of hints of this with Ashley's organ solos from *Atalanta*, which became the middle opera. The project kept growing, and the last part, *Now Eleanor's Idea*, became its own tetralogy of four complete operas. The third opera in that tetralogy, also named *Now Eleanor's Idea*, was performed in the 1994 festival.

The idea of the protagonist, called Now Eleanor, is that the great religions of America—Judaism, Protestantism, Catholicism, and Business—have become one, and that's wrong. Throughout all the operas, normal people in the Midwest and Southwest express big and little thoughts in hypnotically arresting sing-song narrations, underscored by harmonically intricate electronic drones that lure a listener out of normality or understanding. Ashley was not a minimalist in the common sense of the term, but nearly all of the music in the trilogy is recited at the same moderate pulse, the composer's secret ingredient for his lulling his audience into a deceptively quotidian operatic realm that is, in fact, unlike anything before or since in opera.

## Kronos Quartet

An improbable supplement to the mid-1980s infusion of theatrical grandeur was a string quartet from San Francisco infused with its own implausibly grand visions. Kronos Quartet made its Next Wave debut in 1986 with three programs that covered everything from the little-appreciated Los Angeles and Bay Area roots of minimalism to the style's latest West Coast flowering, as well as equally novel string quartet rock and string quartet jazz and—who knew?—South African and Korean minimalism.

Throughout its many Next Wave residencies, Kronos, which has over some four decades given more than 1,000 world premieres, brought to the insular ensemble of four instruments, all in the same string family that had long been the emblem of "pure" music, such startling collaborators as poet Allen Ginsberg and liberal historian Howard Zinn. Bassist Ron Carter joined the quartet for arrangements of Thelonious Monk. In 1995, the group gave premieres of works for string quartet and orchestra by Chinese composer Zhou Long and Uzbek composer Dmitri

Yanov-Yanovsky with the Brooklyn Philharmonic and performed in the 1997 festival with dancers Eiko & Koma in **River**. Kronos celebrated, if that's the word, the quartet's 25th anniversary in the 1998 festival by examining the "Day of the Dead" through a profound prism of cultures, including Tan Dun's **Ghost Opera** that featured pipa player Wu Man; turned a screening of the film, *Dracula*, into live performance art with a new Philip Glass score written not to accompany but to interact with the Bela Lugosi classic in the 1999 festival; commemorated the 10th anniversary of 9/11 with 12 meditative pieces that showed a common thread between us and the Middle East in **Awakening** (2011); helped Laurie Anderson create her evening-long **Landfall** (2014); and collaborated with composer Jonathan Berger and instrumentalist Vân-Ánh Võ in the 2017 festival on **My Lai**, based on the civilian massacre that took place in the eponymous Vietnamese village during the Vietnam War.

OPPOSITE
Philip Glass and Kronos Quartet in *Dracula: The Music and Film*, Philip Glass/Kronos Quartet, 1999. Photo: Stephanie Berger

ABOVE
Laurie Anderson in *Landfall*, included in *Nonesuch Records at BAM*, Laurie Anderson/Kronos Quartet, 2014. Photo: Stephanie Berger

The only generalization that emerges as possible about the 100-plus works that Kronos has presented at BAM over more than three decades is that the quartet defies generalization. Even so, there was a certain West Coast method in the quartet's mission. This was nothing less than to kindle in the ensemble's contemporaries—and particularly Riley, Glass, and Reich—the same profound musical, philosophical, and personal self-reflection that writing for string quartet had for Haydn, Beethoven, Bartók, Shostakovich, and Carter. In order to do so, for a generation lost in the sensory overload of minimalist profusion, was the need for perspective, to go back to the forgotten beginning with La Monte Young's **Five Small Pieces for String Quartet, on Remembering a Naiad**, composed in 1956, to see how we got there.

The mere wisps of string sounds in these short pieces, which Kronos performed in the 1986 festival, are the experiments of a 21-year-old student in Los Angeles, 30 years earlier, studying the reductive music of Webern with pianist Leonard Stein, who had been, like Webern, a student of Schoenberg. Short for Young became long. While a composition graduate student at University of California, Berkeley in the late 1950s, he turned an obsession with gradual processes into excruciatingly slow-moving drones and befriended fellow student composer and jazz pianist Terry Riley. Riley would go on to add a pulse to Youngian stationary tonality, which is how *In C* came to launch minimalism.

Arguably, the greatest contribution of Kronos to string quartet literature has been enticing Riley into the string quartet world, beginning a relationship that has continued into the composer's eighties and resulting in his most substantial body of work. One of Kronos's three 1986 festival programs was devoted to Riley's epic **Salome Dances for Peace**, at two hours one of the most expansive string quartets in the literature, that was based on a fanciful narrative structure new to Riley and to string quartet writing. In the 2004 festival, Kronos performed Riley's even more expansive **Sun Rings**, a multimedia work influenced by the sounds of space and the expanse of the solar system.

Likewise, Kronos budged Glass and Reich out of their musical and demonstrative comfort zones and into each other's worlds. Despite his long ensemble pieces, Glass had proven most adept at creating mood and atmospheric setting for theatrical purposes. Reich, on the other hand, was a contrapuntal master of absolute music, kaleidoscopically elaborating on rhythmic, melodic, or harmonic cells through shifts in phase and timbre. Yet in writing six major string quartets for

Film stills from *Three Tales*, Steve Reich/Beryl Korot, 2002. Courtesy of BAM Hamm Archives

Kronos over a quarter century, Glass—with a couple of diversions, such as the *Dracula* quartet—concentrated on musical abstraction, while Reich, in his first work for Kronos, became downright autobiographical with **Different Trains**, composed in 1988 and performed the following year as part of the Next Wave gala benefit celebrating New Music America.

Incorporating recordings of voices from Reich's childhood, *Different Trains* hauntingly contrasts the composer's early travels across America with the unimaginably gruesome train rides Jewish children were then taking in Germany. In doing so, Reich created a new kind of dramatic music, the rhythms of the voice generating the musical material as well as a dramatic approach, not to mention an openness for political, philosophical, and spiritual expression. *Different Trains* gave Reich a deeply expressive vocabulary that allowed him to make such major large-scale festival pieces, staged and with video, as **The Cave** (1993) and **Three Tales** (2002), both in collaboration with his wife, Beryl Korot.

Glass's string quartets proved oddly personal in the opposite way. He had become a composer so used to constant collaboration, including, besides music-theater, and dance and opera, films (both artsy like *Koyaanisqatsi* or more commercial like the *Candyman* horror movies) and writing music meant for touring to keep his ensemble members in employment. So just as it

had for Beethoven and Bartók, the string quartet became for Glass a personal medium suited to individual self-expression and experimentation with new musical ideas.

## Glass, Reich, and Beyond

Meanwhile, the Glassian big projects kept coming in profusion at the Next Wave. After the portrait operas, the composer turned to a triptych of operas based on Cocteau films: **Orpheé** (1993), a chamber opera that uses the movie script; the more radical **La Belle et la Bête**; and **Les Enfants Terribles** (1996), handled as a dance opera. Glass welcomed the new millennium at the 2000 Next Wave Festival with his immense, evening-long **Fifth Symphony** for chorus, orchestra, and vocal soloists, the texts representing the world's major religions. Later works included **Galileo Galilei** (2002) and **Kepler** (2009), in which he further examined his concerns with and operatic investigations into the intersection of science, religion, and art.

The Next Wave also became the prime place in the United States to hear Glass's symphonies—which have been startlingly absent from the repertoire of most major U.S. orchestras, including until 2017 the New York Philharmonic. Just as with the operas, Glass continually expanded

the scope and intent of his symphonies, beginning with the **"Low" Symphony**, a symphonic metamorphosis on David Bowie's eponymous album. The Brooklyn Philharmonic under Dennis Russell Davies gave the New York premiere at the 1992 Next Wave Festival as part of a three-part program, **Glass Reflections**. Two years later, his **Symphony No. 2** proved more rigorously conventional. In the 2000 festival, Davies offered the *Fifth Symphony*, followed in 2005 by the **Symphony No. 6**, a setting of Allen Ginsberg's "Plutonian Ode" for soprano that moves from outcry against nuclear contamination to epiphany, and the Brucknerian **Symphony No. 8**.

Although Glass and Reich had been friends and composition students at Juilliard together and formed a joint ensemble that greatly helped popularize the nascent minimalism of the 1960s, they soon had a competitive falling out and stood noticeably apart throughout their waves of Next Wave projects and appearances. For many musicians (though far less so for fans), it was, thus, a half-century of either Glass or Reich—Davies was primarily a Glass man; Tilson Thomas, a Reichian. Both composers, however, shared the Nonesuch record label, and at a 2014 Next Wave tribute to Nonesuch, minimalism finally came full circle when Glass and Reich publicly joined forces once more for a conciliatory program.

OPPOSITE
*Kepler*, Philip Glass/ Dennis Russell Davies/ Bruckner Orchester Linz/ Choir of the Upper Austrian State Theatre, 2009. Photo: Jack Vartoogian

ABOVE
John Duykers in *Galileo Galilei*, Philip Glass/Mary Zimmerman/Goodman Theatre/ Eos Orchestra, 2002. Photo: Richard Termine

The real conciliation had, however, come much earlier with the next generations of composers for whom the BAM concert was more like the reuniting of parents after a long bitter divorce. The younger composers, beginning with John Adams, had never had a problem finding things they could use from both Glass and Reich. Indeed, Adams demonstrated that minimalism was but a starting point for creating a vastly expressive musical language capable of voicing Mozartean psychological nuance. In his first opera, **Nixon in China**—a collaboration with poet Alice Goodman, directed by Peter Sellars, with choreography by Mark Morris, staged at the 1987 festival—Adams began a process of treating opera as a means for offering mythic perspective to current events by giving a singular sympathetic voice to inner lives. In this case, Nixon and Mao were shown not as the world leaders that history had come to revile but as vulnerable old men trying to figure out what it had all meant.

Adams's next opera, *The Death of Klinghoffer*, was given its controversial American premiere at BAM in advance of the Next Wave Festival, angering a large part of the audience and press for presuming that terrorists and innocent victims alike had inner lives that led them to act the way they did in the Palestinian hijacking of the *Achille Lauro* cruise ship. It took a full 13 years, but when the Brooklyn Philharmonic presented a semi-staged concert version of the opera for the 2003 Next Wave Festival, *Klinghoffer* could be seen as providing profound post-9/11 insight into the terrorist mindset, troubling though that might be—as was evident in the angry protests and death threats that accompanied the Met's ill-fated first production of the opera 11 years later.

Equally compatible with minimalism had also been pop music, world music, and jazz, the three worlds that Glass, Reich, and Riley looked to when they wanted to create a new music more relevant to American culture than the European avant-garde. What minimalism then gave back, particularly to pop, was the example of usefulness. Rock opera had its roots in the concept album rather than the stage, and proved clumsy theater when tired elements from Broadway or flashy rock psychedelia got in the way. But the new music-theater, especially that pioneered by Glass and Wilson, offered different openings in which the music and the stage could remain independent yet equal. This, in fact, provided exactly the opportunity vital for the more artistically minded pop musicians to grow.

Wilson, here, proved a key figure. He brought in David Byrne, from the Talking Heads, to compose for **The Forest** (1988). He got Tom Waits to write strikingly dark cabaret-style songs for

**The Black Rider: The Casting of the Magic Bullets** (1993), based on the story of Weber's opera *Der Freischütz*, as well as the Lewis Carroll-inspired **Alice** (1995) and **Woyzeck** (2002), adapted from the play by George Büchner, both with Kathleen Brennan. He enticed Lou Reed in **Time Rocker** (1997) to make disconcertingly edgy music for a Wilsonian interpretation of H.G. Wells's novel *The Time Machine* and for **POEtry** (2001) based on the life and work of Edgar Allan Poe. In addition, Wilson enlisted Rufus Wainwright to write the music for **Shakespeare's Sonnets** (2014).

In a rare foray onto the stage, David Lynch mounted a misty, semi-improvisational, alluringly moody theater piece, **Industrial Symphony No. 1** (1989), when BAM helped host New Music America, with music by *Twin Peaks* composer Angelo Badalamenti and starring the smoky chanteuse, Julee Cruise. Velvet Underground members Reed and John Cale memorialized Andy Warhol in a rock song cycle **Songs for 'Drella—a fiction** (1989), which was also a reminder that Cale had the genuine minimalist credentials of having worked with La Monte Young. Cale

Kaya Brüel in *Woyzeck*, Robert Wilson/Tom Waits/ Kathleen Brennan, 2002. Photo: Jack Vartoogian

returned to BAM in the 2017 festival to celebrate his 75th birthday and the 50-year anniversary of the release of the classic debut album *Velvet Underground & Nico*. In the 2016 Next Wave, Stephin Merritt performed his five-hour, two-part **The Magnetic Fields: 50 Song Memoir**, a song for each year of his life that has the scope of a theatrical Robert Wilson or Peter Brook pageant. In a series of works—**One Loss Plus** (2007), **Darwin's Meditation for the People of Lincoln** (2008), and **Symphony for the Dance Floor** (2011)—composer/violinist Daniel Bernard Roumain defied "genrefication" in his mixture of hip-hop and classical.

The atmosphere of acceptance reached its apex with the Bang on a Can collective of composers Michael Gordon, David Lang, and Julia Wolfe, who had studied together at Yale in the 1980s. Each developed into a composer of note—Lang and Wolfe have both won Pulitzer Prizes—with a number of major staged works mounted for the Next Wave. In the 2016 festival, Gordon's **Amplified** offered an hour of polyphonic amplified guitars reaching for weird harmonics, whereas a new Lang opera was all about what can go wrong when we don't amplify our desires. Based on Thomas Bernhard's novel about a peer of Glenn Gould, Lang's **the loser** featured a hushed monologue from baritone Rod Gilfry, hovering above the audience seated only in the mezzanine, as he musically and physically floats into nothingness in an effort to retrieve his

ABOVE
Stefan Kurt and Annette Paulmann in *Time Rocker*, Robert Wilson/Lou Reed/Darryl Pinckney/Thalia Theater, 1997. Photo courtesy of BAM Hamm Archives

OPPOSITE
Aaron Dessner in *The Long Count*, Bryce Dessner/Aaron Dessner/Matthew Ritchie, 2009. Photo: Julieta Cervantes

identity from an artistically overpowering mentor. The previous year, Anne Bogart's SITI Company staged Wolfe's **Steel Hammer** that explored the startling racial, cultural, and musical implications of the folk ballad "John Henry."

The BOAC composers also put on joint theater pieces. But beyond their own work, they have been their generation's leading advocates for everybody else's music with their annual Bang on a Can Marathons, incorporated into the festival in 2000 and 2001—taking a cue from the post-genre Next Wave progenitors of the previous dozen years—and created an evening-length work titled **Road Trip** for the 2017 festival in celebration of BOAC's 30th anniversary. From 1988 through the end of the century, Brooklyn Philharmonic programs under music directors Dennis Russell Davies and Robert Spano surveyed European mystics (1993), Duke Ellington's New York (1993), American Transcendentalists (1994), post-Mahler symphonic music (1997), and put together the dissimilar (and not altogether friendly) likes of John Adams and Elliott Carter. Next Wave venues developed for popular music included New Music America (1989); Jazz: The Next Wave (1995–99), hosted and curated by musician and composer Don Byron; the Next Wave of Song (2001–02, 2010); and the "Red Hot" concerts—**Red Hot + RIOT LIVE!** (2006), **Rio 2** (2008), **New Orleans** (2010), **Cuba** (2012), and **Arthur Russell** (2015).

More multiplicity, however, has meant maybe fewer new ideas in an "anything goes" new millennium. Absorption takes time, and a present-day generation of post-genre artists defies categorization. It barely seems relevant anymore to cite Bryce and Aaron Dessner as coming out of pop, Vijay Iyer out of jazz, or Gabriel Kahane as a folk singer, since they are just as likely to be writing for orchestra, music-theater, or for classical soloists.

Meanwhile audiences have begun to rely more and more on tastemakers such as Robert Hurwitz, the head of Nonesuch Records who curated a 2014 series for Next Wave based on the label's artists and who operates on the hunch that if he likes something someone else will, too. In addition to bringing Glass and Reich back together, Hurwitz put the African musics of Youssou N'Dour and Rokia Traoré, American folk star Rhiannon Giddens, the jazz duo of mandolinist Chris Thile and Brad Mehldau, and a classical art song recital by Dawn Upshaw and Gilbert Kalish on the same musical footing.

Rhiannon Giddens (featured) with Carolina Chocolate Drops, included in *Nonesuch Records at BAM*, 2014. Photo: Jack Vartoogian

But it has been just as easy to get lost in the tangle of this profusion. As wave after wave crashes onto BAM, only time will tell whether a new wave really is a next wave, whether we've reached a new pinnacle or not. The indication is that we have.

## A New Beginning

Almost 35 years to the day that Trisha Brown danced in silence preparing for the first sound waves of the Next Wave—and after all these many years of works beyond category, grand in ambition and resources, none more so or more importantly than Peter Brook's *The Mahabharata*—Brook brought **Battlefield** to BAM. The 91-year-old director had reduced his nine-hour epic to a few pages of script, an hour-long play for four actors and one musician. This is the end of the *Mahabharata* story, the time after hundreds of thousands of warriors have been killed for no other reason than that everything in nature is cyclical, every wave has a next.

Though epilogue to Brook's earlier work, *Battlefield* is just as much provision for a new beginning. The lone musician is the *Mahabharata*'s Toshi Tsuchitori, who had been responsible for the eclectic *Mahabharata* score. He is now an elder in need of only a single drum. Improvising on it, he is once more the heartbeat of the production. Every kind of music seems streamlined into his beating. His drumming exposes the art of storytelling as the art of listening.

*Battlefield* closes with the four actors seated around Tsuchitori as he drums a long, enthralling solo. Their raptness is meant to instruct and infect the audience with the practice of intent listening to the exclusion of all else. By the end, only silence remains, a silence broken seconds, maybe minutes, later with the sound of applause, which sounds strangely like that of the next wave crashing on a beach.

Bebel Gilberto in *Red Hot + Rio 2: The Next Generation of Samba Soul*, 2008. Photo: Jack Vartoogian

Gabriel Kahane (featured)
in *The Ambassador*,
Gabriel Kahane/John
Tiffany, 2014.
Photo: Max Gordon

Darcy James Argue (featured) in *Real Enemies*, Darcy James Argue/Isaac Butler/Peter Nigrini/Secret Society/ Beth Morrison Projects, 2015. Photo: Ed Lefkowicz

OPPOSITE
*Documerica*, Steve Cosson/ ETHEL, 2013. Photo: Jack Vartoogian

ABOVE
Annette Paulmann (featured) in *Alice*, Robert Wilson/Tom Waits/ Kathleen Brennan/Thalia Theater, 1995. Photo: Dan Rest

ABOVE
Caroline Polachek and John Cale (featured) in *John Cale: 50th Anniversary of The Velvet Underground & Nico*, 2017. Photo: Mike Benigno

OPPOSITE
Meshell Ndegeocello in *Red Hot + RIOT LIVE!: The Music and Spirit of Fela Kuti*, 2006. Photo: Jack Vartoogian

Sarah Joy Miller (featured) in *Anna Nicole*, Mark-Anthony Turnage/Richard Thomas/Richard Jones/New York City Opera, 2013. Photo: Stephanie Berger

CBNC

The history of BAM aligns itself with allowing for experimentation from artists working with other disciplines, and we see the interaction between visual art and the creators of other art forms as a significant element in being part of BAM and the Next Wave. The key to understanding BAM is that it has an organic flow to it, and the flow of the Next Wave has different components—performance, cinematic, educational, and visual—and as visual artists, we want and need to work with artists from other disciplines, and BAM makes that happen for us. The new generation of visual artists will have the added benefit of the technology that allows for more diverse experimentation to happen. You've planted the seeds in curating the Next Wave Festival, and now it's going to grow deeper into the visual arts.

**José Parlá**

Artist

Jonah Bokaer (featured) in *ECLIPSE*, Jonah Bokaer/ Anthony McCall, 2012. Photo: Stephanie Berger

# Visual Arts

Dan Cameron

In any discussion about the vanguard role that the BAM Next Wave Festival has played in the flowering of a multidisciplinary contemporary performance culture over the three and a half decades since its inception, it is easy to lose sight of the catalytic role it has also played in the visual arts during the same time period. When the Next Wave Festival launched its first season in the fall of 1983, the New York visual art community was experiencing the final throes of a generational transformation that had been brewing since the late 1950s and early 1960s. Following the trail blazed by Allan Kaprow's artistic concept of "happenings," John Cage's genre-shattering classes at the New School, Judson Dance Theater's radical fusion of the arts, and the unwavering spirit of the experimental arts movement Fluxus, the emergence in the 1960s and 1970s of performance art as a post-object medium now seems all but inevitable.

Visual artists like Carolee Schneemann, Charlotte Moorman, Vito Acconci, and other multidisciplinary practitioners led the way, supplemented by the advent of video that enabled the documentation of otherwise fleeting events; in effect, pushing visual art into the technological age. Despite these advances, performance art attained its legitimacy slowly and often at the considerable professional expense of many of its originators. An important platform for the new art form was the groundbreaking magazine *Artforum*, launched in 1962, which regularly published scholarly essays on experimental dance, theater, film, and music, alongside texts of equal ambition on photography, sculpture, and painting.

By the early 1980s, pioneering BAM figures like Merce Cunningham, Philip Glass, and Trisha Brown had long enjoyed close working relationships with the visual artists of their age, and a new generation of artists born in the 1940s, such as Laurie Anderson, Patti Smith, and Robert Wilson, were the first to enjoy active exhibition careers that unfolded in galleries and museums, while their performance careers evolved onstage. With the epic production of **Einstein on the Beach**, in collaboration with composer Philip Glass—which premiered at BAM in 1984, given a revival in 1992, and remounted with technical advancements in a 2012 rendition—Wilson introduced an essentially new genre of performance that was a mirror-image to opera. It seamlessly fused music, dance, lighting, stagecraft, technology, and choreography, while simultaneously rejecting the traditional constraints of each discipline to become a marathon spectacle of the avant-garde in all its precise, minimalist, non-narrative splendor.

Jennifer Goggans in *RainForest*, included in *The Legacy Tour*, Merce Cunningham Dance Company, 2011. Photo: Stephanie Berger

As befitting a high-profile New York cultural institution, the location of BAM could not have been better. Years prior to the debut of the Next Wave Festival, BAM had already cemented its role as a cultural institution willing to take artistic risks in the name of championing new ideas. Beginning in 1957, when choreographer Merce Cunningham invited artist Robert Rauschenberg to create décor and costumes for an evening-length dance program, this interdisciplinary spirit became a guiding principle of collaboration, further enhanced by the arrival in 1967 of Harvey Lichtenstein as executive producer. It was Lichtenstein who invited Andy Warhol to present his *Silver Clouds* installation of floating mylar pillows as part of Cunningham's production in 1968 of *RainForest*, reprised in the 2011 Next Wave in the Cunningham company's **Legacy Tour**, whose three varied programs also included visual contributions by Roy Lichtenstein and Jasper Johns. Likewise, in 1970, Martha Graham's *El Penitente* featured sets by sculptor Isamu Noguchi, and in 1979, choreographer Lucinda Childs was paired with Philip Glass and conceptual artist Sol LeWitt to collaborate on her performance work titled *Dance*. By the 1980s, Lichtenstein's BAM became a place where the visual art community could consistently find new performance works within a complex idiom that was increasingly familiar to them, and where their contemporaries regularly assumed collaborative roles with the composers and choreographers they were going to see and hear. Increasingly, the works they were experiencing also brought together artists from a variety of media to create a single, unique multidisciplinary artwork commissioned by BAM. This was the case of the Next Wave Festival's inaugural work, **THE PHOTOGRAPHER/Far From the Truth** (1983), originally conceived by the Dutch artist Rob Malasch, which fused the talents of Glass, director JoAnne Akalaitis, choreographer David Gordon, and designers Wendall K. Harrington, Santo Loquasto, and Jennifer Tipton.

Much of this sense of familiarity between BAM and the art world was, in fact, the result of a carefully orchestrated campaign. In 1981, Lichtenstein brought in art consultants Anne Livet and Steve Reichard to help develop the marketing and calendar template for what would become the Next Wave Festival. The Livet-Reichard plan not only emphasized bundling contemporary mainstage performances in a fall subscription package, but included a specific marketing outreach to the art world—partly to broaden BAM's audience, but also to tap into the increasing prominence of the downtown New York art scene. Nothing symbolized this connection more aptly than the iconic deconstructed brushstroke by artist Roy Lichtenstein that formed the basis for the festival's first poster and program. Not only was Lichtenstein a towering figure in American

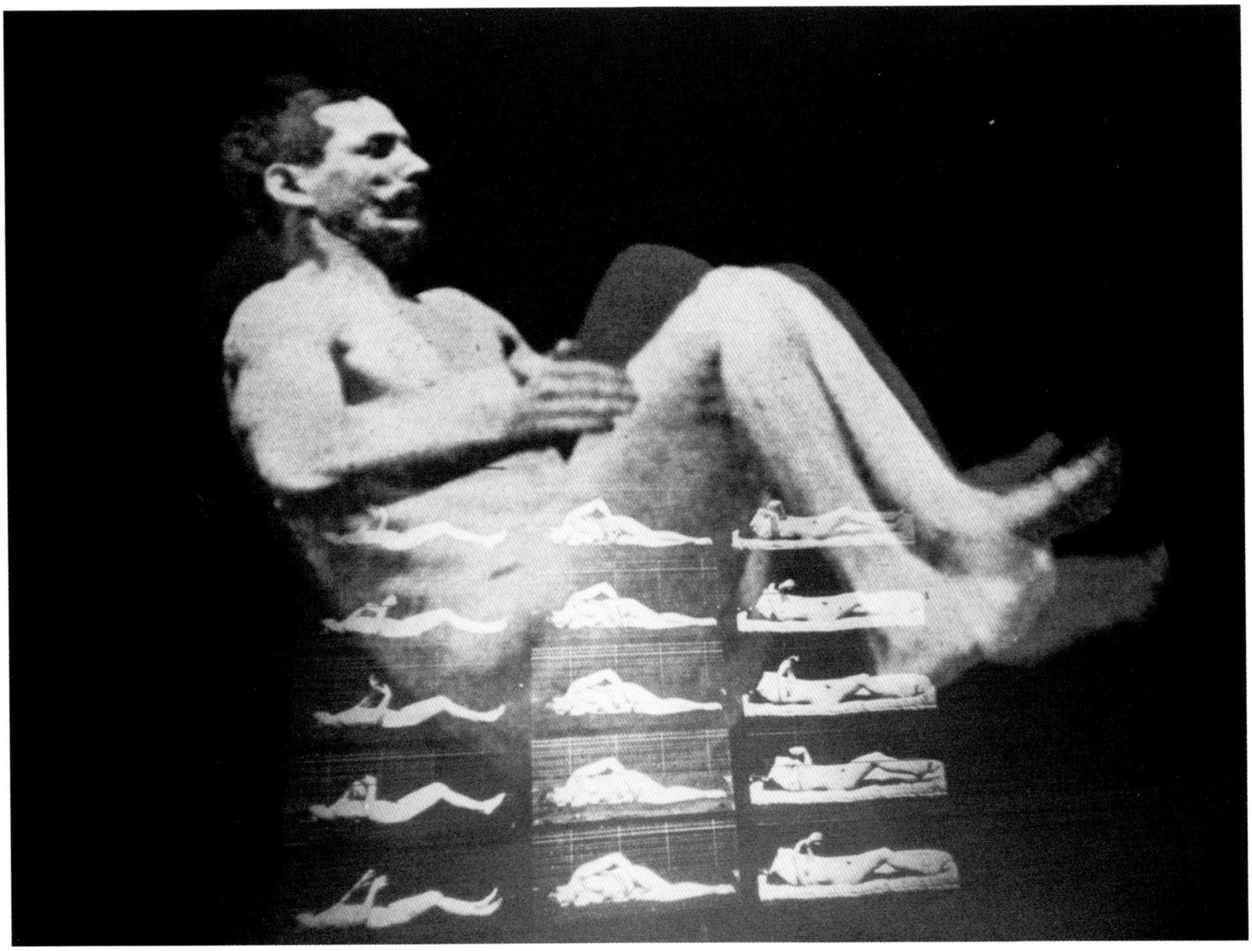

art of the late 20th century and a highly visible New Yorker, but his work possessed the desirable quality of being instantly recognizable, which in turn boosted public awareness of the Next Wave through its association with the New York art world's rising public profile.

It should not be surprising that for its first few seasons, the most evident part of BAM's relationship with the art world existed in the form of copious amounts of visual production generated through posters, programs, and other printed material. Still, from the vantage point of its 35 years of existence, a detail that stands out about the early Next Wave program structure is the clear evidence of visual art at virtually every possible point of engagement. At the marketing and publicity level, for instance, the inspired idea of conceiving the Next Wave Festival's program as the *Next Wave Journal*, sponsored to a large degree by galleries and fashion houses, and

*THE PHOTOGRAPHER/Far From the Truth*, Philip Glass/Robert Coe/David Gordon/JoAnne Akalaitis, 1983. Photo courtesy of BAM Hamm Archives

NEXT WAVE FESTIVAL
4 October-4 December 1983
BROOKLYN ACADEMY OF MUSIC

providing as much coverage to the visual as the performing arts, soon expanded into a series of posters and limited editions that engaged an impressive string of artists during the first decade of the Next Wave, including Francesco Clemente (1984), Frank Stella (1985), Susan Rothenberg (1986), and Willem de Kooning (1987). Aside from providing a consistent revenue stream for the organization, these collaborative engagements with galleries and artists built on and clarified the welcoming environment that many in the art world felt characterized their BAM experience as audience members. The visible intensity of that interchange has continued in the form of the cover art for the BAMbill house program, which engages a different artist each season—among them, Jonathan Lasker, Jim Dine, George Segal, Shinique Smith, and Ellen Carey—and brings with it the prestige and exposure that goes with the BAM imprimatur.

OPPOSITE
Next Wave Festival poster by Roy Lichtenstein, 1983. Courtesy of BAM Hamm Archives

ABOVE, LEFT
Next Wave Festival poster by Francesco Clemente, 1984. Courtesy of BAM Hamm Archives

ABOVE, RIGHT
Next Wave Festival poster by Susan Rothenberg, 1986. Courtesy of BAM Hamm Archives

Today, sifting through the physical evidence from those halcyon years, there are ample opportunities to enjoy some of the fruits of those early and close ties between visual artists and New York's premier institution for new work in the performing arts. Frank Stella's cover is an outstanding example of where painting and graphic design can meet, just as the subtle **Set and Reset** collage that Rauschenberg created for Trisha Brown's Next Wave performance in 1983 is a gem that any art museum would be proud to own, and the vibrant Keith Haring drawing for the poster for Bill T. Jones/Arnie Zane & Company's 1984 performance **Secret Pastures** is a moving gesture of love and admiration from one friend to another. It wouldn't be an exaggeration to propose that a survey exhibition of posters from that era—highlights would be Karel Appel's poster for choreographer Min Tanaka's 1989 production of **Can We Dance a Landscape? (Peut-on**

ABOVE
Next Wave Festival poster by Keith Haring for *Secret Pastures*, Bill T. Jones/Arnie Zane & Company, 1984. Courtesy of BAM Hamm Archives

OPPOSITE, LEFT
Next Wave Festival poster by David Hammons and Papo Colo, 1991. Courtesy of BAM Hamm Archives

OPPOSITE, RIGHT
Next Wave Festival poster for *Can We Dance a Landscape? (Peut-on Danser le Paysage?)*, Karel Appel/Min Tanaka, 1989. Courtesy of BAM Hamm Archives

**Danser le Paysage?)** as well as the Next Wave posters done by Carroll Dunham (1990), David Hammons and Papo Colo (1991), Philip Taaffe (1992), and Robert Moskowitz (1994)—might offer a fairly coherent overview of American art in the 1990s.

Behind the scenes, the embrace of BAM by the New York art community was, if possible, intensifying, particularly in the area of development. In 1987, a three-year grant to BAM from the Luce Foundation to create the BAM Art Fund resulted in the launch of the BAM Collaborative Arts Council, whose membership was filled by such prominent gallerists as Leo Castelli, Barbara Gladstone, Arne Glimcher, and Marian Goodman. The Collaborative Arts Council, in collaboration with a larger art world support group formed as the BAM Producers Council, in turn published three print portfolios—each of which sold out—in 1987, 1988, and 1990, with the participation of such artists as Jennifer Bartlett, Eric Fischl, Alex Katz, David Salle, and Keith Sonnier. What is known broadly today as BAM Visual Art (an expansion of BAMart, used for a period) exists

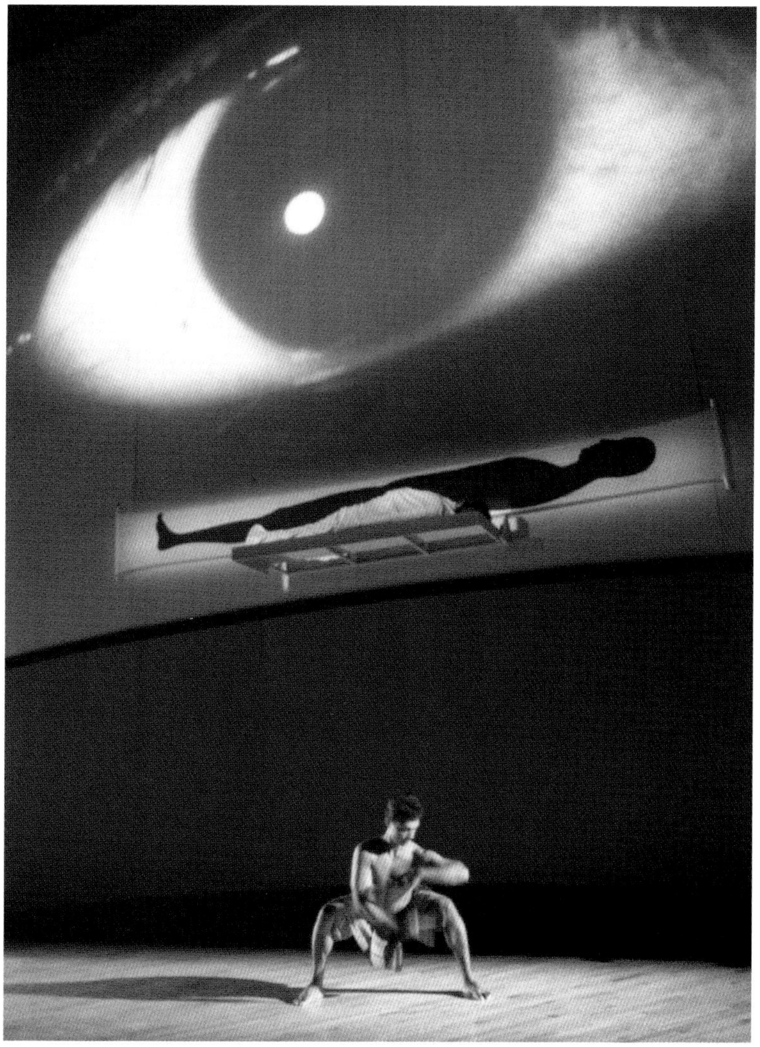

as a direct result of policies devised by Harvey Lichtenstein, whose retirement in 1999 became an occasion marked by the participation of such blue-chip artists as Cecily Brown, Ellsworth Kelly, and Jeff Koons to an exhibition and sale in his honor.

Whether by design or not, an arguably more compelling outcome of BAM's growing interchange with the visual art community in the late 1980s and early 1990s was the gradual transformation of their original role of venue and ideal audience into something more closely resembling a two-way street. Artists, collectors, gallerists, curators, and critics are among BAM's most devoted followers, and that devotion has in turn led the way to BAM's pioneering role in merging the two areas of creative expression into one unique hybrid/composite form: the live work of art. A landmark moment in this trajectory was the award of a grant from the Pew Charitable Trusts organization enabling BAM to debut in 1995 a three-year series titled Artists in Action, which represented the first-ever systematic effort by a cultural institution to provide a platform for live works of art in the form of a program of commissioned performances from visual artists, staged variously at BAM and venues like the Dia Center for the Arts, The Kitchen, and the Queens Museum of Art.

Featuring new works by, among others, Vito Acconci, Kristin Jones, Andrew Ginzel, Chandralekha, Ilya Kabakov, Rona Pondick, Nayland Blake, and Kerry James Marshall, Artists in Action's approach was unapologetically experimental, which in the short term may have driven

ABOVE
*Interim: after the end and before the beginning,* included in Artists in Action, Kristin Jones/Andrew Ginzel/Chandralekha, 1995. Photo: Dan Rest

OPPOSITE
*Victory Over the Sun,* Robert Benedetti/Kazimir Malevich, 1983. Photo: Alma Law

a few patrons to the exits during intermission, but in the long view only furthered the deepening mutual affection and admiration between the art world and BAM. To take one example, Kabakov's **The Flies** (1995), self-described as a "musical phantasmagoria," with choreography by David Dorfman, featured libretto, costumes, and stage design by the artist—a renowned Soviet conceptualist—and a musical score by Vladimir Tarasov that featured violin and a recording of flies buzzing incessantly, a motif that Kabakov had explored throughout his oeuvre. *The Flies* happened at a time when a string of well-received exhibitions by Kabakov, both locally and abroad, drew wide public attention, and reinforced the idea that BAM was paying close attention to the ebb and flow of the mid-1990s art world collective pursuit of global conceptualism.

More fundamentally, the sea change marked by the Artists in Action initiative was that the rightful place of visual artists within the performing arts is in full view onstage, as creative partners with their performing arts colleagues, and in some cases taking on roles as prime movers for the works themselves. In a sense, this shift had been foreshadowed in Next Wave's first season in the form of a new production of the Futurist opera **Victory Over the Sun**, whose pre-

miere in St. Petersburg's Luna Park in 1913 had famously been greeted with aggressively hostile reactions from the public and critics. With its scenography and costumes by the radical abstract painter Kazimir Malevich, which led the critic from the *New York Times* to write that its "primary impulse is visual, not dramatic or musical," *Victory* had long been considered a landmark in the modernist quest for an avant-garde *ménage à trois* between painters, lyricists, and composers.

The matching of artistic collaborators from a range of different disciplines, which rapidly became one of the most recognizable features of the Next Wave Festival's original commissions, also proved the source of one of its earliest, and most infamous, missteps: the evening-long work, **The Birth of the Poet**, a much-touted highlight of the 1985 Next Wave season, which featured the estimable talents of writer Kathy Acker as playwright, Richard Foreman as director, Peter Gordon as composer, and painter David Salle as set and costume designer. Instead of coalescing as a single composition, however, the apparently disjointed overlays of sound, movement, and text came off as completely discordant to the audience, who greeted the opening night curtain calls with loud boos and catcalls. Considering that BAM's public had by that time accustomed itself to the challenges of vanguard performance, and that Salle's growing fame had enabled his dealer Mary Boone to support the production with a contribution of $300,000, the audience's hostility is, in retrospect, somewhat surprising. More than anyone else, they must have been aware that a work's harsh reception at its premiere has often historically led to its fervent embrace by a later generation, which leaves open the possibility for a revival of *The Birth of the Poet* in the not so distant future. Salle returned to BAM for the 1987 festival as the set designer for **The Tarnished Angels** and **The Elizabethan Phrasing of the Late Albert Ayler**, performed by the Armitage Ballet.

LEFT
Stuart Hodes in *The Birth of the Poet*, Richard Foreman/Kathy Acker/Peter Gordon/David Salle, 1985. Photo: Beatriz Schiller

OPPOSITE
*Last Supper at Uncle Tom's Cabin/The Promised Land*, Bill T. Jones/Arnie Zane & Company, 1990. Photo courtesy of BAM Hamm Archives

Although primary or partial authorship by visual artists of BAM's productions was not a regular feature of Next Wave prior to Artists in Action, it did occur with enough regularity that a pattern emerged over the years. In 1989, the acclaimed Dutch painter Karel Appel collaborated with choreographer Min Tanaka to produce the evening-long piece *Can We Dance a Landscape?* in which the visual weight of Appel's participation was comparable to that of Malevich's in *Victory Over the Sun*: scenography and costumes. A similar role was played a year later by the painter Huck Snyder in his collaboration with Bill T. Jones/Arnie Zane & Company in the production, **Last Supper at Uncle Tom's Cabin/The Promised Land.** Employing choppy, primitive gestures with conspicuously perishable materials, Snyder's masks and scenography functioned effectively as another character within the multilayered narrative.

ABOVE
Laurie Anderson in her *Empty Places*, 1989. Photo: Linda Alaniz/ Martha Swope Associates

OPPOSITE
*Griot New York*, Garth Fagan/Wynton Marsalis/ Martin Puryear, 1991. Photo courtesy of BAM Hamm Archives

Slightly less visibility was afforded to visual artist Perry Hoberman, who created projections for Laurie Anderson's **Empty Places** (1989), despite the fact that Hoberman's images, towering over and behind Anderson, have become central to the work's place in its audience's collective memory. Perhaps the most successful of these early collaborations came about as a result of choreographer Garth Fagan's invitation to the sculptor Martin Puryear to create a visual mass that would be the first thing audiences see when the curtain rises for his work **Griot New York** (1991), which also featured an exemplary score by the composer Wynton Marsalis. In each of these cases, the role of the visual artist was to create a literal framework in which the performance unfolded, a task that frequently depended on the newest technologies then in circulation, especially projectors used for video and other digital feeds.

Not only was Artists in Action an ambitious expansion of the definition of performance as it had been previously observed by BAM, but it also opened the possibility of bringing other

cultural institutions into a closer collaborative relationship. In one memorable production, the Dia Center for the Arts in Chelsea was the location for **Theater Project for a Rock Band** (1995), Acconci's collaboration with the band The Mekons, which employed raised platforms to separate band members from each other, while placing the audience on a viewing plane beneath them, so that the spectators gazed upwards at the musicians. Pondick's **MINE** (1996), a collaboration with choreographer Sara Rudner and fellow artist Robert Feintuch, took place in conjunction with an installation by Pondick at the Brooklyn Museum, and wove an elaborated deconstruction of the title word with the visual language of bodily movement relative to the sculpture. At one moment in the performance, a cascade of large ear shapes on the museum's floor becomes an integral part of the space filled by the dancers, who convey on their backs the large image of a human mouth with a full set of grinning teeth. Among the Artists in Action artists whose work was presented at BAM, Nayland Blake's **Hare Follies** (1997) used the physical intimacy of the BAM Harvey Theater to present a short work in which one of the climactic scenes involves a mechanical toy rabbit wheeling its own coffin across the stage.

ABOVE, LEFT
*MINE*, included in Artists in Action, Rona Pondick/Robert Feintuch/Sara Rudner, 1996. Photo: Sidney Janis Gallery

ABOVE, RIGHT
*Hare Follies*, included in Artists in Action, Nayland Blake, 1997. Photo: Nayland Blake

OPPOSITE
Ralph Lemon in his *Geography*, Ralph Lemon/Nari Ward, 1997. Photo: T. Charles Erickson

By the late 1990s, a different philosophy of programming with visual artists began to take shape, as demonstrated by French artist Christian Boltanski's central role in designing and staging the version of Schubert's **Die Winterreise** presented in the 1998 Next Wave Festival, with baritone James Maddalena accompanied by Robert Spano on piano. Boltanski's production featured two elements long associated with his art: bare lightbulbs and accumulated winter coats. Rather than remain in place as static elements, however, bulbs and coats were slowly raised and lowered on separate tracks during the performance, and at the peak of the music, one of the winter coats slides off the pile and falls to the stage with a thud. The experience of a visual artist exerting a significant measure of artistic control over the production of a venerated composition performed by two renowned musicians was still a relatively new phenomenon for BAM audiences, but coming in the wake of increasingly lavish productions through the 1990s by Robert Wilson and Robert Lepage, among others, Boltanski's introduction of stark visual elements—which seemed to operate independently of the activity onstage—suggested that more surprises were in store.

Just as one generation of artists conversant in both the performing and visual arts emerged in the 1980s to straddle the two creative worlds, another generation of artists took the lead in the early 2000s with an approach to live art that took its textual cues from sociocultural reality and its

visual vocabulary from painting and sculpture, while quietly shifting the status quo in dance, theater, or music. Emblematic of this approach is the self-described "conceptualist" Ralph Lemon, whose **Geography Trilogy**, developed over a 10-year span, remains one of the artistic high points of the Next Wave. A crucial aspect of Lemon's working method emerged from his decision, in 1995, to dissolve his dance company and embark instead on a multi-year collaboration with a number of international artists across different disciplines. One memorable result of this working process was artist Nari Ward's remarkable setting of old mattresses and empty liquor bottles, created for **Geography** (1997), the first part of the trilogy, which functioned less as traditional scenography and more like an additional, unique presence within the performance. In Lemon's case, a project can have multiple iterations: as a dance, a book, an exhibition, a film, or some combination thereof, its form ultimately determined by the results of his extended interactions with these hand-picked collaborators.

A related approach can be seen in Meredith Monk's collaborations with the installation artist Ann Hamilton, whose own artistic practice has long been rooted in performance. Beginning with the 2002 Next Wave production of **mercy** and later in **Songs of Ascension** (2009),

ABOVE
Meredith Monk and Ann Hamilton in their *mercy*, 2002. Photo: Jack Vartoogian

OPPOSITE
*Three Tales*, Steve Reich/ Beryl Korot/Bradley Lubman, 2002. Photo courtesy of BAM Hamm Archives

absolutely no s ow of emotion, he turned away

Hamilton's meditative actions are an essential part of Monk's own larger composition of sound and movement, while the videos (also by Hamilton) sustained her presence even when she was not onstage. This long-term collaboration between artists working in distinct media but with kindred sensibilities has a direct precedent in the pair of collaborative works created by composer Steve Reich, working together with video artist Beryl Korot. Their artistic relationship had its world premiere in 1993 when BAM presented **The Cave**, and its most ambitious outcome was the evening-long **Three Tales** (2002), which billed itself as a "digital documentary video opera."

Sometimes the artistic collaborations that Next Wave's performing artists choose don't come specifically from the world of galleries and museums, but nonetheless push the discussion of stagecraft onto potentially risky terrain. Choreographer John Jasperse's 2004 production at the BAM Harvey, enigmatically titled **CALIFORNIA**, featured a multi-tiered canopy created by Chicago architect Ammar Eloueini, which could be manipulated by the dancers and changed into various shapes and configurations of reflective surfaces, until it was dismantled altogether. In a kind of reversal of most of the other cited examples, the elaborately detailed set that choreographer Sarah Michelson and Parker Lutz (who also performed) created for the former's 2006

Next Wave work **DOGS** drew so much attention that it appears to have had the unexpected long-term effect of expanding Michelson's career as a choreographer who collaborates directly with art museums, up to and including a 2014 project with the Whitney Museum for which she produced a sprung dance floor composed of 220 original paintings.

A different sort of multidisciplinary practice came to the world's attention in the work of South African artist William Kentridge, whose New York introduction was through art exhibitions centered on his handmade animations, as well as his genre-defying collaborations with the innovative Cape Town-based Handspring Puppet Company. It was not until 2007, when his production of Mozart's *The Magic Flute*, originally presented in 2005 at Belgium's Royal Opera House, came to BAM that American audiences became aware of something European audiences had known for years—that Kentridge was an opera director of remarkable versatility and invention. His virtuosic control of the opera's staging, within which humans become characters inside a larger swirl of

OPPOSITE
*CALIFORNIA*, John Jasperse Company, 2004. Photo: Julieta Cervantes

ABOVE
Parker Lutz in *DOGS*, Sarah Michelson/Parker Lutz, 2006. Photo: Julieta Cervantes

FOLLOWING PAGE
Dada Masilo in *Refuse the Hour*, William Kentridge/Philip Miller/Dada Masilo/Catherine Meyburgh, 2015. Photo: Stephanie Berger

GIVE US BACK
OUR SUN

events, immediately drew the opera world's attention. While the Metropolitan Opera went on to commission new Kentridge productions of Shostakovich's *The Nose* and Alban Berg's *Lulu*, BAM hosted the artist's more intimately virtuoso work, **Refuse the Hour**, during the 2015 Next Wave Festival. Presented in the form of an elliptical lecture on the vicissitudes of time, Kentridge's chamber opera—with music by longtime collaborator Philip Miller—transforms into a phantasmagoric immersion into physics, colonial history, and personal memory.

Recent years have seen a noticeable uptick in these sorts of collaborations during the festival. In the 2009 Next Wave, Bryce Dessner and Aaron Dessner of the rock group The National developed an evening-long musical work, **The Long Count,** whose flowing, color-saturated visual identity was the result of their creative partnership with the New York painter Matthew Ritchie. In 2012, the sculptor Anthony McCall's stunning light installation functioned as the key visual feature of choreographer Jonah Bokaer's **ECLIPSE**, followed in that same season by artist Derrick Adams, taking an inside-out look at children's television in his interdisciplinary work **The Channel**. BAM also premiered **Brooklyn Bred**, an evening-long showcase of separate performance works by visual artists Coco Fusco and Dread Scott, along with circus artist Jennifer Miller. In addition to its cutting-edge

RIGHT
*Y el mar te hablará (And the Sea Will Talk to You)*, audience view, included in *Brooklyn Bred*, Coco Fusco, 2012. Photo: Rahav Segev

participating artists, the pilot season of *Brooklyn Bred* was curated by Martha Wilson, who helped to pioneer performance art as a genre through her founding in 1976 of the alternative space Franklin Furnace. These events took place in the flexible Fishman Space in the BAM Fisher Building, where artist José Parlá painted a lush, site-specific mural spanning the width of the lobby.

The 2013 Next Wave provided the occasion for an unusual collaboration between visual artist Suzanne Bocanegra and actor Frances McDormand in the form of a lecture-performance based on the former's experience of spending two years in a body cast, formative in her later decision to devote her life to making sculpture. In the 2014 season, a second edition of Wilson's *Brooklyn Bred* featured separate full-length works by Clifford Owens, Dynasty Handbag, and Pablo Helguera. The 2015 Next Wave not only offered Kentridge's *Refuse the Hour*, but a theatrical production by Canadian Stage of the play **Helen Lawrence**, written by Chris Haddock and directed by the Vancouver-based video artist Stan Douglas. Fusing live-action film

ABOVE
Wilmer Wilson IV, Lawrence Graham-Brown, Clifford Owens, and Rocheford Belizaire in *Decision*, included in *Brooklyn Bred*, Dread Scott, 2012. Photo: Ed Lefkowicz

OPPOSITE
Daniel Pettrow and Maira Kalman in *The Principles of Uncertainty*, Maira Kalman/Dance Heginbotham, 2017. Photo: Rebecca Greenfield

with computer-generated simulations, the fast-paced production—inspired by film noir—brought period nostalgia together with cutting-edge digital technology. In the 2016 Next Wave, Jonah Bokaer returned with the work **Rules Of The Game**, this time in collaboration with artist Daniel Arsham, while painter-turned-choreographer Shen Wei revised the theatrical tradition of a hand-made curtain by deploying a massive abstract landscape painted by himself as a visual prelude to **Neither**, an evening of new work by his company, Shen Wei Dance Arts.

The role of visual art as an interdisciplinary link continued to be a significant factor in the 2017 Next Wave, illustrated in **Tesseract**, an evening-length collaboration between video pioneer Charles Atlas and Merce Cunningham alumni Rashaun Mitchell and Silas Riener; **Farmhouse/Whorehouse: An Artist Lecture by Suzanne Bocanegra Starring Lili Taylor**; **The Principles of Uncertainty**, illustrator Maira Kalman's collaboration with choreographer John Heginbotham; and separate programs by "post-Internet society" performance artist Xavier Cha and spoken word poet and playwright Marc Bamuthi Joseph, respectively, **Buffer** and **/peh-LO-tah/**.

The most recent stage in the evolution of BAM Next Wave's collaboration with the visual arts community was originally dubbed *Next*Next Visual Art; the name was soon shortened to Next Wave Art, then BAMart, and finally BAM Visual Art. Projects by participating artists were limited

only by what the crew could physically install, and what BAM audiences could feasibly make their way through or around by curtain time. The first season the exhibition took place, for the 2002 Next Wave Festival, was both tentative, in that most artists lent smaller or medium-scaled works, but also wildly ambitious, to the extent that the exhibition had three completely separate iterations, one for each month of the Next Wave. Other efforts already under way to expand the presence of visual art projects in the Next Wave Festival include Mark Hansen and Ben Rubin's installation **Listening Post** (2001), which used digital technology, then in its infancy, that allowed texts and other information gleaned from online chat rooms to be shared both visually—in the form of 200+ tiny LED screens—and aurally, through speakers scattered around the room. As part of a multi-year collaboration with Lucent Technologies, *Listening Post* fused sound, text, voyeurism, and random data harvesting to provide a spectacle whose Big Brother overtones deepened its appeal.

For more than a decade, through the 2011 season, the annual Next Wave exhibition at BAM became a test laboratory for how visual artworks might function within the spaces that audiences typically use for milling about, meeting friends, picking up tickets, and having a drink or snack before the show. From its inception, Next Wave visual art programming operated semi-clandestinely, by attempting to infiltrate the field of vision of people who had come to experience an artwork of a different nature, but might be open to visual art encounters as well. From precise rows of photographs and drawings hung in the Natman Gallery off the main lobby of the Howard Gilman Opera

House to the series of occasionally oversized sculptures suspended from the ceiling of the Lepercq Space, the art was generally positioned wherever your eye might land, or in the case of Diana Al-Hadid's 2009 lobby sculpture, somewhere you might be passing. Among the more than 100 artists included in the 10 editions of the exhibition, highlights include Wangechi Mutu's stunning collage mural in the upstairs Diker Cafe (2003); Iván Navarro's ghostly furniture assembled from fluorescent lighting fixtures (2005); Shinique Smith's chandelier-like soft sculpture floating over the BAMcafé bar (2009); and Ester Partegàs's hut in homage to Samuel Beckett (2009). Among the most distinctive and dramatic artworks that have since become iconic of BAM was Leo Villareal's LED *Stars* installation in 2007, a series of five 12-foot diameter light sculptures that illuminate the arched windows of the Peter Jay Sharp Building.

Art museums aside, it is probably not an exaggeration to claim that over the course of its 35-year history, the BAM Next Wave Festival has almost certainly done more for the visual arts than any other performance venue in the city, if not the entire country. As the reach and scope of the art world has expanded exponentially within the same time frame, BAM has commissioned more than its fair share of posters and program covers from visual artists, and made them a prominent part of its outreach and development activities. But these are things any astute arts center would have done, as demonstrated by the recent uptick in visual art at places like Lincoln Center. But the Next Wave broke more critical ground far earlier—first by establishing the multidisciplinary collaborative performance work as a programming standard, and later by introducing the practice of commissioning or producing major performance works from artists trained and practicing in the visual arts. As if this were not enough, by inviting studio artists who share its Brooklyn home to present their paintings, sculptures, and video projections throughout the myriad public spaces of its principal venues, BAM has expanded the curatorial conversation about where and in what conditions art can be experienced, such as the fluorescent outdoor KAWS mural across Lafayette Avenue, and David Byrne's functional alphabet bike racks. This consistent dialogue with visual art has yielded the addition of a dedicated art gallery within the BAM campus, to open in the fall of 2019. BAM has acted decisively to break down the historical boundaries that have served to keep the visual and performing arts separated, transferring itself along the way as a creative cauldron where a true fusion of the best creative minds of our time can continue developing what appears to be the quintessential art form of the 21st century.

OPPOSITE
*Listening Post*, sound installation, Mark Hansen/Ben Rubin, 2001. Photo courtesy of BAM Hamm Archives

FOLLOWING PAGE
*Stars*, art installation, Leo Villareal, Brooklyn Academy of Music, Peter Jay Sharp Building, 2007. Photo courtesy of BAM Hamm Archives

1859
THE BROOKLYN

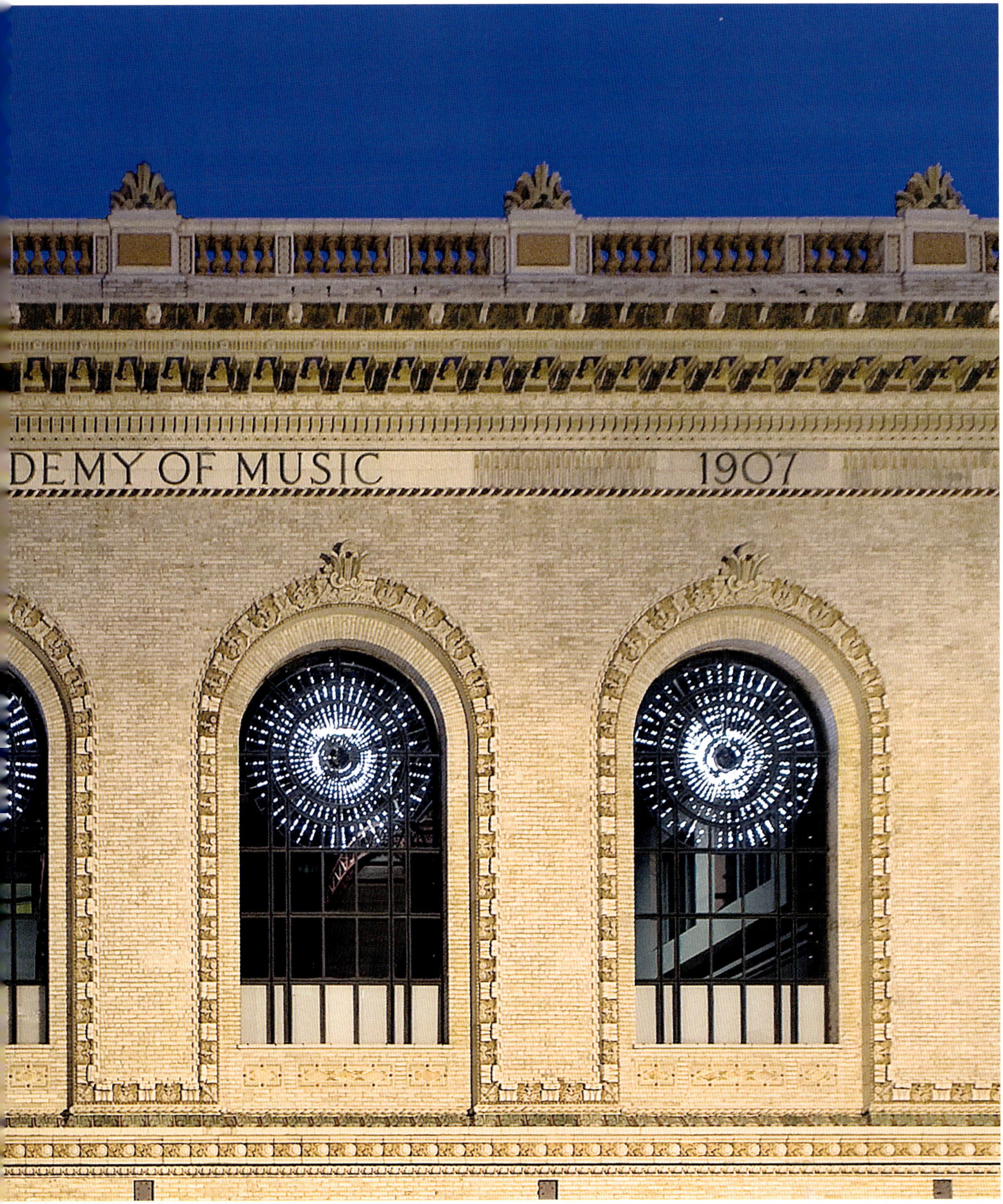
DEMY OF MUSIC 1907

# Chronology

## Next Wave Series 1981

**Glacial Decoy**, **Son of Gone Fishin'**, **Opal Loop/Cloud Installation #72503**
Trisha Brown Company, Robert Ashley, Donald Judd, Robert Rauschenberg, Fujiko Nakaya

**Tympani**, **Dance**, Music from **Night**
Laura Dean Dancers and Musicians

**Satyagraha**
Philip Glass, Constance DeJong, Christopher Keene, Brooklyn Philharmonia

**Relative Calm**
Lucinda Childs Dance Company, Jon Gibson, Robert Wilson

## 1982–83

**Tehillim**; **Drumming**; **Variations for Winds, Strings and Keyboards**; **Vermont Counterpoint**; **Octet**; **Six Pianos**; **Music for 18 Musicians**
Steve Reich and Musicians, Ransom Wilson

**Juggling and Cheap Theatrics**
The Flying Karamazov Brothers

**Symphony No. 3 ("Gloria")**
Glenn Branca

**United States: Parts I–IV**
Laurie Anderson

**Field Papers**
Dana Reitz and Dancers

**Intuitive Momentum**
Bill T. Jones, Arnie Zane, Connie Crothers, Max Roach

## Next Wave Festival 1983

**THE PHOTOGRAPHER/Far From the Truth**
Philip Glass, Robert Coe, David Gordon, JoAnne Akalaitis

**The Way of How**
George Coates Performance Works, Paul Dresher

**Accumulation**, **With Talking**, **Plus Watermotor**, **Son of Gone Fishin'**, **Line-Up**, **Set and Reset**
Trisha Brown Company, Robert Ashley, Donald Judd, Laurie Anderson, Robert Rauschenberg

**Great Black Magic: Ancient to the Future**
Art Ensemble of Chicago

**Mad Rush**, **Available Light**
Lucinda Childs Dance Company, Philip Glass, John Adams, Frank Gehry

**The Gospel at Colonus**
Lee Breuer, Bob Telson

**Underwood**
Carolyn Carlson Dance Theater of La Fenice, René Aubry

**Hemispheres**
Molissa Fenley and Dancers, Anthony Davis, Francesco Clemente, Episteme

Next Wave Festival *In Performance* cover featuring art work by Ed Paschke, 1983. Courtesy of BAM Hamm Archives

**Threads, Silk, Sticks**
Rina Schenfeld

**Victory Over the Sun**
Aleksei Kruchenykh, Mikhail Matiushin, Robert Benedetti, California Institute of the Arts

**Wind Devil**
Nina Wiener and Dancers, Sergio Cervetti, Judy Pfaff

## 1984

**The Games**
Meredith Monk, Ping Chong

**Ten Men**
Remy Charlip

**Democracy in America**
Tim Miller

**The Desert Music**
Steve Reich and Musicians, Michael Tilson Thomas, Brooklyn Philharmonic Symphony Orchestra

**Pigs and Fishes**, **Indoors**, **Set in Stone**, **Treading**, **White Dragon**
Elisa Monte Dance Company

**Brooklyn Solo 1984, In The Middle Of**
Richard Landry

**Secret Pastures**
Bill T. Jones/Arnie Zane & Company, Peter Gordon, Keith Haring

**Gloria, O Rangasayee**, **Championship Wrestling After Roland Barthes**
Mark Morris Dance Group

**Simon Jeffes, Penguin Cafe Orchestra**

**Einstein on the Beach**
Philip Glass, Robert Wilson, Lucinda Childs

## 1985

**Arien**, **Kontakthof**, **Auf dem Gebirge hat man ein Geschrei gehört (On the Mountain a Cry Was Heard)**, **The Seven Deadly Sins**, **Don't Be Afraid**
Tanztheater Wuppertal Pina Bausch

**Inside Outside (Stages of Light)**, **Pedal Steal**
Margaret Jenkins Dance Company, Barbara Kasten, Terry Allen

**The Golden Windows**
Robert Wilson

**Blue Lady**
Carolyn Carlson, René Aubry

**Wo Meine Sonne Scheint (Where My Sun Shines for Me)**
Mechthild Grossmann, Helmut Schäfer

Next Wave Festival program cover, 1984. Courtesy of BAM Hamm Archives

Next Wave Festival program cover, 1985. Courtesy of BAM Hamm Archives

**Sky Light**, **Transformer**, **Impact**
Laura Dean Dancers and Musicians

**Callas**
Reinhild Hoffmann, Tanztheater Bremen

**In Closed Time**
Nina Wiener and Dancers, Meredith Monk, Sergio Cervetti, Elliott Sharp, Arquitectonica

**Russia**
Chris Hardman/Antenna Theater

**The Alchemedians**
Bob Berky, Michael Moschen

**Love of Life Orchestra, Peter Gordon, David Van Tieghem**

**Swans Weigh**, **Bath Tubbing**, **Orient-Occident**, **Flood**
Susanne Linke

**The Birth of the Poet**
Richard Foreman, Kathy Acker, Peter Gordon, David Salle

**Carriage of Sacrifices**
Cecil Taylor, World Saxophone Quartet

## 1986

**Roaratorio**, **Inlets 2**
Merce Cunningham Dance Company, John Cage

**Social Amnesia . . . a live movie**
John Schneider, Impossible Theater

**Jon Hassell Concert Group**

**No Fire Escape in Hell**
Michael Clark & Company

**The Angels of Swedenborg**
Ping Chong, John Fleming, Fiji Theater Company

**Rosas Danst Rosas**
Anne Teresa De Keersmaeker, Thierry de Mey, Peter Vermeersch, Rosas

**Once Upon a Time in the East Village**
Ennio Morricone, John Zorn

**Geologic Moments**
Molissa Fenley and Dancers

**Songs of Innocence and of Experience**
William Bolcom, Lukas Foss, Brooklyn Philharmonic Symphony Orchestra

**Marble Halls, Pièces en Concert**, **Stabat Mater**
Mark Morris Dance Group

**Kronos Quartet**

**New Moon Stories**
Eiko & Koma

**Transparent Means for Travelling Light**, **My Folks (1984–85)**, **The Seasons**
David Gordon/Pick Up Co.

**The Soldier's Tale**
Robert Woodruff, The Flying Karamazov Brothers

**The Animal Trilogy**
Bill T. Jones/Arnie Zane & Company

**the CIVIL warS: a tree is best measured when it is down, Act V—the Rome Section**
Robert Wilson, Philip Glass, Ulysses Dove

## 1987

**The Mahabharata**
Peter Brook, Jean-Claude Carrière, Chloe Obolensky

**Babel Babel**, **Eden**
Compagnie Maguy Marin

**Swing**
Elizabeth Swados

**Elena's Aria**
Anne Teresa De Keersmaeker, Rosas

**The Music of Steve Reich**
Steve Reich, Kent Nagano, Pat Metheny, Lukas Foss, Brooklyn Philharmonic Symphony Orchestra

**Transatlantic Light**, **Fierce Attachments**
Nina Wiener Dance Company, Sergio Cervetti, Lucia Hwong

**Theme, Four Fanfares and Ostinato**; **Five People Taking Long Journeys Separately**; **Radical Filtering**; **Larynx**
Peter Zummo Orchestras, Elliott Sharp and CARBON

**Zangezi: A Supersaga in Twenty Planes**
Velimir Khlebnikov, Peter Sellars, Jon Hassell, Paul Schmidt, George Tsypin

**The Tarnished Angels**, **The Elizabethan Phrasing of the Late Albert Ayler**
The Armitage Ballet, David Salle

**An Artist and Her Music**
Meredith Monk, Bobby McFerrin

**"L" Train to Eldorado**
Stephan Balint, Squat Theatre

**Nixon in China**
John Adams, Alice Goodman, Peter Sellars, Mark Morris

**Run Silent, Run Deep, Run Loud, Run High**
Henry Threadgill and Orchestra

## 1988

**The Warrior Ant**
Lee Breuer, Bob Telson

**Tango Varsoviano**
Alberto Felix Alberto, Teatro del Sur

**The Next Wave in Europe**
Gidon Kremer, Dennis Russell Davies, Brooklyn Philharmonic Symphony Orchestra

**The Power Project (Antic Variations)**
Bob Berky, Mark Harrison, Geoffrey Moss

**The Return of the Native**
Thomas Hardy, Peter Gordon, Kit Fitzgerald

**Michael Moschen in Motion**
Michael Moschen, John Kahn, David Van Tieghem

**Polka from the Fringe**
Guy Klucevsek

**Thirst**, **Tree**
Eiko & Koma

**The Forest**
Robert Wilson, David Byrne

**Interior with Seven Figures**
Susan Marshall & Company, Luis Resto

**M-BASE Jams at BAM**

**My Sex, Our Dance**; **Deep End**
Lloyd Newson, DV8 Physical Theatre

**United States**
David Gordon/Pick Up Co.

**Nonet, The President**
Wayne Horwitz

## 1989

**Empty Places**
Laurie Anderson

**Machandel**
Tanztheater Reinhild Hoffmann

**Avantgarde-Music**, **Herne**
Pöhl Musik

**Hommage à Dore Hoyer**
Susanne Linke

**Can We Dance a Landscape? (Peut-on Danser le Paysage?)**
Karel Appel, Min Tanaka

Next Wave Festival program cover featuring art work by Willem de Kooning, 1987. Courtesy of BAM Hamm Archives

**Woman with Blue Ball**, **The Song on the Bridge**
Tanztheater Christine Brunel

**Nusrat Fateh Ali Khan and Party**

**Stuff As Dreams Are Made On**
Fred Curchack

**Hey, What's All This to Me!?**
Compagnie Maguy Marin

**New Music America**

**Rain**, **Allies**
Bebe Miller and Company

**Songs for 'Drella—a fiction**
Lou Reed, John Cale

## 1990

**Endangered Species**
Martha Clarke

**L'Allegro, il Penseroso ed il Moderato**; **New Love Song Waltzes**; **Wonderland**; **Love Song Waltzes**
Monnaie Dance Group/Mark Morris

**Ninagawa Macbeth**
The Ninagawa Company

**Polygraph**
Robert Lepage, Marie Brassard, Le Théâtre Repère

**Le Dortoir**
Gilles Maheu, Carbone 14

**Next Wave Concert**
William Schuman, Lou Harrison, Henryk Gorecki, Dennis Russell Davies, Brooklyn Philharmonic Orchestra

**Margie Gillis, Christopher Gillis, Stephanie Ballard**

**Last Supper at Uncle Tom's Cabin/The Promised Land**
Bill T. Jones/Arnie Zane & Company, Julius Hemphill Sextet

**Chagall, Don Quichotte**
Ginette Laurin, O Vertigo Danse

**The Greatest Masters of Persian Music**
Ali-Asghar Bahari, Mohammad Esmaili, Jalil Shahnaz, Faramarz Payvar, Mohammad Musavi

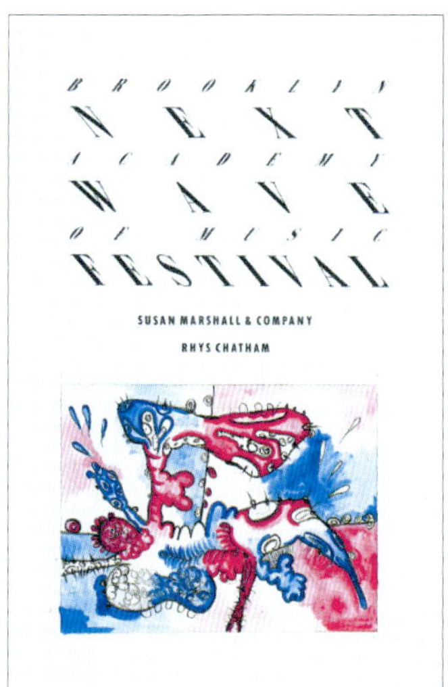


Next Wave Festival program cover featuring art work by Carroll Dunham, 1990. Courtesy of BAM Hamm Archives

**Contenders**
Susan Marshall & Company, Pauline Oliveros

**The Heart Cries with Many Voices**
Rhys Chatham

## 1991

**Palermo Palermo**, **Bandoneon**
Tanztheater Wuppertal Pina Bausch

**Invitations to Heaven (Questions of a Jewish Child)**
Eric Bass/Sandglass Theater

**Maturando**
Marcos Caetano Ribas, Grupo Contadores de Estórias

**1991: A Performance Chronicle of the Rediscovery of America by the Warrior for Gringostroika**
Guillermo Gómez-Peña

**Carmen Miranda**
Arto Lindsay

**Land**
Eiko & Koma, Robert Mirabal

**Next Wave Concert**
Keith Jarrett, Heitor Villa-Lobos, Peggy Glanville-Hicks, Terry Riley, Dennis Russell Davies, Brooklyn Philharmonic Orchestra

**Always the Same Lies**
Wim Vandekeybus, Ultima Vez

**Praise House**
Jawole Willa Jo Zollar, Urban Bush Women

**Griot New York**
Garth Fagan Dance, Wynton Marsalis, Martin Puryear

## 1992

**Frida**
Hilary Blecher, Migdalia Cruz, Robert Xavier Rodriguez

**Native Voices: Music of the Pueblo, Songs of the City**
Pura Fé, Robert Mirabal

**Power Pipes**
Muriel Miguel, Spiderwoman Theater

**Achterland**
Anne Teresa De Keersmaeker

**Dah-Dah-Sko-Dah-Dah**
Saburo Teshigawara/KARAS

**Urban Scenes/Creole Dreams**
David Roussève/REALITY, Ysaye Barnwell

**Glass Reflections**
Philip Glass, Dennis Russell Davies, Brooklyn Philharmonic Orchestra, New York Choral Society

Next Wave Festival program cover featuring art work by Philip Taaffe, 1992. Courtesy of BAM Hamm Archives

**Einstein on the Beach**
Philip Glass, Robert Wilson, Lucinda Childs

**Needles and Opium**
Robert Lepage

**The Hard Nut**
Mark Morris Dance Group, Donald York, Brooklyn Philharmonic Orchestra

## 1993

**The Cave**
Steve Reich, Beryl Korot

**Passage Through the Gong**
Rahayu Supanggah, Sardono Dance Theater

**Orphée**
Jean Cocteau, Francesca Zambello, Philip Glass, Dennis Russell Davies, Brooklyn Philharmonic Orchestra

**The European Mystics**
Dennis Russell Davies, Brooklyn Philharmonic Orchestra

**Billboards**
Gerald Arpino, The Joffrey Ballet

**Light Shall Lift Them**
John Kelly

**The Black Rider: The Casting of the Magic Bullets**
Robert Wilson, Tom Waits, William S. Burroughs, Thalia Theater

**Njinga the Queen King**
Ione, Pauline Oliveros

**Ellington's New York**
Luther Henderson, Duke Ellington Orchestra, Mercer Ellington, Dennis Russell Davies, Brooklyn Philharmonic Orchestra

## 1994

**Radical Graham**
Ronald Protas, Martha Graham Dance Company

**As You Like It**
Declan Donnellan, Nick Ormerod, Cheek by Jowl

**Michael Nyman, Live!**
The Michael Nyman Band

**Noiject**
Saburo Teshigawara/KARAS

**Mirror Images**
Philip Glass, John Zorn, Chen Yi, Dennis Russell Davies, Brooklyn Philharmonic Orchestra

**Jiří Kylián, Nederlands Dans Theater**

**Gaudeamus**
Sergei Kaledin, Lev Dodin, Maly Drama Theatre of St. Petersburg

**American Transcendentalists**
Charles Ives, John Adams, Dennis Russell Davies, Brooklyn Philharmonic Orchestra

**Spectators at an Event, Fields of View**
Susan Marshall & Company

**Now Eleanor's Idea**
Robert Ashley

**Two Cigarettes in the Dark**
Tanztheater Wuppertal Pina Bausch

**Still/Here**
Bill T. Jones/Arnie Zane Dance Company

**La Belle et la Bête**
Jean Cocteau, Philip Glass Ensemble

## 1995

**Alice**
Robert Wilson, Tom Waits, Kathleen Brennan, Paul Schmidt, Thalia Theater

Artists in Action:
**Theater Project for a Rock Band:** Vito Acconci, The Mekons; **Interim: after the end and before the beginning:** Kristin Jones, Andrew Ginzel, Chandralekha; **The Flies: A Musical Phantasmagoria**: Ilya Kabakov, Vladimir Tarasov, David Dorfman

**Alternative Jazz: The Next Wave**
Don Byron

**Salome**
Oscar Wilde, Steven Berkoff

**Nine Songs**
Lin Hwai-min, Cloud Gate Dance Theatre of Taiwan

**The Passion of Joan of Arc**
Carl Theodor Dreyer, Richard Einhorn, Lucinda Carver, Voices of Light

**From Gospel to Gershwin**
Gunther Schuller, Brooklyn Philharmonic Orchestra

**Chinoiserie**
Ping Chong

**Kronos Quartet, Brooklyn Philharmonic Orchestra**

**The Whispers of Angels**
David Roussève/REALITY

**Mark Morris Dance Group, Lou Harrison, Brooklyn Philharmonic Orchestra**

**The Duchess of Malfi**
Declan Donnellan, Nick Ormerod, Cheek by Jowl

## 1996

**Chimère: Equestrian Theater by Zingaro**
Bartabas

**Trisha Brown at 25: Post Modern and Beyond**
Trisha Brown Company, Laurie Anderson, Mikhail Baryshnikov, Robert Rauschenberg

**The Beatification of Area Boy: A Lagosian Kaleidoscope**
Wole Soyinka, Jude Kelly, West Yorkshire Playhouse

**The Politics of Quiet**
Meredith Monk Vocal Ensemble

**The Predators' Ball: Hucksters of the Soul**
Karole Armitage, David Salle, MaggioDanza di Firenze

**Furioso**
Meryl Tankard Australian Dance Theatre

**Global Music**
Joe Killian, The Sabri Brothers, Cornershop

Artists in Action:
**Flatland/A Romance of Many Dimensions**: Jene Highstein, Hanne Tierney; **MINE:** Rona Pondick, Sara Rudner; **Black Fathers and Sons: A US Perspective**: Albert Chong, Johnny Coleman

**Yuragi: In a Space of Perpetual Motion**
Ushio Amagatsu, Sankai Juku

**Aural Histories**, **Medieval to Modern**, **American Mavericks**
Kronos Quartet

**Les Enfants Terribles: Children of the Game**
Jean Cocteau, Philip Glass, Susan Marshall

**Jazz: The Next Wave**
Don Byron Group, Marilyn Crispell, Victor Wooten, J.D. Blair, Dave Holland Quartet

**The Seven Streams of the River Ota**
Robert Lepage, Ex Machina

**A to Z**
Robert Spano, Brooklyn Philharmonic Orchestra

**The Harlem Nutcracker**
Donald Byrd/The Group; 651, An Arts Center

## 1997

**Der Fensterputzer**
Tanztheater Wuppertal Pina Bausch

**Tango: A Tribute to Astor Piazzolla**
Gidon Kremer

**Elsinore**
Robert Lepage

**Cunningham Merce: Forward & Reverse**
Merce Cunningham Dance Company

**Woud (Forest)**
Anne Teresa De Keersmaeker, Rosas

Artists in Action:
**Hare Follies:** Nayland Blake; **Doppler Incident:** Kerry James Marshall; **Take My Breath Away:** Beth B

**Antony & Cleopatra**
Barrie Rutter, Northern Broadsides

**After Mahler**
Robert Spano, Brooklyn Philharmonic Orchestra

**Missionaries**
Elizabeth Swados

**Time Rocker**
Robert Wilson, Lou Reed, Darryl Pinckney, Thalia Theater

**You ANC Nothing Yet!**
Pieter-Dirk Uys

**Journey Beyond the West: The New Adventures of MONKEY**
Fred Ho, Christopher Mattagliano, John Carrafa

**Jazz: The Next Wave**
Don Byron Ensemble, Medeski Martin & Wood

Next Wave Festival BAMbill cover featuring art work by Jim Dine, 1996. Courtesy of BAM Hamm Archives

**River**
Sômei Satoh, Eiko & Koma, Kronos Quartet

**Messiaen/Pärt**
Robert Spano, Wu Han, Brooklyn Philharmonic Orchestra

**Geography**
Ralph Lemon, Nari Ward

## 1998

**Eclipse: Equestrian Theater by Zingaro**
Bartabas

Next Wave Festival BAMbill cover featuring art work by Christian Boltanski, 1998. Courtesy of BAM Hamm Archives

**We Set Out Early . . . Visibility Was Poor**
Bill T. Jones/Arnie Zane Dance Company

**Maria de Buenos Aires**
Astor Piazzolla, Horacio Ferrer, Gidon Kremer, KREMERata Musica

**The World Mysteries: The Mysteries of Eleusis**
Vasilios Calitsis

**Hindenburg/Music for 18 Musicians**
Steve Reich, Beryl Korot

**Romeo and Juliet**
Ballet Preljocaj

**Kronos Quartet: 25th Anniversary Celebration**

**Die Winterreise**
Robert Spano, Christian Boltanski, James Maddalena

**Anna Karenina**
Nancy Meckler, Shared Experience

**A B & C**
Robert Spano, Brooklyn Philharmonic Orchestra, New York Virtuoso Singers

**Raga: In Search of Femininity**
Chandralekha, Anish Kapoor

**Jazz: The Next Wave**
Don Byron, Tito Puente, Hector Martignon and The Foreign Affair Trio

**EIDOS : TELOS**
William Forsythe, Ballett Frankfurt

**Monsters of Grace**
Robert Wilson, Philip Glass

**Powder Her Face**
Thomas Adès, Philip Hensher, Edward Berkeley, Robert Spano, Brooklyn Philharmonic Orchestra

**The Most Dangerous Room in the House**
Susan Marshall & Company, David Lang, Bang on a Can All-Stars

## 1999

**The Whiteheaded Boy**
Gerard Stembridge, Barabbas . . . the company

**Songs and Stories from Moby Dick**
Laurie Anderson, Anne Bogart, Bob Bielecki

**Life Is a Dream**
Pedro Calderón de la Barca, Calixto Bieito, Royal Lyceum Theatre Company

**Carmen & Solo for Two**
Georges Bizet, Mats Ek, Lyon Opera Ballet

**Operation : Orfeo**
Hotel Pro Forma

**Dracula: The Music and Film**
Philip Glass, Kronos Quartet

**Morning Song: No beauty for me there, where human life is rare, part two**
Jan Lauwers, Needcompany

**Danzón**
Tanztheater Wuppertal Pina Bausch

**Hiyomeki (Within a Gentle Vibration and Agitation)**
Ushio Amagatsu, Sankai Juku

**Geometry of Miracles**
Robert Lepage, Ex Machina

**Nixon in China**
John Adams, Alice Goodman, Robert Spano, Brooklyn Philharmonic Orchestra

**Love Songs**
David Roussève/REALITY

**Party at the End of Time: 1999 Live**
Vernon Reid, The Roots

## 2000

**War of the Worlds**
Anne Bogart, Naomi Iizuka, SITI Company

**Symphony No. 5: Requiem, Bardo, Nirmanakaya**
Philip Glass, Dennis Russell Davies, Brooklyn Philharmonic Orchestra

**Parcours**
Lucinda Childs Dance Company

**Máquina Hamlet**
Ana Alvarado, Daniel Veronese, Emilio García Wehbi, El Periférico de Objetos

**A Magic Science: Celebrating Jimi Hendrix**
Vernon Reid, Medeski Martin & Wood, The Gil Evans Orchestra

**Tree: Part 2 of The Geography Trilogy**
Ralph Lemon, Nari Ward

**Uttar-Priyadarshi**
Ratan Thiyam's Chorus Repertory Theatre of Manipur

**Songs of the Wanderers**
Lin Hwai-min, Cloud Gate Dance Theatre of Taiwan

**Requiem for Srebrenica**
Olivier Py, Centre Dramatique National/Orléans-Loiret-Centre

**A Dream Play**
Robert Wilson, Stockholm's Stadsteater

**When Nights Were Dark**
Eiko & Koma

**To Lie Tenderly**
David Dorfman Dance

**Bang on a Can Millennium Marathon**

## 2001

**Cloudstreet**
Neil Armfield, Justin Monjo, Nick Enright, Company B Belvoir, Black Swan Theatre

**Crumpled & Corrupted 2**
Gideon Obarzanek, Chunky Move

**Drumming**
Steve Reich, Anne Teresa De Keersmaeker, Rosas, Ictus

**The Theft of Sita**
Nigel Jamieson, Paul Grabowsky

**Corroboree**
Stephen Page, Bangarra Dance Theatre

**Next Wave of Song**
Beth Orton, Rufus Wainwright, Meshell Ndegeocello

Next Wave Festival program cover featuring art work by Robert Frank, 1998. Courtesy of BAM Hamm Archives

**Bang on a Can Marathon**

**Needcompany's King Lear**
Jan Lauwers

**Masurca Fogo**
Tanztheater Wuppertal Pina Bausch

**Once Upon a Time in Chinese America...**
Fred Ho, Mira Kingsley

**Giant Empty**
John Jasperse Company

**Trace**
Paul Kaiser, Nicolas Tsingos

**POEtry**
Robert Wilson, Lou Reed, Thalia Theater

**Big Love**
Charles L. Mee, Les Waters, Goodman Theatre

**Listening Post**
Ben Rubin, Mark Hansen

**Woolf Phrase, Enemy in the Figure, Quintett**
William Forsythe, Ballett Frankfurt

## 2002

**Galileo Galilei**
Philip Glass, Mary Zimmerman, Goodman Theatre, Eos Orchestra

**Medea**
Euripides, Deborah Warner, Fiona Shaw, Abbey Theatre

**The Next Wave of Song**
Marc Ribot, Ben Folds, Stephin Merritt, Marc Anthony Thompson

**Three Tales**
Steve Reich, Beryl Korot, Bradley Lubman

**Helikopter & Rite of Spring**
Ballet Preljocaj

**21 & O Corpo**
Rodrigo Pederneiras, Grupo Corpo

**La Pasión Según San Marcos**
Osvaldo Golijov, Robert Spano, Brooklyn Philharmonic Orchestra

**Woyzeck**
Georg Büchner, Robert Wilson, Tom Waits, Kathleen Brennan, Betty Nansen Theatre

**Körper**
Sasha Waltz & Guests, Schaubühne am Lehniner Platz

**Hibiki (Resonance from Far Away)**
Ushio Amagatsu, Sankai Juku

**mercy**
Meredith Monk, Ann Hamilton

**Macbeth**
The Ninagawa Company

**Water Passion After St. Matthew**
Tan Dun

**The Hard Nut**
Mark Morris Dance Group, Robert Cole, Brooklyn Philharmonic Orchestra

## 2003

**The Room As It Was**; **Duo**; **(N.N.N.N.)**; **One Flat Thing, reproduced**
William Forsythe, Ballett Frankfurt

Next Wave Festival BAMbill cover featuring art work by Yoshitomo Nara, 2002. Courtesy of BAM Hamm Archives

**Henry IV, Part One**
Richard Maxwell, New York City Players

**The Sound of Ocean**
Liu Ching-ming, U-Theatre

**bobrauschenbergamerica**
Charles L. Mee, Anne Bogart, SITI Company

**Merce Cunningham Dance Company: 50th Anniversary Season**

**Sleeping Beauty and Other Stories**
Susan Marshall & Company

**The New Yorkers**
Barry Edelstein, Michael Gordon, David Lang, Julia Wolfe, Bang on a Can All-Stars

**The Hanging Man**
Phelim McDermott, Julian Crouch, Lee Simpson, Improbable Theatre

**Omega**
Enrique Morente, Lagartija Nick

**Rain**
Steve Reich, Anne Teresa De Keersmaeker, Rosas, Ictus, Synergy Vocals

**Moon Water**
Lin Hwai-min, Cloud Gate Dance Theatre of Taiwan

**Alladeen**
Marianne Weems, Keith Khan, Ali Zaidi, The Builders Association, motiroti

**The Death of Klinghoffer**
John Adams, Alice Goodman, Bob McGrath, Robert Spano, Brooklyn Philharmonic Orchestra

**The Flight Project**
Doug Varone, Warren Spears, Dwight Rhoden, Bebe Miller, Bill T. Jones, Jawole Willa Jo Zollar, Dayton Contemporary Dance Company

## 2004

**Othello**
Declan Donnellan, Nick Ormerod, Cheek by Jowl

**Sun Rings**
Terry Riley, Kronos Quartet

**The Dybbuk**
Krzysztof Warlikowski, TR Warszawa

**Bush**
Stephen Page, Frances Rings, Steve Francis, David Page, Bangarra Dance Theatre

**The Temptation of St. Anthony**
Robert Wilson, Bernice Johnson Reagon

**Come home Charley Patton: Part 3 of The Geography Trilogy**
Ralph Lemon

**A Passage to India**
E.M. Forster, Nancy Meckler, Martin Sherman, Shared Experience

**Near Life Experience**
Ballet Preljocaj

**Nora (A Doll's House)**
Thomas Ostermeier, Schaubühne am Lehniner Platz

**FAUST/How I Rose**
John Jesurun, Martín Acosta

**Für die Kinder von gestern, heute und morgen**
Tanztheater Wuppertal Pina Bausch

**Lost Objects**
David Lang, Julia Wolfe, Michael Gordon, François Girard, Bang on a Can, Concerto Köln

**The Chairs**
Eugène Ionesco, David Gordon, Pick Up Performance Company

**CALIFORNIA**
John Jasperse Company

**Isabella's room**
Jan Lauwers, Needcompany

## 2005

**Orion**
Philip Glass, Michael Riesman

**Tall Horse**
Khephra Burns, Marthinus Basson, Handspring & Sogolon Puppet Companies

**Raise the Red Lantern**
Zhang Yimou, Wang Yuanyuan, Wang Xinpeng, National Ballet of China

**Emilia Galotti**
Gotthold Ephraim Lessing, Michael Thalheimer, Deutsches Theater Berlin

**4.48 Psychose**
Sarah Kane, Claude Régy, Isabelle Huppert

**Carnaval Eletrônico**
Daniela Mercury

**Lecuona and Onqotô**
Rodrigo Pederneiras, Grupo Corpo

**Symphony No. 6 (Plutonian Ode), Symphony No. 8**
Philip Glass, Dennis Russell Davies, Bruckner Orchester Linz

**The Winter's Tale**
Edward Hall, Propeller, Watermill Theatre

**Les Noces & Petrušhka**
Mauro Bigonzetti, Compagnia Aterballetto

**Bright Abyss**
James Thierrée, La Compagnie du Hanneton

**Shelter**
David Lang, Michael Gordon, Julia Wolfe, trio mediæval, musikFabrik

**Mamootot**
Ohad Naharin, Batsheva Dance Company

**Super Vision**
Marianne Weems, The Builders Association, dbox

**Patti Smith: Horses**

**Impromptus**
Sasha Waltz & Guests

**Everywhere**
Wally Cardona Quartet, Phil Kline, Ethel

## 2006

**Steve Reich @ 70**
Steve Reich, Anne Teresa De Keersmaeker, Akram Khan, Rosas, London Sinfonietta

**The End Of Cinematics**
Mikel Rouse

**Mycenaean**
Carl Hancock Rux

**Nine Hills One Valley**
Ratan Thiyam's Chorus Repertory Theatre of Manipur

**DOGS**
Sarah Michelson, Parker Lutz

**Violet Fire: A Multimedia Opera**
Jon Gibson, Miriam Seidel, Terry O'Reilly

**Kagemi: Beyond the Metaphors of Mirrors**
Ushio Amagatsu, Sankai Juku

**The Wild Duck**
Eirik Stubø, National Theatre of Norway

**impermanence**
Meredith Monk Vocal Ensemble

Next Wave Festival BAMbill cover featuring art work by Mary Heilmann, 2005. Courtesy of BAM Hamm Archives

**Twelfth Night**
Declan Donnellan, Nick Ormerod, Chekhov International Theatre Festival

**the 51st (dream) state**
Sekou Sundiata

**underground**
David Dorfman Dance, Alex Timbers

**La Tempête**
Michel Lemieux, Victor Pilon, Denise Guilbault, 4D art

**Hedda Gabler**
Thomas Ostermeier, Schaubühne am Lehniner Platz

**Red Hot + RIOT LIVE!: The Music and Spirit of Fela Kuti**
Andres Levín, Amadou & Mariam, dead prez, Keziah Jones, Les Nubians, Meshell Ndegeocello, John Medeski, Tony Allen, Cheikh Lô

**Still Life with Commentator: An Oratorio**
Vijay Iyer, Michael Ladd, Ibrahim Quraishi

**Nefés**
Tanztheater Wuppertal Pina Bausch

**Don Juan in Prague**
David Chambers, Prague National Theatre

## 2007

**Wild Cursive**
Lin Hwai-min, Cloud Gate Dance Theatre of Taiwan

**Kronos Quartet: More Than Four**
Kimmo Pohjonen, Erik Sanko, Samuli Kosminen, Kronos Quartet

**Hotel Cassiopeia**
Charles L. Mee, Anne Bogart, SITI Company

**Krum**
Hanoch Levin, Krzysztof Warlikowski, TR Warszawa

**Por Vos Muero, Castrati, White Darkness**
Nacho Duato, Compañía Nacional de Danza

**New Voices from Spain**
Buika, Macaco

**Misuse liable to prosecution**
John Jasperse Company

**The BQE**
Sufjan Stevens

**Borrowed Light**
Tero Saarinen Company, Boston Camerata

**Cast No Shadow**
Isaac Julien, Russell Maliphant

**Three**
Ohad Naharin, Batsheva Dance Company

**One Loss Plus**
Daniel Bernard Roumain

**Lulu**
Frank Wedekind, Michael Thalheimer, Thalia Theater

**Ship in a View**
Hiroshi Koike, Pappa Tarahumara

**The Gate**
Tan Dun, Michael Christie, Brooklyn Philharmonic Orchestra

**Au Revoir Parapluie**
James Thierrée/La Compagnie du Hanneton

Next Wave Festival BAMbill cover featuring art work by McDermott & McGough, 1936/2005. Courtesy of BAM Hamm Archives

## 2008

**A Quarreling Pair**
Bill T. Jones/Arnie Zane Dance Company

**Sunken Red**
Guy Cassiers, Dirk Roofthooft, Toneelhuis, ro theater

**New Voices from Spain**
Huecco

**ETHEL's TruckStop™: The Beginning**
ETHEL, Annie Dorsen

**Woyzeck**
Gísli Örn Gardarsson, Nick Cave, Warren Ellis, Vesturport Theatre, Reykjavík City Theatre

**Awakenings**
Stephen Page, Bangarra Dance Theatre

**Steve Reich Evening**
Steve Reich, Anne Teresa De Keersmaeker, Rosas, Ictus

**Darwin's Meditation for The People of Lincoln**
Daniel Bernard Roumain, Daniel Beaty, SymphoNYC

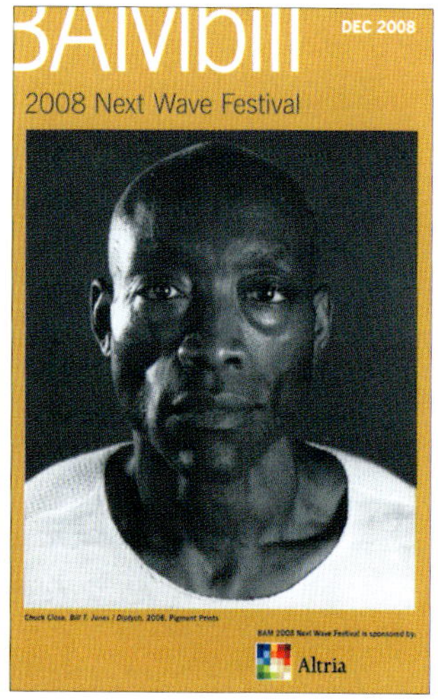


**Meeting with Bodhisattva**
Liu Ruo-yu, U-Theatre

**Arjuna's Dilemma**
Douglas J. Cuomo, John Kelly, Robin Guarino, Music-Theatre Group

**Les sept planches de la ruse (The Seven Boards of Skill)**
Aurélien Bory, Scènes de la Terre, Compagnie 111

**Amjad**
Édouard Lock, La La La Human Steps

**Continuous City**
Marianne Weems, The Builders Association

**Les écailles de la mémoire (The Scales of Memory)**
Jawole Willa Jo Zollar, Germaine Acogny, Urban Bush Women, Compagnie Jant-Bi

**Opening Night**
John Cassavetes, Ivo van Hove, Toneelgroep Amsterdam, NTGent

**Red Hot + Rio 2: The Next Generation of Samba Soul**
Bebel Gilberto, João Parahyba, Curumin, Otto, CéU, José González

**Bamboo Blues**
Tanztheater Wuppertal Pina Bausch

**Lightning at our feet**
Michael Gordon, Ridge Theater

## 2009

**In-I**
Akram Khan, Juliette Binoche, Anish Kapoor

**Lipsynch**
Robert Lepage, Ex Machina, Théâtre Sans Frontières

**Decreation**
The Forsythe Company

**Imaginary City**
Sō Percussion

**Songs of Ascension**
Meredith Monk Vocal Ensemble, Ann Hamilton

**The Long Count**
Bryce Dessner, Aaron Dessner, Matthew Ritchie

Next Wave Festival BAMbill cover featuring art work by Chuck Close, 2008. Courtesy of BAM Hamm Archives

**Itutu**
Armitage Gone! Dance, Burkina Electric

**Quartett**
Heiner Müller, Robert Wilson, Isabelle Huppert, Odéon-Théâtre de l'Europe

**Inside Out**
Tilde Björfors, Cirkus Cirkör, Irya's Playground

**Really Real**
Phil Kline, Wally Cardona Quartet, Brooklyn Youth Chorus

**Kepler**
Philip Glass, Dennis Russell Davies, Bruckner Orchester Linz, Choir of the Upper Austrian State Theatre

**Terra Nova: Sinfonia Antarctica**
Bob McGrath, DJ Spooky

**Mortal Engine**
Gideon Obarzanek, Chunky Move

**The Good Dance—dakar/brooklyn**
Reggie Wilson/Fist & Heel Performance Group, Andréya Ouamba, Compagnie 1er Temps

## 2010

**Delusion**
Laurie Anderson

**Vollmond**
Tanztheater Wuppertal Pina Bausch

**The Deer House**
Jan Lauwers, Needcompany

**How Can You Stay In The House All Day And Not Go Anywhere?**
Ralph Lemon

**A House in Bali**
Evan Ziporyn, Jay Scheib, Bang on a Can All-Stars, Gamelan Salukat

**Brooklyn OMNIBUS**
Heidi Rodewald, Stew, The Negro Problem

**Persephone**
Bob McGrath, Ben Neill, Mimi Goese, Warren Leight, Ridge Theater

**Empty moves (parts I & II)**
Ballet Preljocaj, John Cage

**Gezeiten**
Sasha Waltz & Guests

**Raoul**
James Thierrée, La Compagnie du Hanneton

**Throne of Blood**
Akira Kurosawa, Ping Chong, Oregon Shakespeare Festival

**The Marriage of Maria Braun**
Thomas Ostermeier, Schaubühne am Lehniner Platz

**Metamorphosis**
Franz Kafka, David Farr, Gísli Örn Gardarsson, Nick Cave, Warren Ellis, Vesturport Theatre/Lyric Hammersmith

**Red Hot + New Orleans**
Trombone Shorty and Orleans Avenue, Dr. John, Kermit Ruffins, Ivan Neville, Irma Thomas, Ledisi, Marc Broussard, Roger Lewis, Rebirth Brass Band, Partners-N-Crime

**Gravity Radio**
Mikel Rouse

**The Hard Nut**
Mark Morris Dance Group, Brooklyn Youth Chorus, MMDG Music Ensemble

## 2011

**Awakening: A Musical Meditation on the Anniversary of 9/11**
Kronos Quartet, Brooklyn Youth Chorus

**To the Ones I Love**
Thierry Smits, Compagnie Thor

**The Threepenny Opera**
Robert Wilson, Elizabeth Hauptmann, Berliner Ensemble

**The Speaker's Progress**
Sulayman Al-Bassam, SABAB Theatre

**Water Stains on the Wall**
Lin Hwai-min, Cloud Gate Dance Theatre of Taiwan

**Symphony for the Dance Floor**
Daniel Bernard Roumain, D.J. Mendel

**Haze**
Wang Yuanyuan, Beijing Dance Theater

**Cries and Whispers**
Ingmar Bergman, Ivo van Hove, Toneelgroep Amsterdam

**I don't believe in outer space**
The Forsythe Company

**69°S.**
Phantom Limb, Sophie Hunter, Kronos Quartet, Skeleton Key, Tony Taccone

**Brooklyn Babylon**
Darcy James Argue, Danijel Žeželj, Secret Society, Beth Morrison Projects

**Canyon**
John Jasperse Company

**The Infernal Comedy: Confessions of a serial killer**
Michael Sturminger, Martin Haselböck, John Malkovich

**Supernatural Wife**
Annie-B Parson, Paul Lazar, Big Dance Theater

**Tudo Isto É Fado**
Camané, Deolinda, Amália Hoje, Lisboa Soul

**Krapp's Last Tape**
Samuel Beckett, Michael Colgan, John Hurt, Gate Theatre

**The Legacy Tour**
Merce Cunningham Dance Company

## 2012

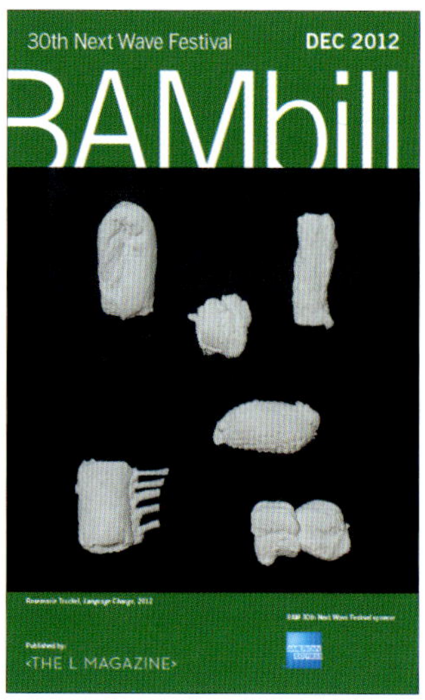


**ECLIPSE**
Jonah Bokaer, Anthony McCall, Aaron Copp

**Miriam**
Nora Chipaumire, Eric Ting, Omar Sosa

**Einstein on the Beach**
Philip Glass, Robert Wilson, Lucinda Childs

**The Channel**
Derrick Adams, Ramon Silva

**Lighthouse/Lightning Rod and Griot New York (excerpts)**
Garth Fagan Dance, Wynton Marsalis Septet, Martin Puryear

**Next Wave of Song**
Ian Axel, Chad Vaccarino, Tamar-kali

**Paris Commune**
Steve Cosson, Michael Friedman, The Civilians

**Rhinoceros**
Eugène Ionesco, Emmanuel Demarcy-Mota, Théâtre de la Ville, Paris

**Political Mother**
Hofesh Shechter Company

**Brooklyn Bred**
Martha Wilson, Dread Scott, Jennifer Miller, Coco Fusco

**ELSEWHERE**
Maya Beiser, Robert Woodruff, Beth Morrison Projects

**The Loves of Pharaoh**
Ernst Lubitsch, Joseph C. Phillips, Jr., Numinous

Next Wave Festival BAMbill cover featuring art work by Rosemarie Trockel, 2012. Courtesy of BAM Hamm Archives

**HOUSE/DIVIDED**
Marianne Weems, The Builders Association

**Out Cold/Zippo Songs**
Phil Kline, Theo Bleckmann, ACME Ensemble

**"...como el musguito en la piedra, ay si, si, si..." (Like Moss on a Stone)**
Tanztheater Wuppertal Pina Bausch

**red, black & GREEN: a blues**
Marc Bamuthi Joseph, Michael Garcés, Living Word Project

**Ímã & Sem Mim**
Rodrigo Pederneiras, Grupo Corpo

**The Shooting Gallery**
Richard Einhorn, Bill Morrison

**Sans Objet**
Aurélien Bory, Compagnie 111

**Donka: A Letter to Chekhov**
Compagnia Finzi Pasca

**DanceMotion USA℠**
Trey McIntyre Project, Korea National Contemporary Dance Company

**Roman Tragedies**
Ivo van Hove, Toneelgroep Amsterdam

**Untrained**
Lucy Guerin

**Trojan Women (After Euripides)**
Anne Bogart, SITI Company, Jocelyn Clarke

**Red Hot + Cuba**
Andres Levín, José Luis Cortés ("El Tosco"), CuCu Diamantes, Alexander Abreu, Kelvis Ochoa, David Torrens, Carlos Varela, Robert Carlos "Cucurucho" Rodriguez Valdés, Osdalgia

**And lose the name of action**
Miguel Gutierrez and The Powerful People

**love fail**
David Lang, Lydia Davis, Anonymous 4

**Faust: A Love Story**
Gísli Örn Gardarsson, Nick Cave, Warren Ellis, Vesturport Theatre, Reykjavík City Theatre

**Timber**
Michael Gordon, Mantra Percussion

**Where (we) Live**
Ain Gordon, Sō Percussion

**All That Fall**
Samuel Beckett, Gavin Quinn, Pan Pan Theatre

**When Past & Future Collide**
John Cale

## 2013

**Anna Nicole**
Mark-Anthony Turnage, Richard Thomas, Richard Jones, New York City Opera

**The Blue Dragon**
Robert Lepage, Marie Michaud, Ex Machina

**The Table**
Karbido

**Not What Happened**
Ain Gordon, Ken Rus Schmoll, Pick Up Performance Co(s)

**We Have An Anchor**
Jem Cohen, Wordless Music

**Documerica**
Steve Cosson, ETHEL

Next Wave Festival BAMbill cover featuring art work by George Segal, 2013. Courtesy of BAM Hamm Archives

**A Rite**
Bill T. Jones/Arnie Zane Dance Company, Janet Wong, Anne Bogart, SITI Company

**The Edge of Heaven**
Gary Lucas, Gods and Monsters

**Sider**
The Forsythe Company, Thom Willems

**DanceMotion USA℠**
Doug Varone and Dancers, Brenda Angiel Aerial Dance Company

**The Sweet Science Suite**
Fred Ho, Emmanuel Brown, Green Monster Big Band

**Come, and Back Again**
David Dorfman Dance

**Goldberg's Variations**
Andy Biskin

**En Atendant, Cesena**
Anne Teresa De Keersmaeker, Björn Schmelzer, Rosas, graindelavoix

**Run Don't Run**
Brian Brooks Moving Company

**Hans was Heiri**
Zimmermann & de Perrot

**Electronium: The Future Was Then**
Ahmir "Questlove" Thompson, Kirk Douglas, Jeremy Ellis, How to Dress Well, Rahzel, Sonnymoon, Emily Wells, Metropolis Ensemble

**Dark Theater**
Dance Heginbotham

**Nosferatu**
Grzegorz Jarzyna, John Zorn, TR Warszawa, Teatr Narodowy

**War Sum Up: Music. Manga. Machine.**
Kirsten Dehlholm, Hotel Pro Forma, Latvian Radio Choir

**Dark Lark**
Kate Weare Company

**An Enemy of the People**
Thomas Ostermeier, Schaubühne am Lehniner Platz

**And then, one thousand years of peace**
Ballet Preljocaj

**Water**
David Farr, Filter Theatre & Lyric Hammersmith

**The Humans**
Alexandre Singh, Witte de With Center for Contemporary Art, Performa

**Sun**
Hofesh Shechter Company

**Play/Pause**
David Lang, Susan Marshall & Company

**La Belle et la Bête**
Michel Lemieux, Victor Pilon, Michael Smith, Pierre Yves Lemieux, Lemieux Pilon 4D Art

**21c Liederabend, op. 3/Festival of Contemporary Art Song**
Paola Prestini, Julian Wachner, NOVUS NY, Trinity Wall Street Choir, Beth Morrison Projects

**Bodycast: An Artist Lecture by Suzanne Bocanegra Starring Frances McDormand**
Suzanne Bocanegra, Paul Lazar, David Lang, Frances McDormand

**Moses(es)**
Reggie Wilson/Fist & Heel Performance Group

**The Rime of the Ancient Mariner**
Samuel Taylor Coleridge, Fiona Shaw, Phyllida Lloyd

**BLEED**
Tere O'Connor Dance

**A Piece of Work: A machine-made Hamlet**
Annie Dorsen

## 2014

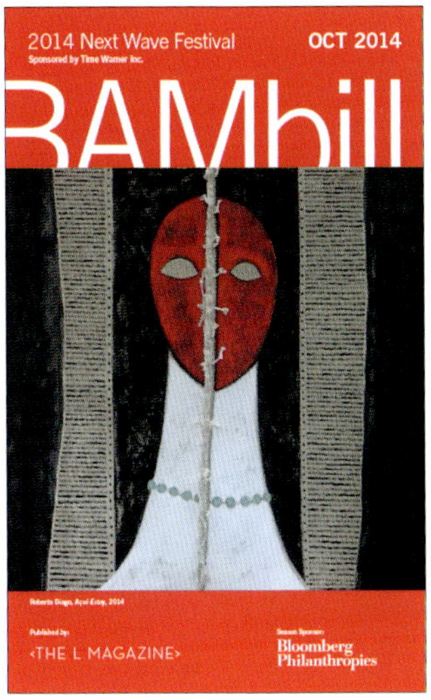


**Nonesuch Records at BAM: Celebrating a Label Without Labels**
Brad Mehldau, Philip Glass and the Philip Glass Ensemble, Steve Reich and Musicians, Chris Thile & Brad Mehldau Duo, Dawn Upshaw, Gilbert Kalish, Youssou N'Dour, Carolina Chocolate Drops, Devendra Banhart, Stephin Merritt, Iron and Wine, Kronos Quartet, Natalie Merchant, Rhiannon Giddens, Sam Amidon, Olivia Chaney, Jeff Tweedy, Laurie Anderson, Rokia Traoré, Toumani Diabaté, Sidiki Diabaté, Caetano Veloso, Robert Plant and the Sensational Space Shifters, John Adams, Tyondai Braxton, Steve Reich, Donnacha Dennehy, Alan Pierson, Alarm Will Sound

**riverrun**
Olwen Fouéré, TheEmergencyRoom, Galway International Arts Festival

**Embers**
Samuel Beckett, Gavin Quinn, Pan Pan Theatre

**ABACUS**
Lars Jan, Early Morning Opera

**Alan Smithee Directed This Play: Triple Feature**
Annie-B Parson, Paul Lazar, Big Dance Theater

**QUANTUM**
Julius von Bismarck, Gilles Jobin Company

**Shakespeare's Sonnets**
Robert Wilson, Rufus Wainwright, Berliner Ensemble

**Not I**, **Footfalls**, **Rockaby**
Samuel Beckett, Lisa Dwan, Walter Asmus, Royal Court Theatre

**Moment Marigold**
Jodi Melnick

**Wild Grass**
Wang Yuanyuan, Beijing Dance Theater

**Brooklyn Bred 2**
Martha Wilson, Clifford Owens, Dynasty Handbag, Pablo Helguera

**L.A. Dance Project**
Benjamin Millepied, Justin Peck, William Forsythe, eighth blackbird

**The Source**
Ted Hearne, Mark Doten, Daniel Fish

**Kontakthof**
Tanztheater Wuppertal Pina Bausch

**Angels in America**
Tony Kushner, Jan Versweyveld, Ivo van Hove, Toneelgroep Amsterdam

**Salt of the Earth**
Zvi Sahar, PuppetCinema/HaZira Performance Art Arena

**Six Characters in Search of an Author**
Luigi Pirandello, Emmanuel Demarcy-Mota, Théâtre de la Ville, Paris

**The Object Lesson**
Geoff Sobelle, David Neumann

**Exposed: Songs for Unseen Warhol Films**
Dean Wareham, Tom Verlaine, Martin Rev, Eleanor Friedberger, Bradford Cox, The Andy Warhol Museum

**BASETRACK Live**
En Garde Arts

Next Wave Festival BAMbill cover featuring art work by Roberto Diago, 2014. Courtesy of BAM Hamm Archives

**Sadeh21**
Ohad Naharin, Batsheva Dance Company

**Oxbow**
Ivy Baldwin Dance

**Birds With Skymirrors**
Lemi Ponifasio, MAU

**Wayfinders**
Holcombe Waller

**Black Mountain Songs**
Bryce Dessner, Richard Reed Parry, Maureen Towey, Brooklyn Youth Chorus

**The Wanderer**
Jessica Lang Dance

**On Behalf of Nature**
Meredith Monk & Vocal Ensemble

**The Etudes**
Philip Glass

**The Ambassador**
Gabriel Kahane, John Tiffany

**Howie the Rookie**
Mark O'Rowe, Landmark Productions, Irish Arts Center

**VIJAY IYER: Music of Transformation**
Vijay Iyer, Prashant Bhargava, International Contemporary Ensemble

## 2015

**Rice**
Lin Hwai-min, Cloud Gate Dance Theatre of Taiwan

**COLLAPSE**
Timur and the Dime Museum, Beth Morrison Projects

**Nufonia Must Fall**
Kid Koala, K.K. Barrett, Afiara Quartet

**TAPE**
K. Kvarnström & Co, Kulturhuset City Theatre, Stockholm

**Antigone**
Sophocles, Anne Carson, Juliette Binoche, Ivo van Hove, Barbican, Les Théâtres de la Ville de Luxembourg

**17 Border Crossings**
Thaddeus Phillips

**Tabac Rouge**
James Thierrée, La Compagnie du Hanneton

**Dream'd in a Dream**
Seán Curran Company, Ustatshakirt Plus

**New Society**
Miranda July

**Reconfiguration: An Evening with Other Lives**
Rebecca Habel, Terry Kinney, Mix Tape Productions

**Helen Lawrence**
Stan Douglas, Chris Haddock, Canadian Stage

**All Vows**
Maya Beiser

**Hallo**
Martin Zimmermann

**texts&beheadings/ElizabethR**
Karin Coonrod, Compagnia de' Colombari

**Refuse the Hour**
William Kentridge, Philip Miller, Dada Masilo, Peter Galison

**Umusuna: Memories Before History**
Ushio Amagatsu, Sankai Juku

Next Wave Festival BAMbill cover featuring art work by Shinique Smith, 2015. Courtesy of BAM Hamm Archives

**The Exalted**
Anne Bogart, Carl Hancock Rux, Theo Bleckmann

**Hagoromo**
Nathan Davis, Brendan Pelsue, Chris M. Green, Wendy Whelan, David Michalek, International Contemporary Ensemble, Brooklyn Youth Chorus

**Epiphany: The Cycle of Life**
Francisco J. Núñez, Michael McQuilken, Ali Hossaini, VisionIntoArt, Young People's Chorus of New York City

**Opus**
Yaron Lifschitz, Circa, Debussy String Quartet

**Savannah Bay**
Marguerite Duras, Didier Bezace, Théâtre de l'Atelier, Paris

**YOU US WE ALL**
Shara Worden, Andrew Ondrejcak, B.O.X. (Baroque Orchestration X)

**Real Enemies**
Darcy James Argue, Peter Nigrini, Isaac Butler, Secret Society, Beth Morrison Projects

**Beyond Time**
Liu Ruo-yu, U-Theatre

**More up a Tree**
Claudia de Serpa Soares, Eve Sussman, Jim White, Performa

**Yimbégré**
Souleymane Badolo

**Steel Hammer**
Anne Bogart, Julia Wolfe, SITI Company, Bang on a Can All-Stars

**Continu**
Sasha Waltz & Guests

**Walking with 'Trane**
Jawole Willa Jo Zollar, Samantha Speis, Urban Bush Women

**Alas, The Nymphs...**
John Jahnke, Hotel Savant

**The Hard Nut**
Mark Morris Dance Group, Colin Fowler, MMDG Music Ensemble, Hard Nut Singers

**Sancho: An Act of Remembrance**
Paterson Joseph, Simon Godwin

## 2016

**Bridge Over Mud**
Verdensteatret, FuturePerfect Productions

**the loser**
Thomas Bernhard, David Lang, Jack Dawson

**Phaedra(s)**
Krzysztof Warlikowski, Isabelle Huppert, Odéon-Théâtre de l'Europe

**Battlefield**
Peter Brook, Marie-Hélène Estienne, Jean-Claude Carrière, C.I.C.T.-Théâtre des Bouffes du Nord

**portrait of myself as my ~~father~~**
Nora Chipaumire, Philip White, 651 ARTS, Théâtre de la Ville, Paris

**monumental**
Dana Gingras, Noam Gagnon, Holy Body Tattoo, Godspeed You! Black Emperor

**The Undertaking**
Steve Cosson, Jessica Mitrani, The Civilians, Théâtre de la Ville, Paris

**Remains**
John Jasperse Company

Next Wave Festival BAMbill cover featuring art work by Ellen Carey, 2016. Courtesy of BAM Hamm Archives

**Songs of Lear**
Grzegorz Bral, Song of the Goat Theatre

**The Hunger**
Donnacha Dennehy, Alan Pierson, Tom Creed, Alarm Will Sound, Irish Arts Center

**Minuit**
Yoann Bourgeois, Centre Chorégraphique National de Grenoble, Théâtre de la Ville, Paris

**Neither**
Samuel Beckett, Morton Feldman, Shen Wei Dance Arts

**Monchichi**
Company Wang Ramirez, Théâtre de la Ville, Paris

**Vortex Temporum**
Anne Teresa De Keersmaeker, Rosas, Ictus

**Letter to a Man**
Robert Wilson, Mikhail Baryshnikov

**Rememberer**
Steven Reker, Open House

**Request Concert**
Franz Xaver Kroetz, Yana Ross, Łaźnia Nowa Theater, TR Warszawa

**Pavement**
Kyle Abraham/Abraham.In.Motion

**Kings of War**
Ivo van Hove, Toneelgroep Amsterdam

**A Star Has Burnt My Eye**
Howard Fishman, Connie Converse, Paul Lazar

**Plexus**
Aurélien Bory, Kaori Ito, Compagnie 111

**Rules Of The Game**
Jonah Bokaer, Daniel Arsham, Pharrell Williams, David Campbell

**Thank You for Coming: Play**
Faye Driscoll

**Memory Rings**
Erik Sanko, Jessica Grindstaff, Ryan Heffington, Phantom Limb Company

**The Tree of Life**
Terrence Malick, Wordless Music Orchestra

**A Gun Show**
Emily Johnson, Ain Gordon, Sō Percussion

**On The Road**
Zvi Gotheiner, Josh Higgason, ZviDance

**The Magnetic Fields: 50 Song Memoir**
Stephin Merritt, Nick Schwartz-Hall, José Zayas, The Magnetic Fields

**The Winter's Tale**
Declan Donnellan, Nick Ormerod, Cheek by Jowl

**Brent Green and Sam Green: Live Cinema**

**The Hard Nut**
Mark Morris Dance Group, Colin Fowler, MMDG Music Ensemble, Hard Nut Singers

**CITIZEN**
Reggie Wilson/Fist & Heel Performance Group

**Amplified**
Michael Gordon, Jim Findlay, Dublin Guitar Quartet, Irish Arts Center

## 2017

**Café Müller, The Rite of Spring**
Tanztheater Wuppertal Pina Bausch

**Olivier Py Sings Les Premiers Adieux de Miss Knife**
Olivier Py, Stéphane Leach, Jean-Yves Rivaud

**My Lai**
Jonathan Berger, Harriet Scott Chessman, Kronos Quartet

**The Principles of Uncertainty**
Maira Kalman, Dance Heginbotham

**A Letter to My Nephew**
Bill T. Jones/Arnie Zane Company, New York Live Arts

**Crossing**
Matthew Aucoin, Diane Paulus, American Repertory Theater

**Mon élue noire (My Black Chosen One): Sacre #2**
Germaine Acogny, Olivier Dubois, Ballet du Nord

**Saudade**
Joshua Beamish, MOVETHECOMPANY

**Richard III**
Thomas Ostermeier, Schaubühne Berlin

**La grenouille avait raison (The Toad Knew)**
James Thierrée, La Compagnie du Hanneton

**Mementos Mori**
Julia Miller, Manual Cinema

**/peh-LO-tah/**
Marc Bamuthi Joseph/The Living Word Project

**boulders and bones**
Brenda Way, KT Nelson, ODC/Dance

**Virago-Man Dem**
Cynthia Oliver

**Road Trip**
Julia Wolfe, Michael Gordon, David Lang, Bang on a Can All-Stars

**Buffer**
Xavier Cha, Performa

**State of Siege**
Albert Camus, Emmanuel Demarcy-Mota, Théâtre de la Ville, Paris

**Man to Man**
Alexandra Wood, Manfred Karge, Wales Millennium Centre

**Aroundtown**
David Dorfman Dance

**Grand Finale**
Hofesh Shechter Company

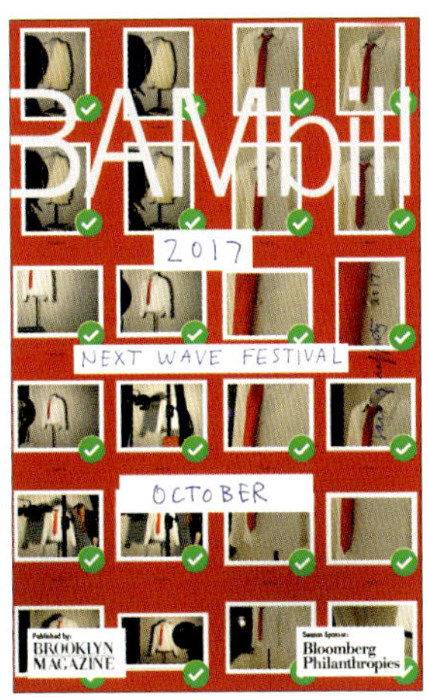


**17c**
Annie-B Parson, Paul Lazar, Big Dance Theater

**A Billion Nights on Earth**
Thaddeus Phillips, Steven Dufala

**John Cale: The Velvet Underground & Nico**
John Cale, Wordless Music Orchestra, BGV Music Choral Group

**The Fountainhead**
Ayn Rand, Ivo van Hove, Toneelgroep Amsterdam

**Sleep**
Haruki Murakami, Rachel Dickstein, Ripe Time, Naomi Iizuka

**8980: Book of Travelers**
Gabriel Kahane

**Suddenly**
Zvi Sahar, Cameri Theatre of Tel-Aviv, PuppetCinema, Etgar Keret

**HOME**
Geoff Sobelle, David Neumann, Steven Dufala

**Farmhouse/Whorehouse: An Artist Lecture by Suzanne Bocanegra Starring Lili Taylor**
Suzanne Bocanegra, Lee Sunday Evans, Lili Taylor

**Tesseract**
Rashaun Mitchell, Silas Riener, Charles Atlas

**Bangsokol: A Requiem for Cambodia**
Him Sophy, Trent Walker, Rithy Panh, Cambodian Living Arts

Next Wave Festival BAMbill cover featuring art work by Sara Greenberger Rafferty, 2016. Courtesy of BAM Hamm Archives

# Contributors

**Anne Bogart** is a cofounder and co-artistic director of the ensemble-based SITI Company, head of the MFA program in directing at Columbia University, and author of *A Director Prepares: Seven Essays on Art and Theatre* (2001), *The Viewpoints Book* (2004), coauthored with Tina Landau, *And Then, You Act* (2007), *Conversations with Anne* (2012), and *What's the Story: Essays about Art, Theater and Storytelling* (2014). With SITI Company, she has directed more than 30 works in venues around the world, including Next Wave productions of *War of the Worlds* (2000), *bobrauschenbergamerica* (2003), *Hotel Cassiopeia* (2007), *Trojan Women (After Euripides)* (2012), *A Rite* (2013), and *Steel Hammer* (2015).

**Dan Cameron** is a New York-based writer, curator, and specialist in global contemporary art. He was senior curator for the New Museum in New York City (1995–2006) and for Next Wave Visual Art at the Brooklyn Academy of Music (2002–11); director of visual arts at the Contemporary Art Center in New Orleans (2007–10); founder and artistic director of the U.S. Biennial in New Orleans (2007–12); and chief curator at the Orange County Museum of Art in Newport Beach, California (2012–15). Internationally, he was the artistic director of the Istanbul Biennial (2003), co-curator of the Taipei Biennial (2006), and curator of the Bienal de Cuenca, Ecuador (2016). Recent exhibitions include *When Jackie Met Ethyl* (2016) at Howl! Happening in New York, which examines the cultural impact of legendary "downtown" performance artists Jackie Curtis and Ethyl Eichelberger, and *Kinesthesia: Latin American Kinetic Art, 1954–1969* (2017), with support from the Getty Foundation, at the Palm Springs Art Museum.

**Kristy Edmunds** is an artist, curator, arts administrator, and frequent lecturer and keynote speaker. She is regarded internationally for her innovation and depth in the presentation of contemporary performing arts and for placing equal emphasis on the support and commissioning of new work. She currently serves as executive and artistic director of UCLA's Center for the Art of Performance, one of the leading presenters nationwide of contemporary performing arts. She has also served as the founding executive and artistic director of the Portland Institute for Contemporary Art and the TBA Festival (Time Based Art) in Portland, Oregon (1995–2005); artistic director for the Melbourne International Arts Festival (2005–08), the head of the School of Performing Arts and deputy dean at the Victorian College of the Arts/University of Melbourne; and consulting artistic director for the Park Avenue Armory in New York City (2009–12). In 2016, she was bestowed with the honor of Chevalier de L'Ordre des Arts et des Lettres by the Republic of France.

**Karen Brooks Hopkins** succeeded Harvey Lichtenstein as president of the Brooklyn Academy of Music from 1999 to her retirement in 2015. During her tenure as president, BAM received the National Medal of Arts, the highest award given to artists and arts organizations by the United States government, presented to her in a White House ceremony by President Barack Obama. For her contribution to the arts, she was appointed Chevalier de L'Ordre des Arts et des Lettres by the Republic of France as well as Commander of the Royal Order of the Polar Star in recognition of her role in solidifying ties between the performing arts communities of Sweden and the United States.

**Colleen Jennings-Roggensack** is the executive director of ASU Gammage, the multipurpose performing arts center at Arizona State University, where she is Vice President for Cultural Affairs. Formerly a dancer and choreographer, she currently serves as a member of the Broadway League Board of Governors. Past president of the Association of Performing Arts Presenters, she is a founding member of the Creative Capital Board, senior advisor to Hermitage Artist Retreat and Women of Color in the Arts, and served on the National Council on the Arts at the behest of President Bill Clinton.

**David Lang** is one of America's most honored composers and his works are performed regularly around the world. In 2008, he was awarded the Pulitzer Prize in Music and received the 2010 Grammy Award for Best Small Ensemble Performance. His work at BAM includes the oratorios *Lost Objects* (2004) and *Shelter* (2005), a collaborative composition with Michael Gordon, Julia Wolfe, and librettist Deborah Artman; his theater work *love fail* (2012) with vocal ensemble Anonymous 4; his opera *the loser* (2016), for which he served as composer, librettist, and stage director; and collaborations with Susan Marshall, Big Dance Theater, L.A. Dance Project, and La La La Human Steps.

**Harvey Lichtenstein** (1929–2017) was president and executive producer of the Brooklyn Academy of Music (1967–99) and was credited with resurrecting the institution into a world-class center for the performing arts. Early in his tenure, he established BAM as a showcase for cutting-edge contemporary performance. In 1981, he launched the Next Wave Series, followed in 1983 by the Next Wave Festival, and the list of artists who performed at BAM under his purview reads like a Who's Who of contemporary performance, among them, Merce Cunningham, Peter Brook, Philip Glass, Laurie Anderson, Pina Bausch, Meredith Monk, Mark Morris, Steve Reich, and Robert Wilson. Iconic BAM productions during his tenure include the Glass/Wilson opera *Einstein on the Beach*, originally staged in 1984, and Peter Brook's *The Mahabharata*, performed in 1987 in the renovated Majestic Theater (now the BAM Harvey Theater). In 1999, he was awarded the National Medal of Arts by President Bill Clinton and in 2013 was presented with the Handel Medallion, New York City's highest award for achievement in the arts.

**Joseph V. Melillo**, executive producer since 1999, is responsible for BAM's artistic direction, overseeing programming in all its performance spaces: the Howard Gilman Opera House, the Harvey Theater, the BAM Fisher, and the Rose Cinemas. He previously served as BAM's producing director and founding director of the Next Wave Festival. He has fostered the work of emerging and established artists, and forged numerous international partnerships. Awards include the Chevalier and Officier de L'Ordre des Arts et des Lettres from the Republic of France, the OBE from Great Britain, and Knight of the Order of Québec from Canada. He currently serves as a member of the International Arts Advisory Committee for the Wexner Prize, and in 2017 served as both a Gish Award panelist and a Heinz Award juror.

**Beth Morrison** is the creative producer of Beth Morrison Projects (BMP), self-described as "the realization of a vision that stems from a deep commitment to nurturing composers and other artists and fostering the development of new opera and other new music-theater works." Acknowledged by the *Los Angeles Times* as a "contemporary opera mastermind," she founded BMP in 2006 as a means to support the work of these composers and their multimedia collaborators, noted by *Opera News* for being at "the edge of innovation." She encourages risk-taking, creating a structure for new work that is unique to the artist and allows them to feel safe to experiment and push boundaries.

**Roger Oliver** is a writer, academician, and theater and film consultant. He created and directed the humanities program for the Next Wave Festival from its inception in 1983 until 1990; in addition, he coordinated humanities activities for the citywide Ingmar Bergman Festival (1995) and for the Classic Stage Company in New York City (1998–2004). He served as research consultant for Next Wave productions of David Gordon's *United States* (1988) and for Steve Reich and Beryl Korot's *The Cave* (1993). Since 1985, he has been Professor of Liberal Arts at the Juilliard School; he also teaches for the Juilliard Drama Division and at New York University. Author of *Dreams of Passion: The Theater of Luigi Pirandello* (1979) and editor of *Ingmar Bergman: An Artist's Journey* (1995), he served as an advisor and contributor to the commemorative volume celebrating the 150th anniversary of the Brooklyn Academy of Music, *BAM: The Complete Works* (2011).

**José Parlá** is a critically acclaimed, multidisciplinary artist in painting, large-scale murals, photography, video, and sculpture. His work has been exhibited at the High Museum of Art and the SCAD Museum of Art, Savannah, Georgia; the Neuberger Museum of Art, Purchase, New York; and the National YoungArts Foundation, Miami, Florida. He is also represented in major public collections, including the British Museum; the Albright-Knox Art Gallery, Buffalo, New York; the POLA Museum of Art, Hakone, Japan; and the National Museum of Fine Arts, Havana, Cuba.

**Wendy Perron** is a former dancer/choreographer turned writer, editor, lecturer, and curator. She danced with the Trisha Brown Company in the 1970s, including performances at BAM in the Lepercq Space (1976–77), and founded and choreographed more than 40 works for her own company, appearing at venues like the Lincoln Center Festival, Jacob's Pillow, and the Joyce Theater. In the early 1990s, she served as associate director of Jacob's Pillow and from 2007 to 2010 was artistic advisor to Fall for Dance at New York City Center. Former editor-in-chief of *Dance Magazine,* she has written extensively for numerous publications and has lectured on contemporary dance across the country. She has taught at Bennington, Princeton, and Rutgers, and currently at NYU Tisch School of the Arts. Author of *Through the Eyes of a Dancer: Selected Writings* (2013), she co-curated *Radical Bodies: Anna Halprin, Simone Forti, and Yvonne Rainer in California and New York, 1955–1972*, an exhibit that originated at the University of California, Santa Barbara, and in 2017 was shown at the New York Public Library for the Performing Arts at Lincoln Center.

**Tom Sellar**, a critic, dramaturg, and curator, is editor of *Theater*, Yale University's international creative journal. Under his editorship since 2003, *Theater* has commissioned and published essays, creative dossiers, reviews, interviews, commentary, polemics, plays, and portfolios by leading global artists and authors. His criticism and reporting have appeared in national publications including *Artforum*, *BOMB*, *American Theatre*, the *Guardian*, and the *New York Times*, and he served as theater critic for the *Village Voice* from 2001 to 2016. He co-curated the 2015 and 2016 Prelude festivals at the Martin E. Segal Theatre Center in New York and has created programming for Philadelphia Fringe Arts, the Prague Quadrennial, and other organizations. He received his Doctor of Fine Arts from the Yale School of Drama, where he is currently Professor of Dramaturgy and Dramatic Criticism.

**Mark Swed** has been the classical music critic for the *Los Angeles Times* since 1996, and before that for more than two decades he was a music critic for both the *Los Angeles Herald Examiner* and the *Wall Street Journal*. He has also contributed to the *New York Times*, the *New Yorker*, the *Economist*, *Opera News*, *Gramophone*, and many other national and international publications. Among his writings are liner notes for recordings, program notes for concerts, and catalogue essays for the Los Angeles Museum of Contemporary Art. From 1992 to 2000, he was the 20th-century music editor of *Musical Quarterly*. He is the author of the 25th anniversary history of the Los Angeles Music Center and is currently completing a biographical study on John Cage. His awards include the ASCAP-Deems Taylor Award, the Letter of Distinction from the American Music Center, and journalism prizes from the Los Angeles Music Center and the Los Angeles Press Club. In 2007, he was a finalist for the Pulitzer Prize in criticism.

**Marianne Weems** is a theater and opera director and cofounder of the award-winning New York-based crossmedia performance ensemble The Builders Association. Since 1994, The Builders Association has toured domestically and internationally to over 80 venues, including Next Wave productions of *Alladeen* (2003), *Super Vision* (2005), *Continuous City* (2008), and *HOUSE/DIVIDED* (2012). The Builders Association has created a significant body of work at the forefront of combining media and performance and collaborated with diverse artistic partners such as the architects Diller + Scofidio, the National Center for Supercomputing Applications, and the innovative arts collective, motiroti.

**Jawole Willa Jo Zollar** is a dancer/choreographer and founder of the Brooklyn-based dance company Urban Bush Women, a performance ensemble dedicated to exploring the use of cultural expression as a catalyst for social change that since 1984 has toured five continents. Her Next Wave productions include *Praise House* (1991), *Les écailles de la mémoire (The Scales of Memory)* (2008), and *Walking with 'Trane* (2015). Featured in the PBS documentary, *Free to Dance*, she is currently the Nancy Smith Fichter Professor in Dance and Robert O. Lawton Distinguished Professor at Florida State University. Still dancing, in 2017 she received the New York Dance and Performance Award for Lifetime Achievement in Dance.

# Acknowledgments

**The Next Wave Festival** was established by Harvey Lichtenstein in 1983 with the support and recognition of the BAM Board of Trustees: Hon. Edward I. Koch, Hon. Howard Golden, Seth Faison, and Paul Lepercq; Honorary Chairmen: Neil D. Chrisman, Chairman; Rita Hillman, I. Stanley Kriegel, Ame Vennema, Franklin R. Weissberg; Vice Chairpersons: Harvey Lichtenstein; Elizabeth D. Bauman, Henry Bing, Jr., Warren Coburn, Chares M. Diker, Jeffrey K. Endervelt, Mallory Factor, Harold L. Fisher, Michael Fuchs, Leonard Garment, David Geffen, Sidney Kantor, Eugene Luntey, Hamish Maxwell, Evelyn Ortner, John R. Price, Jr., Richard M. Rosan, Marion Scotto, and William Tobey. Officers: Harvey Lichtenstein, President and Chief Executive Officer; Judith E. Daykin, Executive Vice President and General Manager; Richard Balzano, Vice President and Treasurer; Karen Brooks Hopkins, Vice President for Planning and Development; John Howlett, Vice President for Marketing and Promotion; Joseph V. Melillo, Festival Coordinator.

Original donors for the Next Wave Festival Production and Touring Fund included the National Endowment for the Arts, the National Endowment for the Humanities, the Rockefeller Foundation, the Howard Gilman Foundation, the Ford Foundation, AT&T, Warner Communications Inc., the New York Council for the Humanities, Willi Wear Ltd., the Dayton-Hudson Foundation, the CIGNA Corporation, and the BAM Next Wave Producers Council. Additional funds for the Next Wave Festival were provided by the New York State Council on the Arts, the Robert Sterling Clark Foundation, Inc., the Emma A. Sheafer Charitable Trust, the Mary Flagler Cary Charitable Trust, Philip Morris Incorporated, Manufacturers Hanover Trust Company, the Tortuga Foundation, Meet the Composer, Inc., the New York City Department of Cultural Affairs, the International Center of Photography, and WNYC.

The Next Wave Producers Council was established February 1983 on the occasion of BAM's world premiere of Laurie Anderson's *United States: Parts I–IV* to provide annual patronage to augment government, foundation, and corporate funding of BAM's Next Wave Festival. In addition, the Council organized and sponsored seminars, exhibitions, publications, and special events to accentuate the role of the festival in relation to the development of the contemporary performing arts.

Founding members of the Council included Roy Lichtenstein, Chairman; Mary Boone, Vice Chairperson; Angela Westwater, Vice Chairperson; Allan Albert, Dr. David Beldengreen, Eddo and Maggie Bult, Jo Ann Caplin, Leo and Toiny Castelli, George D. Clark, Jr., Paula Cooper, Mary Sharp Cronson, Betty Freeman, Stanley and Elyse Grinstein, Miriam Katowitz, Laura Kleege, Gerrit and Sydie Lansing, Sydney and Frances Lewis, Dorothy Lichtenstein, Dr. Philip and Rosanne Livingston, Jacques and Laurie Mallet, Valerie Manuel, Mr. and Mrs. William McKay, Everett and Evelyn Ortner, Arthur Radin, Jonathan Rose, Rudolf, Willi Smith, Daniel Wolf, and Ian Woodner.

# Index



Page numbers in italics indicate photographs and illustrations.

# Gratitude

It is important that I acknowledge the exceptional professionalism of a group of colleagues who have worked with me to bring Next Wave Festival artists and their works to their respective opening nights in one of our three venues: Alice Bernstein, Executive Vice President; Mary Reilly, Director of Artist Services; Patrick Scully, Associate Vice President and General Manager; Amy Cassello, Associate Producer, Next Wave Festival; Stonie Darling, Associate Director, Artistic Programming; and Juan Pablo Siles, Manager of Artistic Programming. To Steven Serafin, Susan Yung, Andrew Sloat, Sharon Lehner, Louie Fleck, Samuel Denitz, and their colleagues who have worked diligently to produce this publication; you all have rendered exemplary service to BAM. I am forever indebted to Harvey Lichtenstein for providing me the opportunity to work with him beginning in 1983 and to my professional partner, Karen Brooks Hopkins, for her devoted commitment to the BAM crusade. —*Joseph V. Melillo*

# Credits

Andrew Sloat, Designer
Sharon Lehner, Archivist

BAM Hamm Archives:
Louie Fleck
Jan Carr

Samuel Denitz, Project Manager

The editors wish to express their appreciation to Shu Chun Xie, Violaine Huisman, and Richard Rothschild.



For reprint requests, media inquiries, and bulk order discounts, please email info@bam.org

ISBN 978-0-9992971-0-0

Manufactured through Asia Pacific Offset Ltd
Printed in China
First Edition
1 2 3 4 5 6 7 8 9 0

FRONT COVER
*Einstein on the Beach*, Philip Glass/Robert Wilson/Lucinda Childs, 2012. Photo: Stephanie Berger

CASE
*Gesture Performing Dance, Dance Performing Gesture*, lobby mural, José Parlá, Brooklyn Academy of Music, Richard B. Fisher Building, 2012. Photo courtesy of BAM Hamm Archives

ENDPAPER, FRONT
*Auf dem Gebirge hat man ein Geschrei gehört (On the Mountain a Cry Was Heard)*, Tanztheater Wuppertal Pina Bausch, 1985. Photo: Beatriz Schiller

ENDPAPER, BACK
*We Set Out Early... Visibility Was Poor*, Bill T. Jones/Arnie Zane Dance Company, 1998. Photo: Dan Rest